D0206291

Software Goes to School

Software Goes to School

Teaching for Understanding with New Technologies

Edited by

David N. Perkins

Judah L. Schwartz

Mary Maxwell West

Martha Stone Wiske

New York   Oxford
OXFORD UNIVERSITY PRESS
1995

Oxford University Press

Oxford   New York   Toronto
Delhi   Bombay   Calcutta   Madras   Karachi
Kuala Lumpur   Singapore   Hong Kong   Tokyo
Nairobi   Dar es Salaam   Cape Town
Melbourne   Auckland   Madrid

and associated companies in
Berlin   Ibadan

Published by Oxford University Press, Inc.,
200 Madison Avenue, New York, New York 10016

Library of Congress Cataloging-in-Publication Data
Software goes to school : teaching for understanding with new technologies /
editors, David N. Perkins . . . [et al.].
p. cm.   Includes bibliographical references and index.
ISBN 0-19-508938-3
1. Educational technology.   2. Science—Study and teaching.
3. Mathematics—Study and teaching.   4. Computer-assisted
instruction.   5. School management and organization.
I. Perkins, David N.
LB1028.3.M335   1995   371.3'078—dc20   94-17671

1 3 5 7 9   8 6 4 2
Printed in the United States of America
on acid-free paper

ACKNOWLEDGMENTS

This book evolved from the collaborative research community formed at the Educational Technology Center (ETC) at Harvard University's Graduate School of Education. ETC was established in 1983, with a grant from the Office of Educational Research and Improvement in the U.S. Department of Education. Its mission was to study ways of using new technologies to improve education in science, mathematics, and computing. Accordingly, the Center was formed as a consortium including four school systems (Cambridge, Newton, Watertown, and Ware, Massachusetts), several educational research, development, and service organizations (Education Collaborative for Greater Boston, Education Development Center, Educational Testing Service, WGBH Educational Foundation, Interactive Training Systems, and Children's Television Workshop), and researchers drawn from many universities. At ETC teachers, researchers, and developers came together to collaborate on specific research projects and gradually to articulate a shared conception of what it means and what it takes to teach for understanding with new technologies. In this book several ETC researchers present ideas and research results that illuminate this conception. All of us are indebted to the wider intellectual community brought together by the Educational Technology Center. Further, we acknowledge with appreciation financial support from the U.S. Department of Education, the National Science Foundation, and the McDonnell Foundation. While each of the authors bears final responsibility for his or her own words, and the work reported here has proceeded in many places over several years, we appreciate the support and resources provided through the Educational Technology Center. In addition, we are indebted to more people than can possibly be listed here. But two of them provided central support to all of us. Ms. Diane Downs assembled the manuscript and managed the process of consulting with potential publishers. Ms. Kristi Hayes oversaw the final preparation of the manuscript, down to the last period.

Contents

3 On Understanding the Nature of Scientific Knowledge, 39
  Susan Carey and Carol Smith

4 History of Mathematics as a Tool for Teaching Mathematics
  for Understanding, 56
  Carlos E. Vasco

5 Inside Understanding, 70
  David N. Perkins, David Crismond, Rebecca Simmons,
  and Chris Unger

II Using Technology to Make a Distinctive Contribution 89

Contributors

Susan Carey, Massachusetts Institute of Technology
David Crismond, Harvard University
E. Paul Goldenberg, Education Development Center
Lorraine Grosslight, Educational Technology Center, Harvard
    University
James Kaput, Southeastern Massachusetts University
Magdalene Lampert, School of Education, Michigan University
Raymond S. Nickerson
David N. Perkins, Project Zero, Harvard University
Judah L. Schwartz, Massachusetts Institute of Technology and
    Educational Technology Center, Harvard University
Steven H. Schwartz, University of Massachusetts/Boston
Rebecca Simmons, Project Zero, Harvard University
Jane Smalley
Carol Smith, University of Massachusetts/Boston and Educational
    Technology Center
Joseph Snir, Haifa University and Educational Technology Center,
    Harvard University
Chris Unger, Project Zero, Harvard University
Carlos E. Vasco, Universidad Nacional de Colombia, Bogota
Margaret Vickers, Harvard University
Marianne Wiser, Clark University and Educational Technology Center,
    Harvard University
Martha Stone Wiske, Educational Technology Center, Harvard
    University

Introduction

The Greek mathematician-philosopher Euclid laid down the foundations of formal axiomatic geometry around the third century B.C., launching one of the most powerful resources for building understandings ever conceived: the formal apparatus of mathematics. Euclid had his special interests, but in many ways he was characteristic of his time, place, and social class—a paragon of the classic Greek commitment to analytical and speculative thought.

Euclid lives on today in the structure of mathematics as a professional discipline . . . and in thousands of classrooms, where students struggle to deal with the model of mathematical inquiry that he established so many centuries ago. While the role of the Euclidean paradigm in mathematics cannot be denied, the Euclidean presence in the classroom is more vexed. The world around, Euclidean geometry has come to be known as a killer subject, widely failed and generally despised, a far cry from the spirit of its origins.

In a few classrooms, however, something different seems to be happening. Always it involves a teacher with special perspective and commitment. And sometimes this resurrection in the teaching of geometry has been sparked by something undreamt of in Euclid's day—a computer. Students of geometry have been dropping perpendiculars for more than two thousand years, their usual tools being the classic instruments of straight edge and compass. But today, dropping a perpendicular can be as easy as striking a few keys. The students can see the results of this and other constructions immediately, with precise rendering. And they can even repeat the same pattern of construction on a fresh triangle, differently proportioned.

A Boost from Technology

These students are using a software package called the *Geometric Supposer*, designed to make the enterprise of geometric construction more accessible, so much more accessible that students can spend serious time finding their own theorems to prove, rather than committing it all to studying the canonical theorems of geometry.

In other classrooms, technology is helping students toward the understanding of other topics—the distinction between heat and temperature, the logic of a programming language, the nature of proportional reasoning. When such interventions go well, as they often do, they illustrate the premise of this book: technology can help with *understanding*. Not just with drill and practice, honing admittedly important skills such as the algorithms of arithmetic to a high level of proficiency; not just with testing, swiftly scoring and tabulating results; not just with classroom management, keeping track of grades, absences, and homework overdue. But with *understanding*.

When technologies help students toward better understanding, inevitably the circumstances illustrate the tripod of concerns that gives this book its organization. The first leg of this tripod is the general challenge of teaching for understanding. Often, the case in point is an ancient one, for example, seeking to understand the structure and properties of Euclidean space. As to the second leg, students are tackling these challenges by using one of the newest instruments available to support human thinking—the computer. And as to the third leg, these events unfold in a setting that, although often vexed and almost always taken for granted, constitutes one of the most foundational inventions of contemporary civilization: the classroom, with its teacher, textbooks, blackboards, curriculum, and surrounding institution. There were, after all, no classrooms in Euclid's day in anything like the modern sense, nor any concept of education on a mass scale.

The Educational Technology Center

This tripod of concern with understanding, technology, and classroom settings has a particular source. In autumn 1983, the Educational Technology Center, an organization of scholars and practitioners committed to exploring the role of technology in education, opened its doors at the Harvard Graduate School of Education. The specific focus of the center—and the focus of this book as well—was education in science, mathematics, and computing. Since that time, with support from the Office of Education and other agencies, associates of the Educational Technology Center have been exploring systematically how technology can help students learn with understanding.

Efforts to reach beyond the immediate staff have involved scholars in different states and nations. Accordingly, while many of the chapters collected here have been authored by individuals on the staff of the Educational Technology Center, others have been invited from colleagues at a distance. So the investigations described and views expressed here represent not just the immediate family but the extended family that has grown up around the Educational Technology Center.

Targets of Difficulty

Serious efforts at educational innovation today inevitably are faced with the daunting vastness of the educational enterprise. Even constraining attention to science, mathematics, and computing, does one work on Newton's laws, chemical equations, the cyclic structure of the periodic table, the quadratic formula? In a virtually endless menu, what basis is there for making a principled choice?

Our solution to this problem lies in the phrase "targets of difficulty." Although the more common version is "targets of opportunity," the "difficulty" variant has proven to be a worthwhile guide in setting directions of inquiry. Both practical classroom experience and ample educational research have shown that there are certain subject matters, and topics within many subject matters, that are particularly troublesome, that confuse generation after generation of students, that befuddle some of the keenest students, and that not uncommonly puzzle the very teachers who have the responsibility of cultivating students' understanding of them.

These topics and concepts are our "targets of difficulty"—not, of course, that we can address them all or even a substantial percentage, but at least that we have sought to tackle problems demonstrably problematic for students and central to the subject matters of mathematics, science, and computing. Such problems include, for example, the whole enterprise of Euclidean geometry, a "killer subject," as noted earlier; the distinction between heat and temperature, a central and widely misunderstood concept in science; the semantics of fractions, an eddy in the development of mathematical understanding that carries many a student into backwaters from which they never emerge; and more.

Good Pedagogy First and Foremost

But how might technology speak to these "targets of difficulty?" One of our most fundamental precepts is that technology is a tool to be used cautiously and selectively in education. All too often, the popular press and other sources have treated technology like the hired gun, called into town to clean up the ills of education. Abundant practical experience shows how inadequate this conception is. For example, a dismayingly high percentage of software constructed in the name of education displays exactly what no "hired gun" could afford: a bad aim—one not directed at substantive educational problems, with sights not aligned on the kinds of pedagogical interactions that are likely to build learners' understanding or stimulate their enthusiasm.

With good pedagogy as the guiding goal, technologies can be employed selectively and sensitively to make a distinct contribution to teaching and learning, for example, to present dynamic visual models of key ideas, to help students gather and display data, to allow them to construct and manipulate screen "objects" such as graphs or geometric figures, and to give teachers and researchers a window on students' thinking and learning.

Following this precept, we have organized the chapters in this book under three broad themes. Part I, "Understanding Understanding," addresses the nature of understanding itself. What constitutes understanding something? What are typical barriers to understanding? What are our principal resources in teaching for understanding? What do the spate of findings concerning students' "misconceptions" about science and mathematics tell us about the enterprise of teaching for understanding? While matters technological figure occasionally in these chapters, they definitely play second string to the exploration of a pedagogy of understanding.

Part II, "Using Technology to Make a Distinctive Contribution," focuses front and center on what technology can offer in teaching for understanding. The chapters examine how technologies afford new ways of representing complex concepts, and make available new means by which students can manipulate abstract entities in a "hands-on" way. Chapters in this Part show how artfully designed software can construct "ramps" from the concrete to the abstract, and underscore how part of the challenge in software design is chunking the information in ways that make it manageable for the learner.

Part III, "Connecting Educational Research and Practice," recognizes the complexities of realistic educational settings, explores what happens when technology-based innovations are introduced, and examines the means by which a pedagogy of understanding can take root and thrive in the often uncongenial climate of public education. Part III honors the point that very few educational innovations actually see wide-scale use in classrooms, and strives to come to terms with the factors that influence educational effectiveness where it really counts—in the day-to-day engagement of youngsters in learning.

The tripod is the minimum number of supports required for a stable structure—a point Euclid would have appreciated. We hope that our tripod of attention to understanding, the contribution of technology, and the texture of classroom realities will afford a perspective on education that stands up too. Since each of Parts I, II, and III has its own introduction, perhaps this is sufficient introduction to lead onward into the heartland of these ideas.

Software Goes to School

I

Understanding Understanding

Whosoever teaches believes that they teach for understanding. Teachers believe it. Authors of textbooks believe it. Designers of worksheets believe it. "What's the point," most would ask, "of teaching anything, unless you're teaching for understanding?"

However, while the will to teach for understanding is plain, the way is far from clear. Looking across a multitude of educational experiences that take this mission for granted, one quickly discovers dramatically different views of what teaching for understanding requires. Some instructional experiences are startlingly reductive—routine, memory-emphatic, narrow in the performances they expect, and sparse in the explanations that they provide. Yet these are as often offered up in the name of understanding as anything else.

Perhaps part of the problem is that understanding is a somewhat mysterious achievement of the human mind. Let us contrast our sense of what it is to understand something with our sense of what it is to know something. If you know the names of the Presidents or the capital of Washington state, you are expected to be able to display that knowledge on call. The display of the knowledge is the operationalization of what it is to have the knowledge. But understanding is a more subtle matter. It is not enough to recite, or deliver canned explanations, or even to solve typical problems. Something more generative seems to be called for—in Jerome Bruner's felicitous phrase, something that goes "beyond the information given."

With such puzzles as these to contend with, first and foremost in this

3

book must be some coming to terms with the character of understanding itself. Each of the chapters in Part I of this volume addresses some facet of understanding, its nature, and its nurture.

In Chapter 1, "Can Technology Help Teach for Understanding?" Raymond Nickerson suggests that the desire to understand—the need for explanations—is a strong one in human beings, adding that understanding understanding is an important aspect of understanding ourselves. He discusses five principles for fostering understanding and examines the ways in which technology can help educators use these principles to advantage.

Nickerson's five principles are: (1) starting where the student is, (2) promoting active processing and discovery, (3) using appropriate representations and models, (4) using simulations, and (5) providing a supportive environment. Nickerson closes his statement by cautioning against the use of technology simply for technology's sake. Nothing about technology, he warns, guarantees its thoughtful application in the service of understanding. Technology is useful in enhancing understanding only if it is applied in ways that are consistent with principles of teaching for understanding.

In the second chapter, Marianne Wiser discusses the importance in science education of addressing students' naive and misconceived, yet *coherent*, systems of explanation. She builds her argument by examining historical developments in science which, though now seen as erroneous, become coherent and plausible when placed in the context of their times. To understand the barriers students face, Wiser urges, it is important to see students' misconceptions as reflecting not shoot-from-the-hip judgments but an entire system of interpretation, not unlike one prominent in seventeenth century thermal physics. From this point of reference, Wiser discusses in some detail her conceptually based computer-modeling intervention, designed to help students toward a more correct conception of heat and temperature.

Susan Carey and Carol Smith address the importance of developing in students an understanding of the nature of science in Chapter 3, "On Understanding the Nature of Scientific Knowledge." They argue against the common textbook practice of portraying science as an inductivist or empiricist activity wherein scientific knowledge is the steady accumulation of a set of confirmed hypotheses.

Instead, the authors suggest, it is important to present students with a more constructivist epistemology of science, one in which students understand that scientists hold theories that underlie the generation and interpretation of specific hypotheses and experiments. Carey and Smith examine the current literature that suggests students come to the classroom with an inductivist epistemology. They then describe their own clinical work, which attempts to change such an epistemology to a more constructivist one.

In Chapter 4, Carlos Vasco argues for the relevance of the history of mathematics to the teaching and learning of mathematics. Writing under the title "The History of Mathematics as a Tool to Understand Children's Understanding of Mathematics," Vasco emphasizes that most proposals for change in the mathematics curriculum derive from a logical, not an historical, sequencing. Among those few mathematicians who do propose curricular changes based on historical criteria, there is an assumption that the historical sequence should dictate the entire pedagogical sequence. Vasco suggests instead that *both* historical and logical sequence have important elements to contribute. He uses examples from arithmetic, algebra, and geometry to show how one might take the best advantage of both in the mathematics curriculum.

"Inside Understanding" is the pointed title of Chapter 5, by David Perkins, David Crismond, Rebecca Simmons, and Christopher Unger. The four authors argue for the importance of explanation to any theory of understanding and define what they term "explanation structures," cognitive structures that mediate understanding. The authors then posit a framework of understanding called the Access Framework. The name comes from a key premise: In order to display understanding (which involves building, extending, and revising explanation structures), the learner needs *access* to the following four broad categories of resources: (1) knowledge, (2) representations, (3) retrieval mechanisms, and (4) construction mechanisms. After discussing each of the four and their interactions, the authors explore the relevance of the Access Framework to current educational practice.

1

Can Technology Help Teach for Understanding?

RAYMOND S. NICKERSON

What it means to understand and how understanding might be enhanced through education are questions that have obvious practical significance. While faulty understanding may be inconsequential in some cases, it can be problematic in others: one who believes a home thermostat acts like a continuously adjustable valve is unlikely to suffer any ill effects as a consequence, but the handyman who decides to replace a defunct light fixture can be in trouble if he does not understand the operation of an electrical circuit. In addition to practical reasons for wanting to understand understanding and how to enhance it, I believe the desire to understand—the need for explanations—is a strong one in most human beings, and motivates the pursuit of scientific knowledge as well as the development and persistence of superstitions and other systems of beliefs. Understanding understanding is an important aspect of understanding ourselves, and learning how to enhance understanding is in the interest of helping to satisfy a fundamental human desire.

Understanding is difficult to define without being quite circular about it. Elsewhere I have noted what appear to me to be some of the important aspects of this concept (Nickerson, 1985). For present purposes let us say that understanding is a matter of degree and that among the evidences that an individual understands something (a concept, principle, structure, process) at a relatively deep level, I would include the abilities to: explain to the satisfaction of an acknowledged expert, apply knowledge appropriately in various contexts, produce appropriate qualitative representations, make appropriate analogies, repair malfunctions, and predict effects of change in structure or process. Understanding as represented by such abilities is a primary objective of education. There is ample evidence, however, that instruction often fails to realize this objective.

It is interesting to reflect on the question of how much the average member of a modern technological society understands of the world and how it works. We are much impressed with what has been learned as a consequence of the scientific enterprise of the last few hundred years. We tend to think, perhaps condescendingly, of our ancestors as having had very limited understanding of nature—by contrast with what is known today. But does the average person of today really understand the world better than the average person of a few centuries ago? I suspect the answer is yes, but I suspect also that current-day "understanding" of the world has a much greater element of superstition—false conception of causation—than we typically assume. Modern-day citizens of an industrialized country come in constant contact with artifacts, the workings of which they understand only vaguely if at all. Radios, televisions, cameras, and microwave ovens are examples. It is conceivable that most people today witness daily more phenomena that they do not understand than did their predecessors of centuries ago.

Examples of what many people do not understand are not limited to products of technology. Wherever researchers have looked for evidences of misconceptions of natural phenomena, they have found them. Nor is lack of understanding limited to individuals who have not had the benefit of formal education. If literacy were defined as the ability to read *comprehendingly*, all of us would have to be considered illiterate with respect to many, if not most, areas of human knowledge. We cannot read comprehendingly in fields we are unfamiliar with because comprehension is a knowledge-based process. If we lack the fundamental knowledge that defines a field, we cannot comprehend what one has to say who takes that knowledge for granted, and very few people acquire the knowledge that is necessary to read comprehendingly in many fields.

Why this is so is an interesting question. Are we, as individuals, inherently incapable of knowing more than a tiny fraction of what there is to know? Or might it be that our failure to acquire more knowledge than we typically do is a consequence, to some significant degree, of limitations in the methods we have developed for informing ourselves? With more versatile representational media, could we do better in this regard? Does modem technology offer the possibility of more effective ways of enhancing understanding? I will try to articulate a number of principles regarding the fostering of understanding that are supported to some degree by educational research and that appear to me to be principles that technology might help apply.

Fostering Understanding

In response to many evidences that students often do not understand the material their schooling is intended to teach, researchers have turned their attention to the question of how to increase the chances that understanding will be achieved. While no one, to my knowledge, has yet devised an educational procedure that guarantees understanding, I will mention five principles for fostering understanding that I believe are consistent with research findings.

Start Where the Student Is

If instruction is to foster understanding, it must meet students, intellectually, where they are. There are at least three ways to miss in this regard. One is to assume that students know what they do not. Another is to overlook misconceptions they have. A third is to ignore what they know.

The problem of imputing knowledge to students that they do not have is brought into focus by a recent analysis by Beck and McKeown (1988), of four widely used fifth-grade American history textbooks that revealed that all the texts "assumed a variety and depth of prior knowledge from target learners that is unrealistic." The texts assumed, for example, that fifth graders already understood such concepts as American identity and representative government and that the significance of such events as the Boston Tea Party, Britain's passage of the "Intolerable Acts," and the convening of the First Continental Congress would be grasped with a minimum of background explanation. Why do writers of texts sometimes produce material that cannot be understood by their readers? One possibility is that they find it easy to assume tacitly that much of what is obvious to them will be obvious to others—even fifth graders—as well. This conjecture is consistent with evidence of a fairly pervasive tendency to assume that one's own knowledge, opinions, and patterns of behavior are more common among other people than they actually are (Kassin, 1981; Mullen et al., 1985; Nickerson, Baddeley, and Freeman, 1987).

The second way to fail to meet students where they are is to ignore the misconceptions they have. Studies of students' understanding of physical phenomena have revealed such commonly held erroneous beliefs as the following:

- That the velocity of a falling object depends on its mass (Champagne, Klopfer, and Anderson, 1980).
- That the natural tendency of an object is to be at rest and that force is required to keep a moving object moving (Clement 1981, 1982; Leboutet-Barrell, 1976; Minstrell, 1984).
- That objects constrained to move along a curved trajectory will continue on a curved path temporarily after the constraint is removed (McCloskey, 1983; McCloskey, Caramazza, and Green, 1980).
- That the downward force on an object at rest is greater than the upward force on that object (Minstrell, 1982).
- That when one moving object passes another moving in the same direction, the two objects must have the same speed at some point (Trowbridge and McDermott, 1980).

- That an object in motion responds to an impulse force (e.g., a kick) by moving off in the direction of the force (diSessa, 1979).
- That one's eyes emit light rays toward objects at which one looks (La Rosa, Mayer, Pratrizi, and Vincentini-Missoni, 1984).

Given that students have preconceived notions about phenomena they study in school, learning with understanding may require the production of conceptual change (Hewson and Hewson, 1984). Investigators have stressed the importance of ensuring that conflicts between old and new ideas are explicated so there is a chance for them to be resolved. Unfortunately, misconceptions sometimes have proven to be exceedingly persistent (Joshua and Dupin, 1987; Leboutet-Barrell, 1976; Rosnick and Clement, 1980). In particular, exposure to standard introductory science courses has not always sufficed to ensure that students acquire accurate conceptions of the phenomena covered (Anderson and Smith, 1987; Champagne, Klopfer, and Anderson, 1980).

A third way to violate the principle of starting where the student is is to fail to relate the relevant knowledge students have to whatever they are expected to learn. This is the complement to the problem of assuming that students know what they do not. Research on mathematics learning has shown, for example, that many children come to school with at least implicit understanding of certain mathematical principles that they are able to apply in practical situations—e.g., commutativity of addition, complementarity of addition and subtraction—but such understanding often is not recognized and built on in the classroom (Resnick, 1987b).

Promote Active Processing and Discovery

Learning—at least learning with understanding—is being viewed more and more as a constructive process in which one imposes structure and meaning on new information, working to integrate that information with what one already knows, and revising one's existing model of reality as a consequence. Researchers have emphasized the active nature of this process (Segal, Chipman, and Glaser, 1985). Wittrock (1974), for example, characterizes learning as a "generative process," and argues that what students learn depends as much on what they construct from what they are taught as on what teachers teach. Motivation and engagement are relevant concepts here. We know that highly motivated learners learn better than poorly motivated ones and we may assume that not much in the way of model construction is likely to occur if one is not intellectually engaged with the task.

Of special interest is the kind of active processing that underlies exploration and discovery. A cardinal rule of learning is that one is more likely to comprehend what one discovers for oneself than what one is taught by someone else (Piaget, 1974). An implication is that an effective way to enhance understanding is to facilitate discovery.

This is not to suggest that there is no room for direction or instruction in education; assuming the acquisition of certain bodies of knowledge as one legitimate educational goal, exploration will require some judicious guidance and discovery will need to be complemented by instruction. While instruction without discovery is likely to be boring and thus ineffectual, exploration without guidance and discovery apart from instruction are likely to yield a very spotty knowledge base. There is a need for balance.

Use Appropriate Representations and Models

Investigators have emphasized the importance to understanding both of representations that teachers use for instructional purposes and those that individuals generate themselves in attempting to solve problems or perform other intellectual tasks. And they are beginning to consider how to ensure that the representations that are used are appropriate to the circumstances (Dupin and Joshua, 1984; Tenney and Gentner, 1984). White and Frederiksen (1987) have argued that the best way to foster understanding of a physical system is to begin with a qualitative causal model that mirrors the system's behavior in its more global respects, and then to elaborate the model as the student's growing understanding permits. Stevens and Collins (1980) have suggested that a way to facilitate understanding of a topic is to teach multiple models explicitly as alternative points of view about a topic.

While representations that are supplied to the learner have considerable pedagogical value, researchers have shown at least as much interest in representations generated by individuals as aids to their own problem solving and other intellectual work. Investigators agree that finding an effective way to represent a problem is not only a help in understanding it, but often the most important step in finding a solution (Bransford and Stein, 1984; Chi, Glaser, and Rees, 1982; Greeno, 1980; Hayes, 1981; Rubenstein, 1975).

The kinds of representations one is likely to produce for a problem depend on how much one knows about the problem area. People untrained with respect to a particular area construct "naive" representations based on entities familiar in everyday life, whereas people trained in the area produce representations composed of entities that have special meanings in the discipline and that help prescribe the kinds of operations that may lead to a solution (Larkin, 1983). Experts typically conceptualize problems in terms of relatively abstract principles, while novices tend to think in terms of concrete surface details (Chi, Feltovich, and Glaser, 1981; Larkin, McDermott, Simon, and Simon, 1980). Unlike novices, experts also tend to attempt to find a qualitative representation before producing a quantitative one, even when working on a problem that requires a quantitative solution (deKleer, 1985; Larkin, 1979; Lesgold, 1984).

An analogy is a particular kind of representation whose explanatory utility for teaching purposes, and especially for dealing with misconceptions, is widely recognized (Joshua and Dupin, 1987; Tenney and Gentner, 1984). A caveat with respect to the use of analogies is that their limitations should be made clear. A hydraulic system, for example, is a useful analogue to an electrical system for some purposes but is misleading for others.

Use Simulations

There are at least two ways to attempt to understand a natural process. One is to observe it as it occurs in nature; the other is to try to simulate it with artifacts. The effectiveness of careful observation has been appreciated for a long time; the usefulness of the second approach has become recognized more recently, but people who use it have little question of its power. As proponents are fond of pointing out, in spite of centuries of observing birds, relatively little was learned about the aerodynamics of flight until successful efforts were made to build machines that could fly.

One result of efforts to give computers the ability to do some of the intelligent things that humans can do has been a better understanding of how humans do these things. Not infrequently, the better understanding has meant a keener appreciation of the complexity of some types of behavior. This has been true, for example, of the considerable efforts to provide computers with the ability to understand speech and natural language; attempts to give machines this ability have forced investigators to address problems that might never be recognized as problems if one were content to observe the process of language acquisition as it occurs in a child.

A caveat is also in order here. A simulation of a process that occurs in nature is a demonstration of one way in which it could occur, but it is in no sense proof either that that is the only way it could happen or that it is the way it does occur. This is an important point. Simulation of a natural process can facilitate the understanding of that process, but, as in the case of analogies, simulations can be pressed too far. One must be careful in using them to make clear what aspects of a process are believed to be reflected faithfully in a simulation and what aspects are not.

Provide a Supportive Environment

If one accepts the idea that active processing and discovery are important contributors to understanding, one must also recognize the importance of providing students with an atmosphere that encourages them to think for themselves and supports their efforts to do so. This means providing an environment that is rich in information resources and aids to exploration and discovery, as well as maintaining an atmosphere in which ideas can be expressed freely and without fear of ridicule.

Understanding sometimes requires more effort than some students are willing to make. A major challenge facing the teacher is that of motivating students to put out the required effort. We know that motivation is easily stifled. Effort that goes unrewarded is not likely to be repeated many times. It is important, therefore, that efforts to understand be reinforced. The teacher who would motivate a student to sustain the effort required to understand difficult material must find a way to turn the "failures" into useful learning experiences, and to demonstrate by both attitude and action that not only does effort pay off but that without it one's ability to understand complex concepts is likely to be limited.

The importance of an atmosphere in which students can express ideas without fear of "showing one's ignorance" has been stressed by Hutchinson (1980), who provided a remedial education course for military veterans returning to school. The course drew methods and materials from Whimbey and Lochhead (1979) and from the Instrumental Enrichment Program of Feuerstein, Rand, Hoffman, and Miller (1980). In reporting his results, Hutchinson stressed the importance of recognizing the affective as well as the cognitive demands placed on students by learning tasks. He noted in particular that students with a history of academic failure may feel threatened by situations in which their academic inadequacies are exposed to others. The problem that any student faces in this situation is that of maintaining an acceptable self-image, and the strategies that are adopted to accomplish this end can be counterproductive with respect to educational goals.

Using Technology to Help Foster Understanding

I have suggested that, as a consequence of the many technological artifacts that surround us, people today may witness more phenomena from day to day that they do not understand than did their predecessors of several centuries ago. Whether this is true or not, there can be no doubt that technology is responsible for the existence of many devices and processes that we encounter frequently in our daily lives that few of us understand well if at all. So, regarding the need to find more effective ways to teach for understanding, technology and its products are a significant part of the problem. But might they also be part of the solution? Can technology be useful in helping to foster understanding—of itself and its products, of natural phenomena and the laws that govern them, and of whatever else we wish to understand?

One does not solve serious educational problems simply by moving more and more technology into the classroom; technology can be used as unproductively as anything else. I believe, however, that technology provides some opportunities for developing new approaches to teaching that are informed by what is being discovered about how learning with understanding comes about. I will comment briefly on what I see as a few of the ways in which technology can be employed to support each of the principles previously mentioned.

Dealing with Misconceptions

One of the more exciting directions that recent attempts to apply technology to education have taken involves the development of explorable microworlds—software systems, usually graphically oriented, that are used to simulate how specific aspects of the world work. Microworlds have been built to facilitate the study of mechanics (diSessa, 1982), electricity (Bork, 1985; Brown, Burton, and deKleer, 1981), electronics (Lesgold, Lajoie, Bunzo, and Eggan, 1992), economics (Shute, Glaser, and Rahgavan, 1989), and relativity (Horwitz and Barow, in press), among other topics.

Microworlds can be made to behave in accordance with laws that are consistent with common misconceptions as well as with laws that represent current scientific views. One can define a microworld, for example, in which the rate of acceleration of a free-falling body in a vacuum is proportional to its mass, or one in which continuing motion is dependent on continuing application of force, or one in which objects constrained to move along a curved trajectory continue to do so for some time after the constraint is removed. The point of using microworlds that behave in accordance with specific misconceptions would be to make explicit the difference between that behavior and the behavior of the same systems when governed by laws that are consistent with what is currently known. The objective would be not only to identify misconceptions as misconceptions, but to help one understand how they differ from valid principles.

Microworlds can also be used to address misconceptions by providing vehicles for observing behavior under conditions constrained to highlight the principle(s) of interest. The point is illustrated by White's (1984) use of diSessa's (1979) microworld to teach Newtonian mechanics. White wished to address the common belief that objects always move in the direction of the most recently applied force (diSessa, 1979). This misconception is revealed in students' failure to take into account the speed of an object in motion when trying to predict how the application of an impulse force would alter its trajectory. White constrained the microworld developed by diSessa by permitting the application of force only at 0, 90, 180, or 270 degrees relative to the object's trajectory. This was to preclude application of force at sufficiently small angles to the direction of movement of the object that the resulting new direction could be mistakenly interpreted as the same as the direction of the force. The intent was to provide the kind of feedback that would make clear to the student the untenability of the "same-direction-as-last-force" misconception. The use of microworlds for instructional purposes permits one to begin with highly simplified situations and complicate them progressively as increases in the student's understanding warrant their complication.

Promoting Active Processing and Discovery

Investigators have noted the strong attraction that computers and their use seem to have for young people (Feurzeig, 1988; Papert, 1980; Turkle, 1984), especially use that involves controlling devices, such as a robot turtle, or making things happen on a visual display. Certainly, there can be little doubt of the holding power of many computer-based games. This attraction is sufficiently strong to have caused some observers to worry about the compulsive user behavior that it sometimes yields (Roszak, 1987; Weizenbaum, 1967). While I do not wish to claim that all computer-based systems that are capable of keeping an individual's attention focused on a particular activity have educational merit, I do see significant educational potential in the fascination that many students have for these systems; the trick will be to design environments that can exploit that fascination for educational ends.

Especially attractive possibilities are environments—such as the microworlds mentioned above—that can facilitate exploration and discovery. Consider a program that permits a user to define, say, any polynomial function, to display the function over a specified range of the independent variable, and then, with a simple menu or command language, to select any of the various operations, or combinations thereof, that one might want to perform on a polynomial (e.g., multiplication by a constant, differentiation, integration, addition or deletion of real roots). By exploring with such a tool, one can discover much about polynomial functions that is difficult to acquire from reading a book. Or consider a program that permits one to design a planetary system by positioning points on a visual display, specifying their masses and initial velocities, and setting the whole system in motion in accordance with one's choice for a law of mutual attraction (e.g., an inverse square law, an inverse cube law, a linear law). Again there is the possibility for discovery by experimentation (e.g., conditions under which a planetary system is stable). Such computer programs have existed for several years, but only recently have the economics of computing begun to make their widespread use feasible. Among the most exciting possibilities associated with the use of interactive microworlds in education is that of the occurrence of bona-fide discoveries, unanticipated by either teacher or microworld builder (Horwitz, 1988; Horwitz and Eisenberg, 1992).

Dynamic and Interactive Representations

The computer makes feasible the development of representations that are dynamic and interactive to a degree not practical, if possible, before. Current technology provides the means for developing systems that can show the user on demand a dynamic visual representation of an unfolding process (e.g., cell mitosis, supernova explosion, restructuring of the atomic bonds in a chemical reaction) at various levels of detail and on different time scales. Such facilities can be interactive in the sense of permitting the user to specify the level of detail, time scale, and other parameters of the representation and thereby observe the same process from a variety of vantage points. Gott (1988–89) describes in some detail several systems that use interactive graphics to instructional advantage.

Systems are beginning to appear that provide an assortment of representational resources that facilitate and enrich the process of reading for either information or pleasure. Consider being able, while reading Tolstoy's *War and Peace,* to call up kinship diagrams, maps, historical chronologies, drawings of uniforms and attire of the day, pictures of weaponry, dynamic diagrams of changing battle formations, drawings or schematics of buildings or rooms, and so on. "Hypertext" systems with such capabilities are beginning to be used in educational settings (Landow, 1988).

Simulation

Computers are general-purpose machines and therefore very well suited to simulation. The use of microworlds, which are simulations, and simulated laboratories for teaching purposes is being actively explored by several investigators and has been noted in preceding paragraphs. Extensive information on many of these efforts can be found in several collections of project reports, including Lajoie and Derry (1993), Larkin and Chabay (1992), and Psotka, Massey, and Mutter (1988).

What has not yet received much attention from researchers is the possibility of having students develop simulations themselves as a way of fostering a greater understanding of the processes they attempt to simulate. Building a microworld is undoubtedly a more difficult task than manipulating one built by someone else; but it is only difficult, not impossible, and the work that goes into the successful building of a microworld is likely to deepen one's understanding of whatever the microworld is intended to simulate. One can build simulations with the various general-purpose programming languages that exist, but to do so requires facility with those languages and some high-level programming skills. For student-developed simulations to be practical for educational purposes, it will probably be necessary to develop tools that are designed to facilitate the building of simulations by people without such language facility and programming experience.

Supportive Environments

Technology has the potential of providing students access to a wide variety of information resources and information-handling tools. Electronic access via computer networks to libraries, museums, databanks, and information services of various sorts is technically feasible today and will become a practical reality in the future. This should make it much easier for students to access information when they need it and to pursue questions of interest when they arise. These ideas are beginning to be explored experimentally (Ruopp, Gal, Drayton, and Pfister, 1993; Tinker and Kapisovsky, 1992).

Technology has the potential of helping to provide an environment that is supportive in the sense of being nonthreatening as well. To be sure, technology can be intimidating, but it can also, in some cases, be comfortingly impersonal. To the extent that learning is sometimes inhibited by reluctance on the part of the learner to seek information or reveal ignorance or tentative ideas for fear of ridicule or rebuff, technology may provide a nonthreatening alternative medium of instruction.

Concluding Comments

Understanding should be an aim of education. Probably nobody disagrees with that. What it means to understand is not easy to say. For the most part, researchers seem to have taken the concept as an intuitively meaningful one and have not attempted explicit definitions. Perhaps it is just as well; definitions can convey a sense of clarity and conceptual precision that may not be justified. One gets a sense of what writers consider to be involved in understanding, however, by the frequent occurrence of certain themes in discussions of understanding or the need to teach for it. These include the importance of relating new ideas to those that already exist in the learner's mind, the need for knowledge to be structured in a meaningful way, the characterization of the knowledge that supports understanding as a rich conceptual network, usefulness of knowledge as an aspect of understanding, and the idea that understanding is less a state of mind that occurs than the result of an act of meaning construction or integrative sense-making (Bransford and Franks, 1976; Reif, 1985; Resnick, 1987a; Smith, 1975). Integrative in this context carries the notion not only of relating what one is learning to what one already knows but also of making whatever adjustments of old ideas are necessary to accommodate the new knowledge. The goal is to come up with a model of whatever it is one is trying to understand that is more adequate, functionally, than the model with which one began.

An overarching idea that emerges from these discussions is the idea of the importance of connections: connections between old concepts and new ones, connections among the concepts that define a field of inquiry, connections between what is being studied in the classroom and what one has learned without formal instruction in everyday life, connections between what one is learning in school and the problems one is likely to face in the workplace. The implied model of learning is often contrasted with the learning of disconnected facts, which may permit one to answer specific questions on scholastic exams, but does little to deepen one's understanding of a subject or increase its utility. We know that it is possible to learn related principles in isolation and remain oblivious to the fact that they are indeed related, or to learn procedures that would be useful in various contexts but fail to make the connection between those procedures and the conditions for applying them. Such isolated knowledge is of dubious value; it is a bit like a neurosurgeon who is very good at brain surgery but poor at recognizing the conditions under which it should be done.

The practical question for educational purposes is the question of how to promote understanding effectively in the classroom. Results of research provide the basis for at least some tentative answers to this question. I have indicated what I believe a few of these tentative answers to be. I have suggested too that while technology amplifies the problem of understanding, in a way, by increasing the number of entities people come in daily contact with that they do not understand, it also opens up new possibilities for the development of instructional approaches through which understanding might be enhanced. However, the potential that technology has to enhance teaching for understanding is still just potential, for the most part; while systems exist that give us glimpses of what is possible, on the whole technology has so far had little impact on the day-to-day business of education. Moreover, it is probably good for us—especially those of us who are enthusiasts for using technology in education—to remind ourselves that the potential is also there for applying technology in ways that do little to enhance understanding or that even hinder learning. Only if technology is applied in ways that are consistent with principles that promote teaching for understanding will it have the desired beneficial effect. Some of these principles are becoming reasonably clear as a result of research; undoubtedly others remain to be discovered. Looking forward, there is the possibility of an effective synergism here, with further research on understanding and continuing efforts to use technology in education informing and reinforcing each other, yielding a better understanding of what it means to understand and of how to teach in such a way that understanding is the result.

References

Anderson, C. W., and E. L. Smith. 1987. Teaching science. In *Educators' handbook: A research perspective,* edited by V. Richardson-Koehler. New York: Longman.

Beck, I. L., and M. McKeown. 1988. Toward meaningful accounts in history texts for young learners. *Educational Researcher* 17: 31–39.

Bork, A. 1985. *Personal computers for education.* New York: Harper & Row.

Bransford, J. D., and J. J. Franks. 1976. Toward a framework for understanding learning. In *The psychology of learning and motivation: Advances in research and theory,* edited by G. H. Bower. Vol. 10. New York: Academic Press.

Bransford, J. D., and B. S. Stein. 1984. *The IDEAL problem solver.* New York: Freeman.

Brown, J. S., R. R. Burton, and J. deKleer. 1981. Pedagogical, natural language and knowledge-engineering techniques in SOPHIE I, II, and III. In *Intelligent tutoring systems,* edited by D. Sleeman and J. S. Brown, pp. 227–80. London: Academic Press.

Champagne, A. B., L. E. Klopfer, and J. H. Anderson. 1980. Factors influencing the learning of classical mechanics. *American Journal of Physics* 48: 1074–79.

Chi, M. T. H., P. J. Feltovich, and R. Glaser. 1981. Categorization and representation of physics problems by experts and novices. *Cognitive Science* 5: 121–52.

Chi, M. T. H., R. Glaser, and E. Rees. 1982. Expertise in problem solving. In *Advances in the psychology of human intelligence*, edited by R. Stemberg. Vol. 1. Hillsdale, NJ: Erlbaum.

Clement, J. 1981. Students' preconceptions in physics and Galileo's discussion of falling bodies. *Problem Solving* 3: 3–5.

———. 1982. Students' preconceptions in introductory mechanics. *American Journal of Physics* 50: 66–71.

deKleer, J. 1985. How circuits work. In *Qualitative reasoning about physical systems*, edited by D. G. Bobrow, pp. 205–80. Cambridge, MA: MIT Press.

diSessa, A. A. 1979. Dynamics: learning physics with a dynaturle. In *Final report of the Brookline Logo project. Part II: project summary and data analysis*, by S. Papert, D. Watt, A. diSessa, and S. Weir. Memo 545, pp. 6.1–6.20. Cambridge, MA: MIT, AI Laboratory.

———. 1982. Unlearning Aristotelian physics: A study of knowledge based learning. *Cognitive Science* 6: 37–75.

Dupin, J. J., and S. Joshua. 1984. Teaching electricity: Interactive evolution of representations, models, and experiments in a class situation. In *Aspects of understanding electricity*, edited by R. Duit, W. Jung, and C. V. Rhoneck, pp. 331–42. Kiel, West Germany: Institute fur die Padogogik der Naturwissenshaften.

Feuerstein, R., Y. Rand, M. Hoffman, and R. Miller. 1980. *Instrumental enrichment: An intervention program for cognitive modifiability*. Baltimore: University Park Press.

Feurzeig, W. 1988. Apprentice tools: Students as practitioners. In *Technology in education: Looking toward 2020*, edited by R. S. Nickerson and P. P. Zodhiates. Hillsdale, NJ: Erlbaum.

Gott, S. P. 1988–89. Apprenticeship instruction for real-world tasks: The coordination of procedures, mental models, and strategies. *Review of research in education*. Edited by E. Z. Rothkopf. Washington, DC: American Educational Research Association.

Greeno, J. G. 1980. Trends in the theory of knowledge for problem solving. In *Problem solving and education: Issues in teaching and research*, edited by D. T. Tuma and F. Reif. Hillsdale, NJ: Erlbaum.

Hayes, J. R. 1981. *The complete problem solver*. Philadelphia: Franklin Institute Press.

Hewson, P. W., and M. G. Hewson. 1984. The role of conceptual conflict in conceptual change and the design of science instruction. *Instructional Science* 13:1–13.

Horwitz, P. 1988. Interactive simulations and their implications for science teaching. *AETS 1988 Yearbook*.

Horwitz, P., and W. Barowy. In press. Designing and using open-ended software to promote conceptual change. *Journal of Science Education and Technology*.

Horwitz, P., and M. Eisenberg. 1992. MultiMap: An interactive tool for mathematics experimentation. *Interactive Learning Environments* 2: 141–179.

Hutchinson, R. T. 1980. *Teaching problem solving to developmental adults: A pilot project*. Paper presented at the NE-LRDC Conference on Thinking and Learning Skills, October, University of Pittsburgh.

Joshua, S., and J. J. Dupin. 1987. Taking into account student conceptions in instructional strategy: An example in physics. *Cognition and Instruction* 4(2): 117–35.

Kassin, S. M. 1981. Distortions in estimating consensus from sequential events. *Personality and Social Psychology Bulletin* 7:542–46.

Lajoie, S. P., and S. J. Derry, Editors. 1993. *Computers as cognitive tools*. Hillsdale, NJ: Erlbaum.

Landow, G. P. 1988. *Hypertext in literary education, criticism, and scholarship*. Technical Report. Providence, RI: Institute for Research in Information and Scholarship, Brown University.

Larkin, J. H. 1979. Information processing models and science instruction. In *Cognitive process instruction: Research on teaching thinking skills*, edited by J. Lochhead and J. Clement. Philadelphia: Franklin Institute Press.

———. 1983. The role of problem representation in physics. In *Mental models*, edited by D. Gentner and A.S. Stevens. Hillsdale, NJ: Erlbaum.

———, and R. W. Chabay, Editors. 1992. *Computer-assisted instruction and intelligent tutoring systems: Shared goals and complementary approahces*. Hillsdale, NJ: Erlbaum.

———, J. McDermott, D.P. Simon, and H.A. Simon. 1980. Expert and novice performance in solving physics problems. *Science* 208: 1335–42.

LaRosa, C., M. Mayer, P. Pratrizi, and M. Vincentini-Missoni. 1984. Common sense knowledge in optics: Preliminary results of an investigation into the properties of light. *European Journal of Science Education* 6:387–97.

Leboutet-Barrell, L. 1976. Concepts of mechanics in young people. *Physics Education* 11:462–66.

Lesgold, A. M. 1984. Acquiring expertise. In *Tutorials in learning and memory*, edited by J. R. Anderson and S. M. Kosslyn, pp. 31–60. San Francisco, CA: Freeman.

Lesgold, A., S. Lajoie, M. Bunzo, and G. Eggan. 1992. SHERLOCK: A coached practice environment for an electronics troubleshooting job. In *Computer-assisted instruction and intelligent tutoring systems: Shared goals and complementary approahces*. Edited by J. H. Larkin and R. W. Chabay. Hillsdale, NJ: Erlbaum.

McCloskey, M. 1983. Intuitive physics. *Scientific American* 248 (4): 122–30.

———, A. Caramazza, and B. Green. 1980. Curvilinear motion in the absence of external forces: Naive beliefs about the motion of objects. *Science* 210:1139–41.

Minstrell, J. 1982. Explaining the 'at rest' condition of an object. *Physics Teacher*, 10–14.

———. 1984. Teaching for the understanding of ideas: Forces on moving objects. In *Observing science classrooms: Perspectives from research and practice*, edited by C. W. Anderson. 1984 Yearbook of the Association for the Education of Teachers in Science. Columbus, OH.

Mullen, B., J. L. Atkins, D. S. Champion, C. Edward, D. Hardy, J. E. Story, and M. Verderklok. 1985. The false consensus effect: A meta-analysis of 115 hypothesis tests. *Journal of Experimental Social Psvchology* 21:262–83.

Nickerson, R. S. 1985. Understanding understanding. *American Journal of Education* 93 (2):201–39.

———, A. Baddeley, and B. Freeman. 1987. Are people's estimates of what other people know influenced by what they themselves know? *Acta Psychologica* 64:245–59.

Papert, S. 1980. *Mindstorms*. New York: Basic Books.

Piaget, J. 1974. *To understand is to invent*. New York: The Viking Press.

Psotka, J., L. D. Massey, and S. A. Mutter, Editors. 1988. *Intelligent tutoring systems: Lessons learned*. Hillsdale, NJ: Erlbaum.

Reif, F. 1985. Acquiring an effective understanding of scientific concepts. In *Cognitive structures and conceptual change*, edited by L.H.T. West and A. L. Pines. New York: Academic Press.

Resnick, L. B. 1987a. *Education and learning to think*. Washington, DC: National Academy Press.

———. 1987b. The development of mathematical intuition. In *Minnesota symposium on child psychology*, edited by M. Permutter. Vol. 19, 159–94. Hillsdale, NJ: Erlbaum.

Rosnick, P., and J. Clement. 1980. Learning without understanding: The effect of tutoring strategies on algebra misconceptions. *The Journal of Mathematical Behavior* 3: 3–27.

Roszak, T. 1987. *Cult of information: The folklore of computers and the true art of thinking*. New York: Pantheon Publishing.

Rubenstein, M. F. 1975. *Patterns of problem solving*. Englewood Cliffs, NJ: Prentice-Hall.

Ruopp, R., S. Gal, B. Drayton, and M. Pfister, Editors. 1993. *LabNet: Toward a community of practice*. Hillsdale, NJ: Erlbaum.

Segal, J. W., S. F. Chipman, and R. Glaser, Editors. 1985. *Thinking and learning skills: Vol 1. Relating instruction to research*. Hillsdale, NJ: Erlbaum.

Shute, V., R. Glaser, and K. Raghavan. 1989. Inference and discovery in an exploration laboratory. In *Learning and individual differences*, edited by P. Ackerman, R. Sternberg, and R. Glaser. San Francisco: Freeman.

Smith, F. 1975. *Comprehension and learning: A conceptual framework for teachers*. New York: Holt, Rinehart and Winston.

Stevens, A. L., and A. Collins. 1980. Multiple conceptual models of a complex system. In *Aptitude, learning, and instruction,* edited by R. E. Snow, P. A. Federico, and W. E. Montague. Vol. 2. Hillsdale, NJ: Erlbaum.

Tenney, Y., and D. Gentner. 1984. What makes water analogies accessible: Experiments on the water-flow analogy for electricity. In *Aspects of understanding electricity*, edited by R. Duit, W. Jung, and C. V. Rhoneck, pp. 311–18. Kiel, West Germany: Institute fur die Padogogik der Naturwissenshaften.

Tinker, R. F., and P. M. Kapisovsky, Editors. 1992. *Prospects for educational telecomputing: Selected readings*. Cambridge, MA: TERC.

Trowbridge, D. E., and L. C. McDermott. 1980. Investigation of student understanding of the concept of velocity in one dimension. *American Journal of Physics* 48 (12): 1020–28.

Turkle, S. 1984. *The second self: Computers and the human spirit*. New York: Simon and Schuster.

Weizenbaum, J. 1967. Contextual understanding by computers. *Communications of the ACM* 10 (8): 474–80.

Whimbey, A., and J. Lochhead. 1979. *Problem solving and comprehension: A short course in analytic reasoning.* Philadelphia: Franklin Institute Press.

White, B. Y. 1984. Designing computer games to help physics students understand Newton's laws of motion. *Cognition and Instruction* 1:1–4.

White, B. Y., and J.R. Frederiksen. 1987. Qualitative models and intelligent learning environments. In *AI and education.* Edited by R. Lawler and M. Yazdani. Norwood, NJ: Ablex.

Wittrock, M. C. 1974. Learning as a generative process. *Educational Psychologist* 11:87–95.

2

Use of History of Science to Understand and Remedy Students' Misconceptions About Heat and Temperature

MARIANNE WISER

Science Learning as Theory Change

Science students come to the classroom with numerous mlsconceptions, that is, interpretations of physical phenomena, that differ, often radically, from those accepted by the scientific community. Misconceptions make it difficult for students to learn the accepted view ("textbook theory") and are often left unchanged by classroom instruction. The need to target instruction to misconceptions or, more generally, to take the knowledge students bring to the classroom into account is now well established (Driver and Erikson, 1983; Driver and Oldham, 1986) and various strategies have been proposed to that effect. The use of bridging analogies to teach mechanics has yielded encouraging results (Clement, 1987; Minstrell, 1989), as has introducing students to a series of microworlds in which the laws of dynamics become increasingly complex (White, 1993).

Our own classroom interventions are based on the assumption that, at least in some scientific domains, students' misconceptions are part of naive theories, that is, systems of interpretation that differ from the scientifically accepted ones but which, like them, have internal and external coherence, so that misconceptions should be viewed as alternative, rather than erroneous, beliefs about physical phenomena. To replace students' misconceptions with the textbook theory amounts to effecting a theory change in students because the perspective offered by a naive theory is generally so different from the textbook theory's that the information presented in class cannot be assimilated without major restructuring.

Naive Theories and History of Science

This view of science learning in general and misconceptions in particular is very much inspired by historians of science, especially by Kuhn (1964, 1977) and Toulmin (1963), who have argued that if statements by scientists of the past often appear wrong and irrational, it is because they are taken in isolation and interpreted from the point of view of modern science; but, when they are placed in the context of the theory and world view within which they were developed, they usually become coherent and plausible. Among the examples both Kuhn and Toulmin chose to illustrate their point is the following Aristotelean principle: "The amount a body can be displaced by a given effort will vary in inverse proportion to the size of the body to be moved, and also, that a given body can be displaced in a set time through a distance directly proportional to the effort available" (Toulmin, 1963). Interpreted in Newtonian terms, this principle becomes $F = W * V$ (where F is force, W weight, and V velocity) and appears to violate directly Newton's first and second laws. But terms such as "velocity" and "weight" had a very different meaning in Aristotle's physics, partly because its ontologically primary elements were qualities, not material bodies, and the questions to be answered were about changes in quality, so that a Newtonian interpretation of Aristotle's statement is misleading and unjustified.

Toulmin also explains that the paradigm at the heart of Aristotle's analysis was fundamentally different from Newton's; Aristotle focused on motions against appreciable resistance, his prototypical motion being that of a cart drawn by a horse: Motion depended on the balance between an external agent (the horse) and the resistance (friction exerted by the road), and the rate at which an object (the cart) moved depended on its weight. For Toulmin, a paradigm exemplifies what is taken for granted ("ideal of natural order") and what is in need of explanation (by means of laws); Aristotle and Newton had different ideals of natural order. Consider, for example, an object coming to a stop on a rough horizontal surface. In Aristotle's mechanics, objects naturally come to a stop when not acted on by an agent, so the phenomenon is "natural"; why objects keep moving is what needs explaining. Newton's mechanics, on the other hand, takes for granted that a moving object will keep moving if no force is exerted on it, so that one needs to find the reason for the object stopping. Within the domain of motions against appreciable resistance that Aristotle thought typical and worth studying, his principle still has its place in twentieth-century physics (Stokes's law).

Another of Kuhn's tenets about historical development is extremely useful in understanding the difference in concepts from one theory to another: Not only are concepts different in different theories, they are different *because* they belong to different theories. Concepts are not definitions, they are "legislative," that is, they act in part as laws of nature because they embody hypotheses about the characteristics of phenomena to which they apply, as well as fundamental relations with other concepts within and outside the theory; as a result, they constrain the regularities that can be established on the basis of observations. Thus, in order to understand scientific concepts, it is not enough to record what is said about them; one has to establish the different contexts in which they are used, the phenomena to which they apply, and their relations to other beliefs. In Kuhn's words (1977): "those concepts were not intended for application to any possible world, but only to the world as the scientist saw it. Their use is one index of his commitment to a larger body of law and theory. . . . That is why . . . their meaning and their criteria for use have so often and so drastically changed in the course of scientific development."

This view is particularly informative in the case of undifferentiated concepts, such as the concept of speed in Aristotelean mechanics. Aristotle's concept of speed is undifferentiated with respect to the modern variables instantaneous and average speeds but, says Kuhn, it is in no way a confused or illogical concept, as paradoxical as it may appear at first to a modern physicist. It is contradictory only in the sense that there are situations in which its two components lead to incompatible judgments. Such situations are rare in nature, however, and there is evidence that Aristotle kept them at the periphery of his consciousness. His concept of speed both fitted and constrained the kinds of motion he thought worth studying (which a modern scientist would describe as uniformly accelerated).

Assuming similar considerations apply to the study of students' misconceptions, the researcher's tasks are to map out the students' theory in a given domain (rather than individual beliefs), to understand how it prevents learning the textbook theory, and to design teaching interventions that can overcome those obstacles. In my research I have focused on thermal physics, an important but difficult topic. Students' fundamental misconception in thermal physics is a lack of differentiation between heat and temperature (Erikson, 1979, 1980; Rosenquist, Popp, & McDermott, 1982a, 1982b; Strauss, Stavy, & Orpaz, 1976). Most students come to the classroom believing that heat and temperature are basically the same, typically distinguishing them only in the sense that heat is hotness and temperature tells you how hot the heat is, and most leave the classroom holding those same beliefs. Because the distinction between heat and temperature underlies most of the concepts, laws, and principles of basic thermal physics (e.g., heat measurement, freezing points, specific and latent heat, law of mixtures, and so on), it is important that students' difficulties be addressed directly at this basic level.

I will argue that students' undifferentiated concept of heat is indeed part of a naive theory, differing from the textbook theory in some of the same ways as two theories differ in the history of science. That is, students have a structured network in which thermal concepts, paradigms (in Toulmin's sense), explanatory schemata, and ontological beliefs differ from those involved in the textbook theory but constrain each other as they do in more sophisticated theories. I will then document some of the obstacles that the naive theory presents to the assimilation of the textbook theory and especially to the differentiation of heat and temperature. Finally, I will present computer conceptual models designed to foster the differentiation by facilitating the overall switch from naive to textbook theory.

A Parallel with History: Students' Conceptualization of Thermal Phenomena and Seventeenth-Century Thermal Physics

Up to now I have shown how an approach borrowed from history and philosophy of science could help make sense of students' misconceptions and guide us toward teaching interventions that are more effective than the traditional ones. History of science can be a guide in another respect: It offers a model for the students' naive theory about heat and temperature.

Most research about heat and temperature has presented piecemeal data, often focusing on mistakes students make during problem solving or on isolated misconceptions (Erikson, 1979, 1980; Rosenquist et al., 1982a, 1982b; Strauss et al., 1976). Those mistakes and misconceptions are generally interpreted from the teacher's point of view, that is, in textbook theory terms. This leads to a confusing state of affairs, with some researchers claiming that students lack a concept of heat, others that they lack a concept of temperature, and still others that they confuse the two. As explained before, I believe that the origin of students' errors is not confused textbook notions but rather alternative conceptions that have internal coherence and fit the phenomena they are meant to explain. But that coherence is not apparent when the problems posed to the students are formulated and their answers interpreted from the expert's rather than student's point of view.

As researchers, we are embedded in our own paradigms and it is often difficult for us to probe students' conceptualizations with an open mind, to ask questions that are not rooted in the textbook theory and to allow students to express their beliefs in their own terms, using their own concepts. My studies of students' ideas about heat and temperature were guided by a historical model—the thermal theory held by the Experimenters (who were members of the Accademia del Cimento in Florence) at the beginning of the seventeenth century. The Experimenters did not differentiate between heat and temperature; they had a single concept—*heat*—with some elements of modern concepts of both heat and temperature but otherwise embedded in a very different theory, the Source-Recipient model (Wiser and Carey, 1983). In agreement with Kuhn's analysis of Aristotle's concept of speed, the Experimenters' concept of heat does not appear confused or illogical; it created some paradoxes for the Experimenters, just as the undifferentiated speed concept had done for Aristotle, but the contradictions were clearly between the concept and the world, not within the concept, and they were very rare.

Given that similarities between modern students' naive conceptions and early scientific ideas had been found in other scientific areas such as mechanics (Clement, 1983; diSessa, 1983; McCloskey, 1983), I explored the possibility that the similarity between modern students' views about heat and temperature and those of the Experimenters might go beyond sharing an undifferentiated concept of heat (Wiser, 1987). The Source-Recipient model suggested a whole range of demonstrations and questions to probe students' thermal knowledge in a way not contaminated by the modern expert's view. The model also guided protocol analysis by providing hypotheses about the concepts, principles, paradigms, and ontological knowledge implicit in students' answers. Strong structural and content similarities were found between the students' and the Experimenters' theory (e.g., ideas about the relation between heat and temperature and about thermal equilibrium), but also differences (e.g., students have ideas about the effect of heat on molecules whereas the Experimenters did not). More relevant to the present topic is that the kind of questions and problems borrowed and derived from the Source-Recipient model were fertile ones in that they generated a lot of information about students' thinking. This is probably because the Experimenters, being the first scientists to investigate thermal phenomena systematically, had concerns and interpretations that were still very close to a layperson's, and thus to modern students'. The students' theory presented below was inferred from the results of several studies using clinical interviews based on the Source-Recipient model (Wiser, 1986, 1987).

Students' Naive Theory About Thermal Phenomena

Students think of heat basically as an intensive quality that is measured with a thermometer: the stronger the heat, the higher the level in the thermometer. Many think of heat as having force and actually pushing the thermometer up. Cold is an entity separate from and opposite to heat. Like heat, it has force and is measured with a thermometer. Thus, temperature (the thermometer reading) is seen either as the synonym of heat, or as a superordinate term for both heat and cold, or as the measure of heat and cold. Students conceive of thermal phenomena as produced by sources of heat (or cold) acting on passive recipients ("passive" in the sense that the state of the recipient has no influence on the heat transfer). Hot sources emit heat spontaneously: they apply more or less intense heat depending on their temperature. (For example, the heat emitted by a stove burner on a high setting is hotter than the heat emitted by a burner on a low setting.) The students have *no concept of amount of heat* in the extensive sense. They rarely use the words, and, when they do, it is in the sense of heat intensity. They account for extensivity through a causal scheme: Larger sources have more effect not because they give off more heat but because they have more contact area with the recipient, thereby applying their heat to a larger portion of the recipient. A source will also have more effect the longer it stays in contact with the recipient. For example, a large amount of boiling water has the same heat as a small amount but will melt more snow because it covers more of the snow and/or because it stays hot longer. Such causal schemata are at the center of students' explanations whereas they are not part of modern physics (deKleer and Brown, 1985).

The naive and textbook theories differ in other ways as well. Some concepts are part only of the textbook theory and not of the naive theory and vice versa. For example, *specific* and *latent heat* are not part of the naive theory; conversely, *cold* has the status of a variable in the naive theory but not in the textbook theory. Moreover, the principles shared by the two theories have different status. Consider, for example, thermal equilibrium. In the textbook theory, thermal equilibrium states the conditions under which heat is exchanged (two objects exchange heat until their temperature is the same); as such it is a principle central to the theory. Since it is based on a concept of heat distinct from temperature, it is not available in the naive theory. But the naive theory has no need for such a principle because heat exchanges do not have to be explained: Sources emit heat spontaneously; it is in their nature to make other objects warm. Some students have their own version of thermal equilibrium, based on a single concept: They know that, eventually, an object placed in contact with a source will reach the temperature of the source but that belief is not central to the naive theory—it is seen a consequence of the fact that a heat source communicates heat of a certain degree to the recipient and cannot make it hotter than itself, not as expressing the conditions for heat exchange. Finally, the domains of the two theories do not coincide: for example, the relation between heat and work is not in the domain of the naive theory.

Placing the students' concept of heat within the context of their naive theory makes it clear that, although undifferentiated, it is not confused or illogical. It is undifferentiated with respect to the textbook concepts of heat and temperature in the sense that it contains elements from both but it is otherwise a very different concept, embedded in and partially embodying a very different theory. The undifferentiated concept and naive theory are well adapted to the everyday experiences from which they were derived (e.g., keeping a pot of water on a fire makes the water hotter and there is nothing paradoxical about using an undifferentiated concept to interpret such a situation) and they also constrain the phenomena a person holding the naive theory would explore. Phenomena that make the undifferentiated concept paradoxical are not within the domain of the naive theory; they are, for example, laboratory experiments about specific and latent heat in which heat and temperature are measured separately; but there is obviously no reason for someone who thinks that temperature measures heat to try to contrast them. Moreover, I will show that the naive theory can assimilate most of those phenomena without fundamental revisions; one could say that the naive theory is self-preserving.

The traditional classroom approach of telling students that heat and temperature are different ("More heat is provided by ten matches than by one match but their temperature is the same" or "There is more heat in an iceberg than in a cup of hot coffee"), and then teaching thermal physics on the assumption that students are now clear about the two concepts, is far from optimal. To differentiate between heat and temperature and to learn the textbook theory are one and the same thing, and it is an arduous task because it involves theory change. This is because the differentiation involves much more than splitting one concept into two: The different components of the theory (concepts, beliefs, laws, and the types of phenomena to which they apply) provide constraints for each other so that they have to change concurrently. Our own classroom interventions are adapted not only to students' initial lack of differentiation but to their whole naive theory and take into consideration the scope and depth of the reconceptualization students have to undergo.

The Controversy About the Existence of Naive Theories

The claim that students hold theories is a controversial one; it stands at one extreme of a continuum where it is supported, although probably not in its strongest form, by McCloskey's (1983), and Clement's work (1983). The coherence of children's beliefs in a domain and the constraint that different beliefs place on each other are advocated by theorists such as Carey (1985), Brewer (e.g., Chinn and Brewer, 1993), and Welman and Gelman (1992). At the other end of the continuum, one finds positions such as that held by diSessa (1983), who believes that people who are naive in a domain of science have only local, piecemeal, phenomenological intuitions.

The controversy gets at the heart of the issue of knowledge restructuring involved in science learning and is explored in more detail elsewhere (Wiser, 1989; see also Chinn and Brewer, 1993). Several factors must be considered, one of them being one's criterion for holding a theory and another being students' familiarity with a given domain. If one's criterion involves metaconceptual awareness, for example, knowing that theories are built in order to be tested, then students do not hold theories (Carey et al., 1989; Kuhn, Amsel, and O'Loughlin, 1988), but if the issue is the structure of conceptual systems, then I believe that students can be shown to hold theories, at least in familiar domains. Naive knowledge about thermal phenomena exhibits high consistency within and between students: the core ideas are found in almost all students, the beliefs of each student are interconnected, stable, consistent, and constrain each other, and a limited number of explanatory schemata are used to account for both familiar and novel phenomena in predictable ways.

Moreover, the differences between students' and textbook conceptualizations parallel the differences between scientific theories discussed by Kuhn and Toulmin: differences in concepts, in ontology (heat as quality versus heat as mechanical energy), in what needs to be explained (why heat is exchanged is taken for granted in the students' theory), in paradigms (heat front making its way through a resisting medium versus molecular kinetic model), in domains, and in explanations. Finally, the resistance of misconceptions to instruction and the misassimilation by students of instructional material (see below) is more consistent with an organized network of beliefs than with piecemeal knowledge.

Other findings (e.g., Driver and Oldham, 1986) do not support the view that students' knowledge is stable and coherent, but the discrepancy may be due at least in part to differences in methods of investigation and interpretation; I have previously argued that approaching students' beliefs from within the textbook paradigm was likely to produce inconsistent and incoherent data because the conceptual system students use to interpret and solve problems is different from the system researchers used to formulate them. Moreover, the problems and phenomena used to probe students' knowledge may not belong to the domain of the naive theory. If students' concepts, like scientists', are legislative and embody hypotheses about the contexts to which they are to be applied, then using those concepts to account for phenomena outside their domain of application is likely to generate inconsistent answers.

Obstacles to Students' Reconceptualization

According to Kuhn, differentiation takes place in the history of science when scientists become (sufficiently) aware of inconsistencies not within the concept itself but in the concept as applied to the physical world (when the undifferentiated concept fails "to fit the fine structure of the world to which it was expected to apply"). In our initial classroom studies we integrated that notion into our curricula by relying on specific and latent heat phenomena to drive the differentiation (this is an instantiation of exposing students to what science educators call "discrepant events") but found no effect on reconceptualization. One reason may be that, like scientists, students are reluctant to give up familiar ideas, especially for others that lack intuitive appeal (Posner et al., 1982). A second reason may be that, unlike scientists, students do not appreciate the distinction and relation between theory and empirical evidence (Carey et al., 1989) nor the revisability of theories, probably in part because they are not aware of the theories they hold.

A third reason and, I think, a major one, is that many phenomena believed to be discrepant turn out to be easily assimilated into the naive theory so that they provide no incentive for revising beliefs. For example, in a typical specific heat experiment, students are asked to keep a hot coil heater in water and an identical heater in an equal mass of alcohol for the same amount of time. They record a higher temperature rise in the alcohol. Within the teacher's framework this experiment "proves" that temperature does not measure heat since (approximately) the same amount of heat is absorbed by the two liquids; it also demonstrates that water has a higher specific heat than alcohol (more heat is necessary to raise the temperature of water than alcohol). For students, the fact that the same heat was applied to the two liquids does not mean that the same heat was absorbed; in fact, the alcohol's higher temperature means that it absorbed more heat. Students conclude from the experiment that specific heat is related to density, a conclusion that fits well within their framework: less dense substances such as alcohol absorb heat faster than denser substances such as water because they let heat through more easily. They also "learn" that alcohol has a higher specific heat than water (because it absorbs more heat), the exact opposite of what is stated in the textbook. This case illustrates both why misconceptions resist instruction and how they proliferate.

Finally, even if students understood that they have to construct a new interpretive framework and were willing to do so, it is unlikely that they could do so by themselves. Here, the historical analogy breaks down in that students are not able to create a new theory. It should be clear by now that differentiating between heat and temperature involves much more than rejecting a false belief ("I was wrong, temperature does not measure heat."); it involves constructing almost entirely new meanings for those concepts, including developing a sense for the extensivity and mechanical nature of heat and for the molecular mechanisms underlying heat transfer, establishing new principles (such as the relation among heat, mass, and temperature), as well as using a much more quantitative approach to the study of thermal phenomena. Students' beliefs should be challenged but, at the same time, the textbook theory should be made explicit and understandable in spite of the students' initial misconceptions. Students have to be shown, for example, *how* heat and temperature differ and relate, and *how* substances differ in specific heat, not simply *that* they do. They should also be given a *framework* in which to integrate the different components of the theory. Once students understand the new theory and that it is an alternative to theirs, they can be shown that the textbook theory gives a more thorough and unified account of thermal phenomena and, one would hope, be convinced to adopt it.

To meet the goals outlined above, we have developed computer-implemented models, which we call "conceptual" because they represent concepts rather than phenomena. (The term is coined after the "conceptually enhanced models" developed by Snir, Smith, and Grosslight in Chapter 7) for weight and density, which inspired and informed our own work.)

Conceptual Models and Theory Change

Using models to teach thermal physics is not new, of course. Most curricula about heat and temperature include a molecular model but do not exploit it systematically to dispel misconceptions or to give students a structured framework into which they can integrate new information. The core notion of the model is that molecular velocity and distance between molecules increase with temperature. Using the distinction drawn by Snir et al. (in Chapter 7), one can say that the model presents the behavior of *objects* (here, molecules) instead of representing *concepts*. More specifically, it does not help students construct the meaning of the textbook concepts because it does not show what temperature and heat are or how they are related. Moreover, the ideas presented in the model are easily assimilated into the naive theory (molecules move faster because the heat they receive pushes them); not only do they offer no incentive for theory revision, but they generate an additional misconception—that the object gets hotter because molecules moving faster means they collide more often, generating more heat by rubbing against each other. Although the model could be used to account for several aspects of the textbook theory (e. g., conduction, thermal dilation, and thermal equilibrium) and therefore give them a certain unity, textbooks and curricula tend to present each topic separately instead, with little cross-reference or even reference to the model itself; this is especially true in the earlier grades. Finally, the molecular model is not quantitative nor is it rich enough to account for many other important elements of the textbook theory.

In contrast, our computer-based models[1] visually depict the nature and relationships of the core concepts in the textbook theory, especially the aspects of the concepts that students' misconceptions make hard to grasp: the extensivity of heat, the difference between heat and temperature, and the idea that heat is mechanical energy. Other advantages will be reviewed after the models have been introduced.

In HEAT & TEMPERATURE, the main model, the amount of heat in an object is represented on the screen by a discrete number of "energy dots" in a rectangle; each dot represents one unit of heat and the size of the rectangle represents the mass of the object. Consequently, temperature is correlated with the density of the energy dots (for a given substance). (See Figure 2-1.) The values for amount of heat, mass, and temperature are also presented numerically (in arbitrary units) above the object. Thus, the difference and the relation between heat and temperature are explicit visually because the spatial properties of the visual representations of heat and temperature are analogues of the distinguishing properties of the concepts —the representation of heat (total number of dots) is extensive and the representation of temperature (dot density) is intensive—and the quantitative relation of heat, mass, and temperature is represented by the spatial relation between their visual representations (total number of dots = dot density ∗ rectangle area).

The COLLISIONS model (see Figure 2-2) gives a sense that energy dots represent the mechanical energy exchanged when the molecules collide whereas the VIEW option of the HEAT & TEMPERATURE program allows users to view the molecules in motion and thus to verify that higher temperature means faster moving molecules. The quantitative relation of heat, mass, and temperature is explicated at the molecular level by the ENERGY IN MOLECULES program (Figure 2-3), in which molecules are represented by open circles, mass is proportional to number of molecules in a rectangle, heat is represented by total number of dots, and

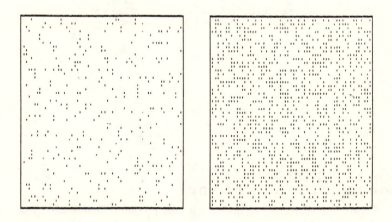

Mass units   = 3
Temperature = 20
Energy units = 360

Mass units   = 3
Temperature = 80
Energy units = 1440

Thermal   equilibrium

Zap   Contact   View   Esc

Figure 2-1   Screen from the HEAT & TEMPERATURE program showing two containers with the same mass. The container on the right has more heat (more energy dots) and a higher temperature (greater dot density).

temperature by number of dots per circle (molecule). The additional option CIRCLES ON/OFF allows the user to remove the circles representing the molecules from the screen, and to think in terms of amount of heat (total number of energy dots) and temperature (dot density), thereby establishing the link with the HEAT & TEMPERATURE model. In both HEAT & TEMPERATURE and ENERGY IN MOLECULES programs, the option ZAP allows users to heat the object, that is, to put more energy dots into it. In the HEAT & TEMPERATURE program, the added energy dots appear at the bottom of the object (to simulate heating on a hot plate) and the dots gradually spread upward until thermal equilibrium is established, whereas in the ENERGY IN MOLECULES program, the dots are distributed among the circles representing the molecules.

By allowing students to move from the representation of variables at the macrolevel (e.g., heat input, temperature change) to their interpretation at the molecular level (e.g., change in energy per molecule) within a single display, and by using a single format (energy dot), the models give students a sense of the nature of the variables and provide an explanatory mechanism for the laws and principles they need to learn. In doing so, the models give these principles a necessity and a unity they do not have at the

**Press   RETURN   to
Choose new positions**

Figure 2-2   Screen from the COLLISIONS program. On the left are the numbers that represent the energy of the molecules after collision. On the right are molecules and their trajectories before and after collision; the dots inside the molecules represent their energy. On the screen the molecule that appears dark gray in this figure is red and the light gray molecule is green.

phenomenological level. For example, the ENERGY IN MOLECULES program allows students to understand that the reason temperature increases less in a larger mass for a given heat input is that each molecule receives fewer energy units. And the VIEW option in the same program shows that the reason molecules move faster at higher temperature is that they have more energy.

We believe that our models help students learn the textbook theory because they present the textbook theory as a "free-standing" network of concepts, relations, and explanatory schemata, which constrain each other, and do so transparently enough that students can construct a new understanding of heat and temperature without "borrowing" and thus interference from the naive theory. Links between the models' microworld and the phenomenological world are to be provided during instruction but are also present in the models themselves; for example, ZAPping mimics heating on a hot plate.

Conclusions

We have conducted a study based on our models among eleventh-grade Honors students; the effects of our intervention were evaluated by com-

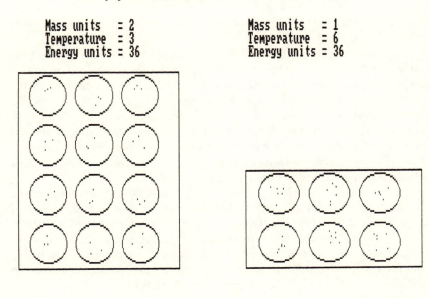

Mass units   = 2
Temperature = 3
Energy units = 36

Mass units   = 1
Temperature = 6
Energy units = 36

Zap   View   Circles on/off   Data on/off   Esc

Figure 2-3   Screen from the ENERGY IN MOLECULES program. The container on the left has twice the number of molecules as the container on the right. The dots represent the energy of each molecule.

paring a group of students taught with the models (the "Model" students) to a comparable group taught the same topics for the same amount of time (two weeks) in a traditional manner (the "Control" students). Reconceptualization was assessed using individual clinical interviews administered before and after the teaching intervention. (For details, see Wiser and Kipman, 1988.)

The interviews showed that the conceptual models were quite helpful. In the posttest, the Model students displayed a firmer grasp than the Control students of the various thermal concepts, laws, and principles, both at the theoretical and applied levels. Their knowledge formed a more integrated whole, and they showed fewer remaining misconceptions. For example, the Model group students demonstrated a much better grasp of the difference between heat and temperature and greater willingness and ability to articulate those differences explicitly both when they were asked theoretical questions or posed qualitative problems. They showed a deeper understanding of the extensivity of heat, of the concept of amount of heat, and of thermal equilibrium. Moreover, they were able to integrate those concepts into predictions about novel situations. They also assimilated the concept of specific heat much better than the Control group at the level of qualitative problem solving, and especially at the explanatory level. Finally, they were more able to relate phenomena at the macrolevel to molecular events.

Very encouraging results have been obtained also with average to low-ability ninth graders, although some aspects of the models were misinterpreted by a majority of students and the scope of their conceptual restructuring was more limited (Wiser and Grosslight, 1992). Typically, these students reified the models, interpreting the dots as molecules, and, although they learned to differentiate between heat and temperature and were able to solve qualitative problems accordingly, our teaching intervention did not lead them to revise their beliefs about the nature of heat or about the mechanism of heat transmission.

Results such as these have led us to apply the same research approach to students' conceptualization of the molecular structure of matter as we had used to study their conceptualizations of thermal phenomena (Wiser, Grosslight, O'Connor, and Thibodeau, in preparation). Preliminary results suggest that in the domain of matter, as in the domain of heat and temperature, students' beliefs are organized in theory-like structures, in which concepts, principles, explanatory mechanisms, and ontological commitments constrain each other. Our findings also suggest that a full-scale theory change in the domain of thermal phenomena cannot take place in the absence of a concurrent theory change in the domain of matter.

Finally, it is becoming more and more evident that close attention should be paid to students' mental models, in both the thermal and the molecular domains (Wiser, 1992). Mental models embody meaningful "chunks" of theory by integrating several concepts (e.g., heat, temperature, molecules) and their interrelations (at a qualitative or semi-quantitative level), as well as causal mechanisms and time-dependent behaviors of physical entities, in units of thoughts that can be "run" to explicate phenomena or solve problems. Some of our findings suggest that mental models play a role in learning thermal physics, as they do, for example, in learning astronomy (Vosniadou and Brewer, 1992). As such, they appear to be intermediaries between theory and phenomena and may play roles similar to those that philosophers of science attribute to scientific models in "normal science" (Giere, 1988) and in scientific discovery (Nersessian, 1992).

Note

1. The models were written by Daphna Kipman (see Wiser and Kipman, 1988, and Wiser, Kipman, and Halkiadakis, 1988, for details).

References

Carey, S., R. Evans, M. Honda, E. Jay, and C. M. Unger. 1989. An experiment is when you try it and see if it works: A study of seventh grade students' understanding of the construction of scientific knowledge. *International Journal of Science Education*.

Chinn, C. A., and W. F. Brewer. 1993. The role of anomalous data in knowledge acquisition: A theoretical framework and implications for science instruction. *The Review of Educational Research* 63: 1–49.

Clement, J. 1983. A conceptual model described by Galileo and used intuitively by physics students. In *Mental models*, edited by D. Gentner and A. L. Stevens. Hillsdale, NJ: Erlbaum.

———. 1987. Overcoming students' misconceptions in physics: The role of anchoring intuitions and analogical validity. In *Proceedings of the Second International Seminar on misconceptions and educational strategies in science and mathematics,* edited by J. Novak. Ithaca, NY: Cornell University.

deKleer, J., and J. S. Brown. 1985. A qualitative physics based on confluences. In *Qualitative Reasoning about Physical Systems*, edited by D. G. Bobrow. Cambridge, MA: MIT Press.

diSessa, A. A. 1983. Phenomenology and the evolution of intuition. In *Mental models*, edited by D. Gentner and A. L. Stevens, pp. 267–98. Hillsdale, NJ: Erlbaum.

Driver, R., and G. Erikson. 1983. Theories-in-action: Some theoretical and empirical issues in the study of students' conceptual frameworks in science. *Studies in Science Education* 10: 37–60.

Driver, R., and V. Oldham. 1986. A constructivist approach to curriculum development in science. *Studies in Science Education* 13: 105–22.

Erikson, G. 1979. Children's conceptions of heat and temperature. *Science Education* 63: 221–30.

———. 1980. Children's viewpoints of heat: A second look. *Science Education* 64: 323–26.

Giere, R. N. 1988. *Explaining science. A cognitive approach*. Chicago: University of Chicago Press.

Kuhn, D., E. Amsel, and M. O'Loughlin. 1988. *The development of scientific thinking skills*. San Diego, CA: Academic Press.

Kuhn, T. S. 1964. *The structure of scientific revolutions*. Chicago: University of Chicago Press.

———. 1977. A function for thought experiments. In *The essential tension* edited by T. S. Kuhn. Chicago: University of Chicago Press.

McCloskey, M. 1983. Naive theories of motion. In *Mental models*, edited by D. Gentner and A. L. Stevens, pp. 299–324. Hillsdale, NJ: Erlbaum.

Minstrell, J. 1989. *Building an environment for thinking about physics ideas*. Paper presented at the annual meeting of the American Association for the Advancement of Science, San Francisco, January 1989.

Nersessian, N. J. 1992. How do scientists think? Capturing the dynamics of conceptual change in science. In *Cognitive models of science. Minnesota studies in the philosophy of science*, edited by R. N. Giere. Minneapolis: University of Minnesota Press.

Posner, G. J., K. A. Strike, P. W. Hewson, and W. A. Gertzog. 1982. Accommodation of a scientific conception: Toward a theory of conceptual change. *Science Education* 66: 211–27.

Rosenquist, M., B. Popp, and L. McDermott. 1982a. *Some elementary conceptual difficulties with heat and temperature*. Paper presented at the national meeting of the American Association of Physics Teachers, San Francisco, January 27, 1982.

————. 1982b. *Helping students overcome conceptual difficulties with heat and temperature*. Paper presented at the meeting of the American Association of Physics Teachers, Ashland, MA, June 23, 1982.

Snir, J., C. Smith, and L. Grosslight. 1994. Conceptually enhanced simulations: A computer tool for science teaching. Chap. 7 in *Making sense: Teaching for understanding with technology*, edited by D. Perkins, J. Schwartz, M. Wiske, and M. West. New York: Oxford University Press.

Strauss, S., R. Stavy, and N. Orpaz. 1976. The child's development of the concept of temperature. Unpublished manuscript, Tel Aviv University.

Toulmin, S. 1963. *Foresight and understanding*. New York: Harper & Row.

Vosniadou, S., and W. F. Brewer. 1992. Mental models of the earth: A study of conceptual change in childhood. *Cognitive Psychology* 24: 535–85.

Welman, H., and S. Gelman. 1992. Cognitive development: Foundational theories of core domains. *Annual Review of Psychology* 43: 337–75.

White, B. 1993. *ThinkerTools*: Causal models, conceptual change, and science education. *Cognition and Instruction* 10: 1–100.

Wiser, M. 1986. The *differentiation of heat and temperature: An evaluation of the effect of microcomputer teaching on students' misconceptions*. Tech. Report 87–5. Cambridge, MA: Harvard Graduate School of Education, Educational Technology Center.

————. 1987. The differentiation of heat and temperature: History of science and novice-expert shift. In *Ontogeny, phylogeny, and historical development,* edited by S. Strauss. Norwood, NJ: Ablex.

————. 1989. *Does science learning involve theory change*? Paper presented at the biannual meeting of the Society for Research in Child Development, Gas City, April 1989.

————. 1992. *Mental models and computer models in thermal physics*. Paper presented at the NATO Advanced Study Institute on Psychological and Educational Foundation of Technology based Environments, Kolymbari, Crete.

Wiser, M., and S. Carey. 1983. When heat and temperature were one. In *Mental models*, edited by D. Gentner and A. L. Stevens. Hillsdale, NJ: Lawrence Erlbaum.

Wiser, M., and L. Grosslight. 1992. Differentiation and theory change in thermal physics: The role of conceptual models and metaconceptual understanding. Grant MDR-8950333. First year report submitted to the National Science Foundation.

Wiser, M., L. Grosslight, K. O'Connor, and R. Thibodeau. In preparation. What is a molecule? : Students' views about molecular phenomena.

Wiser, M. and D. Kipman. 1988. *The differentiation of heat and temperature: An evaluation of the effect of microcomputer models on students' misconceptions*. Tech. Report 88–20. Cambridge, MA: Harvard Graduate School of Education, Educational Technology Center.

Wiser, M., D. Kipman, and L. Halkiadakis. 1988. *Can models foster conceptual change?: The case of heat and temperature*. Tech. Report 88–7. Cambridge, MA: Harvard Graduate School of Education, Educational Technology Center.

3

On Understanding the Nature of Scientific Knowledge

SUSAN CAREY and CAROL SMITH

One important curricular goal of science education is to help students understand the nature of the scientific enterprise itself. This goal is important for several reasons. First, students can master only a small fraction of scientific knowledge in the course of their schooling, but as citizens they must adopt positions on public issues that turn on controversial points. Hence, the successful science curriculum will have fed an interest in science that underlies lifelong learning, a valuing of the kind of knowledge that is acquired through a process of careful experimentation and argument, as well as a critical attitude toward the pronouncements of experts. Involving students in the process of doing science and talking with them explicitly about its nature are thought to be central to cultivating these interests, values, and attitudes.

In addition, another quite different reason for teaching students about the nature of science has recently come to the fore. Because students come to science class with theories and concepts that are different from the scientists', the successful science curriculum will have involved students in making difficult conceptual changes. An open question is the relation between student understanding of the nature of scientific knowledge and student success in learning from curricula designed to foster conceptual change. Making students aware of the process of conceptual change may help them succeed at it.

Exactly what view of the nature of science do we wish to give to students? It is common practice for current textbooks to portray scientists as engaged in a process that depends on careful observation and experiment and to teach students some of the skills involved in careful experimentation. However, overlooked in these accounts is any discussion of the role of the scientists' theories in this process. Instead, mention is only made of scientists' specific hypotheses or beliefs about the world. In some accounts, these hypotheses are seen to be a simple consequence of unbiased observation and experiment, whereas in others it is acknowledged that scientists may have hypotheses that motivate their doing a particular experiment. However, in both cases, these hypotheses are thought to be tested in unproblematic and straightforward ways by the data of critical experiments, and scientific knowledge is portrayed as the steady accumulation of a set of confirmed hypotheses. As Hodson (1985, 1988), Nadeau and Desautels (1984), and Strike and Posner (1985) claimed, such a view is essentially an inductivist or empiricist view: The origin of scientific knowledge lies solely in data about the world.

We argue (along with these authors) that it is important to present students with a more constructivist epistemology of science: one in which students develop an understanding that scientists hold theories that can underlie the generation and interpretation of specific hypotheses and experiments. We want them to come to understand that our knowledge of regularity in nature is a consequence of successful conjecture, rather than its precursor, and that an adequate theoretical perspective is essential to both observation and experimentation. Thus, without challenging students' faith that theories may ultimately reflect reality, we may be able to help them see that theories are large-scale intellectual constructions that constitute the scientists' understanding and guide the day-to-day activities of scientists. This would help students understand why scientists do experiments, why there can be legitimate controversies in science, and even why learning science is difficult.

In this chapter, we first review the evidence that seventh-grade students come to science class with a naive empiricist epistemology. We then go on to consider how that epistemology is changed as a consequence of an explicit attempt to teach them about the constructive nature of science.

Student Epistemology

Hodson (1985, 1988) and Nadeau and Desautels (1984) assumed that the existing science curricula reinforce students' own common-sense views about the nature of scientific knowledge—one that sees knowledge acquisition driven solely by the data at hand. But what is the evidence for this assumption? Surprisingly, most of the evidence regarding this point is indirect. In this section, we review the evidence from three quite separate literatures that potentially can bear on this issue.

Common-Sense Epistemology

The first literature concerns common-sense epistemology in general, not particularly an epistemology of science. Several authors have used clinical interviews to probe adolescent and adult views of the nature of knowledge and its source and justification (e.g., Broughton, 1978; Chandler, 1987; Kitchener and King, 1981; Kuhn, Amsel, and O'Loughlin, 1988; Perry, 1970). Emerging from these clinical interview studies is some consensus on the stages that ordinary people go through in developing their epistemological views, although the exact number of stages and the timing of transitions has been subject to some dispute. In reviewing this literature, we focus on two related developments that we regard as important: a conception of a theory or interpretative framework and an appreciation that theoretical knowledge is acquired through indirect arguments from evidence.

Relating to the first theme, some have claimed that young children begin with a common-sense epistemology in which they view knowledge arising unproblematically (and directly) from sensory experiences and view knowledge as simply the collection of many true beliefs (e.g., Chandler, 1987; Kitchener and King, 1981; Kuhn et al., 1988). At this point, there is no notion that beliefs themselves are organized in intuitive theories or interpretative frameworks or that one's intuitive theory can influence one's beliefs and observations.

A study by Kuhn et al. (1988) provides support for this claim. They presented subjects with two accounts of a fictitious war called the Fifth Livian War, told by a historian from each of the different sides. In each account, the two historians, among other things, each claimed victory for their side. Subjects were then asked to describe in their own words what happened in the Fifth Livian War, whether the two historians' accounts were different in any important ways, and whether both accounts could be right.

Responses were coded into six stages. All sixth graders and over three-quarters of the ninth graders were at the lowest three stages. A key feature of the lowest stages is that students show no awareness of "theoretical interpretation as having played a role in the construction of the accounts and as a vehicle for reconciling them" (Kuhn et al., 1988, p. 213). Instead they deal primarily on the level of objective fact, at most seeing the accounts as differing in the facts chosen for presentation. This may be due to the historians being in different places at different times or having had different motives or purposes (i.e., they may have lied or exaggerated to make their side look good). However, students at this point still assume there is a simple truth to the situation, which can be known to a careful impartial observer.

In contrast, older adolescents, college, and graduate students tended to be at the highest three stages. At these stages, students are increasingly aware that the two historians have different points of view and that determining the reality of the situation is not so simple as determining who lied and who told the truth. Some believe there may in fact be multiple individual realities, whereas others acknowledge an elusive objective reality that can only be known approximately.

At the same time that children are moving from a common-sense epistemology that sees knowledge arising unproblematically from observations to one that sees a role for interpretative frameworks in knowledge acquisition, they are also developing more complex conceptions of how beliefs are justified. This point is nicely illustrated in Kitchener and King's studies (1981). Like Kuhn et al. (1988), Kitchener and King presented students with dilemmas about differences of opinion; one difference was that they then probed students about how they would decide what to believe. They found that the younger adolescents justified beliefs primarily in terms of perceptual experiences or what they were told by authorities. Sometime in late adolescence (especially for students who go to college), students become aware of genuine differences in the interpretation of the same facts and, consequently, that even authorities may disagree. This leads to an epistemological crisis, a period in which students are radical relativists and hold there is no true knowledge and everybody is free to believe whatever they want. Finally, in the college years, some people reach a mature epistemology that not only recognizes the relativity of belief to interpretative frameworks, but also recognizes that there are canons of rational justification for belief. Beliefs need to be justified in terms of arguments from patterns of data, and some beliefs are better justified than others.

Although these data certainly indicate likely differences between the epistemological beliefs of young adolescents and adults, other data indicate that these authors may not have done full justice to the complexity of the beliefs of young adolescents. For example, in Kuhn et al.'s earliest stage (1988), it is asserted that students fail to make a distinction between the account of an event and the event itself; similarly, in Kitchener and King's earliest stage (1981), there is no awareness that one's own beliefs can be false or different from an expert's. Both of these stages are thought to characterize a number of young adolescent children. Yet there is now very good evidence (using a different methodology that calls for less formal and verbalized understandings) that even 3 year olds can make distinctions between their beliefs about reality and reality itself and understand that people can have false beliefs (see, e.g., the work of Wellman, 1990).

Another example of an oversimplification in Kitchener and King's account (1981) of early adolescent epistemology concerns their claims that students view perceptual experience and expert testimony as the sole sources of belief and that students do not realize that the same facts can be given different interpretations or that there can be legitimate differences in opinion. Again, however, there is now good evidence that even 6 year olds understand that inference is a genuine source of knowledge (Sodian and Wimmer, 1987). In addition, Taylor, Cartwright, and Bowden (1991) showed that, by age 6, children are beginning to understand that the same visible stimulus might be interpreted differently by different people, depending on their background knowledge (although presumably only one interpretation is right; the other interpretations are wrong due either to misinformation or ignorance.) Finally, Flavell, Flavell, Green, and Moses (1990) demonstrated that even 3 year olds are aware that people can have differences of opinion especially about questions of value.

An adequate characterization of young students' epistemology must integrate findings from these diverse methodologies. Appendix A at the end of the chapter sketches our preliminary attempt to give a richer account of students' early epistemology and contrast it with a later epistemology that makes clear use of a notion of theory. Both are constructivist epistemologies in the sense that they acknowledge that one's present beliefs can affect one's observations and subsequent knowledge. And both are realist in the sense that both assume the existence of an objective reality. However, in the first (dubbed *knowledge unproblematic*), it is assumed that knowledge of reality can be obtained with enough diligent observation, whereas in the second (dubbed *knowledge problematic*), reality can be known only through successive approximations via a process of critical inquiry. We offer these, tentatively, as the beginning point and one relatively sophisticated possible endpoint for school-aged children's epistemologies. Clearly, there are many intermediate steps between these two points.

Process Skills

The second literature that bears indirectly on students' epistemology of science concerns attempts to construct scientific arguments. These are studies of the so-called science process skills (e.g., Dunbar and Klahr, 1989; Inhelder and Piaget, 1958; Kuhn et al., 1988). Many studies show that preadolescents and young adolescents do not appreciate the logic of argumentation from experimental results. Dramatic deficiencies in designing experiments and drawing conclusions from experimental evidence are amply documented in Inhelder and Piaget's classic work (1958) exploring the development of scientific reasoning and in more recent work by Kuhn et al. (1988) and Dunbar and Klahr (1989).

There may be at least two distinct deficiencies underlying children's problems on such tasks. On the one hand, students may genuinely lack knowledge about aspects of the logic of hypothesis testing. For example, Kahneman, Slovic, and Tversky (1982) documented errors in statistical reasoning that are made even by quite sophisticated adults. On the other hand, students' difficulties may in part reflect their commitment to a naive epistemology that makes no clear distinction between theory, specific hypothesis, and evidence. Such an epistemology leads them to expect a more direct relation between hypothesis and experiment than exists, to overlook the role of auxiliary assumptions in testing hypotheses, and to reach more certain conclusions from their data than the data in fact allow. In this way, some of the literature on deficiencies in process skills may indirectly support the existence of the knowledge unproblematic epistemology of young children.

Kuhn et al. (1988) reported a series of studies in which they looked at students' abilities to modify their initial theories (e.g., about the causes of colds) in light of experimental evidence that was presented to them. Subjects of all ages, even adults, found their tasks difficult. That is, even lay adults were poor at drawing proper conclusions from patterns of statistical evidence. However, Kuhn et al. also argued that the way young children responded indicated that they did not have a clear notion of theory that they distinguished from evidence. In particular, they noted that fewer than one third of the sixth graders spontaneously referred to evidence when answering whether the scientist's data showed that a given variable makes a difference to some outcome. What subjects did instead of referring to the evidence was to restate their theory or elaborate it with a mechanism. When the evidence was at odds with their theory, only graduate students were likely to distinguish what they thought from what the scientists' evidence showed. Instead, subjects changed their hypotheses and only later mentioned evidence. When their theory was compatible with the evidence, Kuhn et al. (1988) described the subjects as regarding the evidence as "equivalent to *instances* of the theory that serve to illustrate it, while the theory in turn serves to explain the evidence. . . . The two meld into a single representation of 'the way things are'" (p. 221).

We believe Kuhn et al.'s (1988) findings are consistent with young adolescents' knowledge unproblematic epistemology—one in which they do not yet distinguish between theory and belief and do not yet see the importance of indirect, multistepped arguments in specific hypothesis testing. At the same time, note that the kinds of finding just presented, although consistent with this hypothesis, do not provide strong evidence for it, for two reasons. First, it is hard to disentangle how much of their difficulty is with the specific statistical inferences they are asked to draw and how much is because of their holding the more limited epistemology, which makes it hard for them to appreciate what it means to test a hypothesis. Second, note that·the studies do not assess a concept of "theory" in the sense of an interpretative framework; the theories tapped by these studies are simply beliefs about causal relations among single variables.

Epistemology of Science

A third literature derives from more direct study of students' verbalizable epistemology of science. Two of the most ambitious standardized tests (Test of Understanding Science, Klopfer and Carrier, 1970, and the Nature of Scientific Knowledge Scale, Rubba and Anderson, 1978) probe for an understanding of science as a set of theories built up through a process of critical inquiry. Results reveal that young adolescents have much to learn about science in this regard but make steady progress toward such understanding throughout secondary school and college, especially as a result of specific instruction (Rubba and Anderson, 1978). However, these standardized tests were not designed to probe for the existence of an alternative epistemology in students. To remedy this limitation, two clinical interviews of seventh-grade students' epistemology of science were conducted.

In the first study, students were asked about the nature and purpose of science, the role of experiments in a scientist's work, and the relations among ideas, experiments, and results/data (see Carey, Evans, Honda, Jay, and Unger, 1989, for further details). Interview questions were divided into six sections, and students' responses on each section were coded into categories that reflected three general levels of understanding. Appendix B summarizes the three general levels that were coded in this study, ranging from Level 1, in which the goal of science is seen simply in terms of gathering specific facts about the world, to Level 3, in which the goal of science is seen in terms of a process of generating ever deeper explanations of the natural world.

Twenty-seven of the seventh-grade students were interviewed prior to their curriculum unit on the nature of science, and the overall mean level was 1.0. Only 4 students had an overall mean score over 1.5. Perhaps the most critical feature of Level 1 is the absence of an appreciation that ideas are distinct, constructed, and manipulable entities that motivate the scientist's more tangible experimental work. In Level 1 understanding, nature is there for the knowing. Accordingly, scientists "discover" facts and answers that exist, almost as objects "out there." Scientists' ideas themselves, however, are never the object of scrutiny.

In the second interview study (Grosslight, Unger, Jay, and Smith, 1991), researchers probed students' conceptions of science in quite a different manner, but the results were quite similar. Students were asked such questions as, "What comes to mind when you hear the word *model*?, What are models for?, What do you have to think about when making a model?, How do scientists use models?," and "Would a scientist ever change a model?" In addition, a number of physical items such as a toy airplane, a subway map, and a picture of a house were presented, and the students were asked to explain whether these could be called models. As in the nature of science interview, three general levels of thinking about models were identified. These differ in how students talk about the relation of models to reality and the role of ideas in models. Appendix C describes the main ideas at each level, ranging from a Level 1 conception of models as little replicas to a Level 3 understanding of models as tools used in the construction and testing of scientists' theories.

In this study (Grosslight et al., 1991), both seventh and eleventh graders were interviewed. Levels were assigned based on six separately scored dimensions (the role of ideas, the use of symbols, the role of model makers, communication, testing, and multiplicity of models). Each student was given six scores, corresponding to each dimension. A student scoring at the same level across five or six dimensions was assigned that level; all students with mixed levels straddled two adjacent levels and were assigned mixed levels (e.g., Level 1/2). Using this scheme, Grosslight et al. found that the majority (67%) of seventh graders were at Level 1. Only 12% of the seventh graders were at Level 2, and 18% had Level 1/2 scores. Turning to the eleventh graders, Grosslight et al. found that only 23% were pure Level 1's. More were split evenly between Level 1/2 (36%) and Level 2 (36%).

Overall, the reliability in scoring the levels was moderate in Study 1 (74%) and quite high in Study 2 (84%). One problem in the first study was that the interview was not designed to clearly probe the difference between Level 2 and Level 3 understandings. In retrospect, this is a significant shortcoming, because both Level 1 and 2 understandings may fall within the knowledge unproblematic epistemology (described in Appendix A), whereas Level 3 calls for a more mature constructivist epistemology, closer to the knowledge problematic epistemology (described in Appendix A). Currently, revisions are being made to the interview and scoring system to handle these shortcomings. Although in both studies no students gave evidence of Level 3 epistemology, some validation of its existence came from interviews of a group of expert scientists using the nature-of-models interview. All the scientists clearly showed Level 3 understanding.

Certainly further work is needed to clarify the nature of these levels and to determine how consistent student epistemology is, both within and across domains. For example, it is possible that students may be more advanced in their common-sense epistemology than in their epistemology of science. Yet the results from the three different literatures are all consistent with the claim that seventh-grade students have an alternative epistemology that they bring to science class that is at odds with the constructivist epistemology that we wish to teach.

Levels and Development

Suppose that we have correctly characterized the junior high school students' common-sense epistemology of science. Two questions of urgent importance to educators now arise. First, in what sense are these levels developmental? Is there something else we know about 12 year olds that would help us understand these levels? Second (and distinctly), do these levels provide barriers to grasping a constructivist epistemology if it is made the target of science curricula?

We do not believe these levels reflect stages in Piaget's sense (see Carey, 1985a, for a review of these issues). That is, they are unlikely to reflect some other, more abstract, cognitive failing of the child. The approach we favor is to characterize knowledge acquisition and knowledge reorganization within cognitive domains. So, for example, we have characterized changes in the child's intuitive biology (Carey, 1985b) and in the child's intuitive theory of matter (Carey, 1991; Smith, Carey, and Wiser, 1985). We see epistemology as part of one such domain—an intuitive theory of mind—that has a specific developmental history (e.g., Wellman, 1990). Understanding why junior high school students have these particular epistemological views consists of understanding their construction of a theory of mind, a process that begins in infancy.

That the levels probably do not reflect stages in Piaget's sense does not mean that they do not provide important constraints on student understanding. Domain-specific knowledge acquisition often involves large-scale reorganization and genuine conceptual change (Carey, 1985b, 1991). It is an open question whether a transition from Level 2 to Level 3 epistemology requires such a reorganization. The levels are not yet well enough characterized to even hazard a guess. One source of evidence relevant to the issue is the success of curricula designed to foster this transition. Insofar as the curricular ideas are sound, the students' failure to grasp Level 3 ideas would suggest that Level 1 and Level 2 epistemologies provide constraints on understanding Level 3 points.

Effects of Curricular Intervention on Student Epistemology

At the junior high school level, curricular interventions concerning meta-conceptual lessons about science have focused primarily on process skills. Although such skills are an important component of scientific inquiry, their mastery constitutes only a small part of the goals for student understanding of scientific knowledge just outlined. In this section, we first contrast two approaches to teaching seventh-grade students about the nature of science: a traditional approach with its emphasis on teaching process skills out of context and our approach with its emphasis on teaching these skills in the context of genuine scientific inquiry. We argue that only the latter approach has a chance at challenging the entrenched knowledge unproblematic epistemology that students bring with them to science classes. Then we discuss briefly the results of using this more innovative unit with seventh graders and raise a series of questions that need to be addressed in subsequent research.

The Standard Curricular Approach to Teaching About Inquiry

Much of current educational practice grows out of curriculum reform efforts that have emphasized the teaching of the process skills involved in the construction of scientific knowledge with such diverse skills as observation, classification, measurement, conducting controlled experiments, and constructing data tables and graphs of experimental results. These skills are typically covered in the junior high school science curriculum, beginning with the introduction of the scientific method in the seventh grade. The standard curricular unit on the scientific method, for example, contains many exercises to teach students about the design of controlled experiments, such as identifying independent and dependent variables in experiments and identifying poorly designed experiments in which variables have been confounded. Although in the best of these curricula, students go on to design and conduct controlled experiments, typically, the possible hypotheses and variables for a given problem are prescribed by the curriculum. Indeed, because students are testing disembodied hypotheses, this curriculum would be expected to move students toward Level 2 understanding on the nature of science interview (i.e., toward an understanding of the role of experimentation in testing hypotheses) but not toward Level 3 understanding with its notions of theory and indirect argument.

Certainly, process skills are important elements of a careful scientific methodology. Junior high school students do not spontaneously measure and control variables or systematically record data when they first attempt experimental work. Yet the standard curriculum fails to address the motivation or justification for using these skills in constructing scientific knowledge. Students are not challenged to utilize these process skills in exploring, developing, and evaluating their own ideas about natural phenomena. Instead, instruction in the skills and methods of science is conceived outside the context of genuine inquiry or the nature of scientific knowledge.

A Theory-Building Approach to Teaching About Inquiry

We assume, but at present have no evidence for our assumption, that process skills will be more easily and better learned if they are embedded in a wider context of metaconceptual points about the nature of scientific knowledge. Such metaconceptual knowledge is important in its own right, and can be gained only by actively constructing scientific understanding and reflecting on this process. These assumptions motivate a curricular approach that emphasizes theory building and reflection on the theory-building process. Carey et al. (1989), therefore, developed and tested an instructional unit to replace the typical junior high school unit on the scientific method.

This instructional unit begins with the question of what makes bread rise and ends with designing a research program aimed at discovering why combining yeast, sugar, and water produces a gas, and, ultimately, the nature of yeast. The metaconceptual points in this curriculum concerned how scientists decide what experiments are worth doing, how the answer to each question we ask raises still deeper questions, how one's theories of chemistry and biology constrain the experiments one does and the interpretations of results, and how unexpected results require changes in those theories.

As a result of the yeast unit, seventh-grade students' overall mean score on the nature of science clinical interview increased from 1.0 on the preinstruction interview to 1.55 on the postinstruction interview ($p < .001$, Wilcoxon Signed Ranks Test). Every student improved, and improvement averaged one-half a level. Now 16 of the 27 students achieved overall scores of 1.5 or better (as opposed to 4 students on the preinterview), and 5 scored Level 2 or better—a score nobody achieved on the preinterview. Although these results are certainly in the right direction, movement was toward consolidating Level 2 responses; there was little evidence that students appreciated the Level 3 metaconceptual lessons included in the curriculum that called for a notion of theory and indirect argument.

The results of curricular interventions aimed at changing students' conceptions of models have been even more limited. At Harvard's Educational Technology Center, Smith and Wiser have developed curricula using computer-implemented interactive models to foster conceptual change in two domains: the theory of matter, especially weight/density differentiation (Smith, Snir, and Grosslight, 1992); and thermal theory, especially heat/temperature differentiation (Wiser, Kipman, and Halkiadakis, 1988). Of course, conceptual change in the respective domains of physics was the main purpose of these model-based curricula, and the two curricula were highly successful in this regard. However, discussion of various metaconceptual points about the nature and use of models in science was also included in each of the curricular units: in particular, the ideas that models can be used to develop and test ideas, that multiple models are possible, and that models are evaluated in terms of their usefulness or how well they serve a given purpose. Unfortunately, there was no noticeable effect of this discussion on students' overall level of thinking about models in the post-instruction clinical interviews. The seventh graders scored at the same overall level on the postinstruction interviews as on the preinstruction interviews. And although the eleventh graders improved significantly to a solid Level 2 understanding, the improvement was just as great in a control group that did not have the modeling curriculum. Apparently, simply having thought about the issues as a result of the preinterview was sufficient to lead eleventh graders to better articulate their views on the postinterview.

Conclusions and Further Questions

It may be that it would be impossible for junior high school students to attain Level 3 understanding of the nature of scientific knowledge. Such understanding may have to await developments in more general epistemological beliefs and may require confronting head-on the relativism that characterizes the transition between the first and second senses of constructivism in the normal, untutored course of development. However, we do not take our failures to date as warranting this conclusion. We feel it is possible that scientific knowledge could well be an arena in which young adolescents could acquire some aspects of a constructivist epistemology in the knowledge problematic sense, in an optimal curricular environment. The curricular interventions we tried so far are far from optimal. They were both designed before we had fully appreciated the differences between students' starting epistemology and the epistemology we wished to teach, and the modeling curriculum had much less metaconceptual content than it would be possible to include. We take it to be very much an open question whether junior high school students can grasp the more sophisticated constructivism depicted in Appendix A.

Another extremely important issue for exploration is the relation between students' epistemological beliefs and conceptual change in science content. Although many have speculated that students' epistemological beliefs interfere with successful learning of science and mathematics, there is little empirical evidence on this point. We know of no studies, for example, that show that changes in students' epistemological views affect their success in learning content. Of course, such studies will not be possible until the research program just outlined is brought to further fruition. That is, we will need accurate and detailed descriptions of student epistemology, as well as curricula that advance their epistemological views, before such studies will be possible.

References

Broughton, J. M. 1978. Development of concepts of self, mind, reality, and knowledge. In *Social cognition: New directions for child development*, edited by W. Damon. Vol. 1, pp. 75–100. San Francisco: Jossey-Bass.

Carey, S. 1985a. Are children fundamentally different thinkers and learners from adults? In *Thinking and learning skills*, edited by S.F. Chipman, J.W. Segal, and R. Glaser. Vol. 2, pp. 485–517. Hillsdale, NJ: Erlbaum.

———. 1985b. *Conceptual change in childhood*. Cambridge, MA: Bradford Books/ MIT Press.

———. 1991. Knowledge acquisition: Enrichment or conceptual change? In *Epigenesis of mind: Studies in biology and cognition,* edited by S. Carey and R. Gelman, pp. 257–91. Hillsdale, NJ: Erlbaum.

———, R. Evans, M. Honda, E. Jay, and C. M. Unger. 1989. 'An experiment is when you try it and see if it works': A study of grade 7 students' understanding of the construction of scientific knowledge. *International Journal of Science Education* 11: 514–29.

Chandler, M. 1987. The Othello effect: Essay on the emergence and eclipse of skeptical doubt. *Human Development* 30: 137–59.

Dunbar, K., and D. Klahr. 1989. Developmental differences in scientific discovery processes. In *Complex information processing: The impact of Herbert A. Simon*, edited by D. Klahr and K. Kotovsky, pp. 109–43. Hillsdale, NJ: Erlbaum.

Flavell, J., E. R. Flavell, F. J. Green, and L. Moses. 1990. Young children's understanding of fact beliefs versus value beliefs. *Child Development* 61: 915–26.

Grosslight, L., C. M. Unger, E. Jay, and C. Smith. 1991. Understanding models and their use in science: Conceptions of middle and high school students and experts. *Journal of Research in Science Teaching* 28: 799–822.

Hodson, D. 1985. Philosophy of science, science and science education. *Studies in Science Education* 12: 25–57.

———. 1988. Toward a philosophically more valid science curriculum. *Science Education* 72: 19–40.

Inhelder, B., and J. Piaget. 1958. *The growth of logical thinking from childhood to adolescence*. New York: Basic.

Kahneman, D., P. Slovic, and A. Tversky, eds. 1982. *Judgment under uncertainty: Heuristics and biases*. New York: Cambridge University Press.

Kitchener, K. S., and P. M. King. 1981. Reflective judgment: Concepts of justification and their relationship to age and education. *Journal of Applied Developmental Psychology* 2: 89–116.

Klopfer, L. E., and E. D. Carrier. 1970. *TOUS: Test of understanding science (Form*

JW). Pittsburgh: Learning Research and Development Center, University of Pittsburgh.

Kuhn, D., E. Amsel, and M. O'Loughlin. 1988. *The development of scientific thinking skills*. Orlando, FL: Academic.

Nadeau, R., and J. Desautels. 1984. *Epistemology and the teaching of science*. Ottawa: Science Council of Canada.

Perry, W. G. 1970. *Forms of intellectual and ethical development in the college years*. New York: Academic.

Rubba, P., and H. Anderson. 1978. Development of an instrument to assess secondary students' understanding of the nature of scientific knowledge. *Science Education* 62 (4): 449–58.

Smith, C., S. Carey, and M. Wiser. 1985. On differentiation: A case study of the development of size, weight, and density. *Cognition* 21 (3): 177–237.

Smith, C., J. Snir, and L. Grosslight. 1992. Using conceptual models to facilitate conceptual change: The case of weight-density differentiation. *Cognition and Instruction* 9: 221–83.

Sodian, B., and H. Wimmer. 1987. Children's understanding of inference as a source of knowledge. *Child Development* 58: 424–33.

Strike, K. A., and G. J. Posner. 1985. A conceptual change view of learning and understanding. In *Cognitive structure and conceptual change*, edited by L. West and A. L. Pines, pp. 211–31. New York: Academic.

Taylor, M., B. Cartwright, and T. Bowden. 1991. Perspective taking and theory of mind: Do children predict interpretive diversity as a function of differences in observer's knowledge? *Child Development* 62: 1334–51.

Wellman, H. 1990. *The child's theory of mind*. Cambridge, MA: MIT Press.

Wiser, M., D. Kipman, and L. Halkiadakis. 1988. *Can models foster conceptual change? The case of heat and temperature*. Tech. Report TR88-7. Cambridge, MA: Harvard Graduate School of Education, Educational Technology Center.

Appendix A

Two Contrasting Constructivist Epistemologies

Knowledge Unproblematic

Knowledge consists of a collection of true beliefs. The sources of beliefs are perception, testimony, and one-step inference. Individuals may draw different conclusions from the same perceptual experience because of differences in prior knowledge or motives; individuals may have different opinions in matters of value and personal taste. Individuals with this epistemology believe there is only one objective reality that is knowable in a straightforward way by making observations. Hence, when individuals disagree about reality, it is possible for only one of them to be correct. Ultimately, ignorance, misinformation, or deceit are the causes of having false beliefs.

Knowledge problematic

Knowledge consists of theories about the world that are useful in providing a sense of understanding and predicting or explaining events. Individuals actively develop their theories through a process of critical inquiry. Conjectures derived from interpretative frameworks merit testing; the results constitute evidence for or against the interpretative framework and associated specific beliefs. Different people may draw different conclusions from the same perceptual experiences because they hold different theories that affect their interpretation of evidence. Reality exists, but our knowledge of it is elusive and uncertain. Theories are judged to be more or less useful, not strictly right or wrong. Canons of justification are framework relative. In addition to false beliefs resulting from ignorance and misinformation, beliefs can be in error for much deeper reasons: Theories can be on entirely the wrong track, positing incorrect explanations of accurate beliefs and positing entities and causal mechanisms that do not even exist.

Appendix B

Three Levels of Understanding in the Nature of Science Interview

Level 1

Students make no explicit distinction between ideas and activities for generating ideas, especially experiments. A scientist tries "it" to see if it works. The nature of "it" remains unspecified or ambiguous; "it" could be an idea, a thing, an invention, or an experiment. The motivation for an activity is the achievement of the activity itself, rather than the construction of tested ideas. The goal of science is to discover facts and answers about the world and to invent things.

Level 2

Students make an explicit distinction between ideas and experiments. The motivation for experimentation is to test an idea to see if it is right. There is an understanding that the results of an experiment may lead to the abandonment or revision of an idea. However, an idea is still a guess; it is not a prediction derivable from a general theory. (Indeed, students may not yet have the general idea of a theory.) There is no appreciation that the revised idea must now encompass all the data, the new and the old, and that if a prediction is falsified, the theory may have to be revised.

Level 3

As in Level 2, students make a clear distinction between ideas and experiments, and they understand that the motivation for experiments is verification or exploration. Added to this is an appreciation of the relation between the results of an experiment (especially unexpected ones) and the theory leading to the prediction. Level 3 understanding recognizes the cyclic, cumulative nature of science, and identifies the goal of science as the construction of ever deeper explanations of the natural world.

Appendix C

Three Levels of Understanding in the Nature of Models Interview

Level 1

Models are thought of as either toys or as simple copies of reality. Models are considered useful because they can provide copies of actual objects or actions. If students acknowledge that aspects or parts of objects can be left out of the model, they do not express a reason for doing so beyond the fact that one might not want or need to include it.

Level 2

The student now realizes there is a specific, explicit purpose that mediates the way the model is constructed. Thus, the modeler's ideas begin to play a role, and the student is aware that the modeler makes conscious choices about how to achieve the purpose. The model no longer needs to match the real-world object exactly. Real-world objects or actions can be changed or repackaged in some limited ways (e.g., through highlighting, simplifying, showing specific aspects, adding clarifying symbols, or creating different versions). However, the main focus is still on the model and the reality modeled, not the ideas portrayed. Tests of the model are thought of as tests of the workability of the model itself, not of the underlying ideas.

Level 3

A Level 3 understanding is characterized by three important factors. First, the model is now constructed in the service of the development and testing of ideas, rather than as serving as a copy of reality itself. Second, the modeler takes an active role in constructing the model, using symbols freely and evaluating which of several designs could be used to serve the modeler's purpose. Third, models can be manipulated and subjected to testing in the service of informing ideas.

4

History of Mathematics as a Tool for Teaching Mathematics for Understanding

CARLOS E. VASCO

Starting from Zero

A common question in teachers' workshops is the following: "Do natural numbers start from zero, or from one?"

What would you answer? Supposedly, natural numbers are to be associated with finite sets: If you accept the empty set as the minimal finite set, that's a good reason to start from zero. But nobody starts counting "Zero, one, two . . ." There you have a good reason to start from one. What do we do now? What should we teach children? Zero or one?

My favorite answer to that question is quite unsettling to the workshop participants, who expect a final authoritative decision from the expert. My answer simply points out that for the Pythagoreans, Plato, Aristotle, Euclid, on through the Middle Ages, the Rennaissance and up to the late nineteenth century, natural numbers started from two. Why not teach children that number starts from two? After all, you wouldn't say that "a number of people" think that number starts from two, if I were the only one to think so.

My answer "two" to the question "zero or one?" is not only a Zen-style conundrum: It aims to be a pointer to what understanding number might mean, and a sample of what a style appropriate to teaching for understanding might look like.

Can we decide what understanding mathematics is, and how to teach mathematics for understanding today, on the basis of the historical sequence of the social construction of mathematics?

Mathematicians and Amnesia

Most mathematicians think that history is irrelevant for mathematics, and also for mathematics teaching and learning. In their opinion, once a demonstration of a theorem is found, the author, the motivation, the circumstances, the historical milieu, all that can be dispensed with. The proved proposition will never be disproved. It enters into the perennial stock of mathematical truths, and its history deserves at most a footnote with a name and a date.

Proposals for changes in the math curriculum come often from eminent mathematicians who have a highly refined and abstract conceptual map of their discipline, based on the logic of theorem deduction from axioms, undefined terms, and definitions. Their criteria to decide a particular pedagogical sequence are mostly logical (though, to their credit, also sometimes esthetic). To draw a clear mental picture, I will say that those proposals for pedagogical sequencing are derived from *the dogma of logical sequence*.

The few mathematicians who propose curricular changes based on historical criteria assume that the historical sequence should dictate the pedagogical sequence. According to them, history shows the way mathematical concepts and propositions were actually learned by our species. They propose to guide children through the same steps. Let us say that their proposals are derived from *the dogma of historical sequence*.

This chapter looks first to the dogma of historical sequence, and then listens to the arguments from the opposite side. After that, a way of handling the pedagogical problem of content sequencing in the mathematics curriculum is derived from the discussion, and a few specific curricular sequences in arithmetic, algebra, and geometry are developed from the proposed way of searching for alternatives.

The Dogma of Historical Sequence

Since the twenties, a patient Swiss biologist turned psychologist had worked painstakingly on tracing the development of logical and mathematical thinking in children. Like the embryologists of the nineteenth century, Jean Piaget detected a clear pattern. Every child's individual development as a human being—its ontogenesis—seemed to repeat the evolution of the human species, genus, family, order or phylum—our phylogenesis. The creative blend of biology, psychology, and philosophy Piaget called "genetic epistemology" opened up new avenues of research. History, anthropology, and sociology could show the development of new forms of thinking in logic, mathematics, and the natural sciences: their sociogenesis, which paralleled the developments found by psychology in each child: their psychogenesis. (See Piaget and García, 1982).

From this theory, a new dogma could be opposed to the dogma of logical sequence: The fast development of the history of mathematics in the twentieth century could provide the clue for the most efficient teaching and learning of mathematics. If we only followed the historical sequence in presenting the topics and the concepts, every child could become an acceptable mathematician.

Piaget did not propose this type of parallelism as a new dogma, but it is interesting to see what happens if we take it as such. How would a pedagogical sequence of mathematical instruction look if derived from the dogma of historical sequence?

Let's look only at the beginning of the kindergarten and first-grade curriculum. Arithmetic could start from base-free rote counting; fingers and hands could form the simplest units and groupings, and tens, dozens, and perhaps twenties could be tried before developing fixed-base numbering systems. Concrete numbers would come first, abstract numbers after that, starting from two. In this scenario, one is not a number, because earlier it was not a number, only the origin of number. It wasn't even or odd, prime, or composite. (Somewhat inconsistently, we still maintain the second statement, not the first.) The different types of counting found in ancient cultures should be revisited by each child. (See Gelman and Gallistel, 1978; Steffe, von Glasersfeld, Richards, and Cobb, 1984). Zero would be just a coding trick, not a number. Much later it could be incorporated into number. And addition would come slowly as a recoding of counting, "from counting-all to counting-on" as cleverly stated by Secada, Fuson, and Hall (1983). (See also Carpenter, Moser, and Romberg, 1982; Fuson, 1992).

Parallel syllabi could be drawn up for every branch of mathematics by simply taking the historical development of that discipline as the main criterion for a didactically optimal exposition of the given subject.

Before attempting to evaluate these proposals, let us hear the arguments of the opposition.

The Dogma of Anti-Historical Sequence

Some psychologists, mathematicians, math teachers, and math historians fought back. Their reasons were manifold. Piaget was wrong in some of his reconstructions of history. Children do not follow spontaneously the same historical phases as our human species. Too much time was wasted by humankind in pursuing dead-end streets, and too much time would be wasted by children learning useless historical curiosities. If anything, a sharp reading of the history of mathematics could provide the basis for just the opposite guideline: The concepts and theories that explicitly appeared later in the development of mathematics seem to be deeper and more powerful; hence, they should be explicitly taught earlier. I would say that these proposals of pedagogical sequencing rather reinforce the dogma of logical sequence through *the dogma of anti-historical sequence*.

Piaget himself saw the power of this type of argument, and tried to contrast it with his own findings. He thought he had found a good example of anti-historical sequencing: Topology is the last form of geometry in the history of mathematics. Also called "analysis situs," rubber-sheet geometry, or combinatorial modeling of space, topology as a new discipline had consolidated from the days of Euler's promenades through the bridges of Königsberg, to the works of Poincaré less than a hundred years ago. Topology was here to stay, if only at the most advanced college level courses.

But children seemed to understand topological relations better than their metric counterparts, much more intuitive to adults. If a child draws a square room or a square playpen, he or she probably draws a closed line closer to a circle than to a square. Neighborhoods, open and closed curves, inside and outside, nonrupturing deformations, all those ideas could be found in children before they even acquired the conservation of length (Piaget and Inhelder, 1948. For a survey of research in this area, see Mandler, 1983; see also the summary in Clements and Battista, 1992).

An anti-historical proposal for a pedagogical sequencing of geometry should not start from pre-Euclidean geometric explorations, but rather from the most advanced branch of modern geometry: topology; then, projective and affine geometry; our usual metric geometry would be the last step. That anti-historical sequence would conform to the latest global rethinking of geometry done by Felix Klein a hundred years ago—the Erlangen Program of 1872.

A good example of the combined power of the logical and the anti-historical dogmas was the development of the "New Math" in the fifties and sixties.

The Rise of the New Math and the Fall of the Old

The need for a radical reform of school mathematics in the fifties, made acute by the launch of *Sputnik* by the Soviets in 1957, found a good theoretical booster in the works of Nicolas Bourbaki. This pseudonym of a brilliant group of French and American mathematicians supposedly comes from a French officer with a Russian first name and a Greek last name (Bourbaki, 1968). But little or nothing remains of Greek mathematics in the architectural reconstruction of mathematics achieved by the Bourbakists (Bourbaki, 1950). In fact, "Death to Euclid!" was one of their battle cries.

The latest rereading of history and the finest logical restructuring of all the mathematical disciplines combined forces to propose a rewriting of mathematics in the language of sets, with the help of a few logical concepts.

Logic, except for some forgotten pages in Leibnitz' manuscripts, had been a purely philosophical discipline until George Boole's *Mathematical Analysis of Logic* in 1847 and his *Laws of Thought* of 1854. Suddenly, through the works of Boole, de Morgan, Hamilton, Venn, Jevons, and Lewis Carroll in England, Peirce in America, and Frege and Schröder in

Germany, mathematical logic was flying free in its own orbit (Kneale and Kneale, 1961).

Set theory, except for a few forgotten pages in Boole's works, was nowhere to be found until the German mathematicians decided to attack Fourier and Cauchy's proposals to develop functions in trigonometric series, and needed a new language to talk about points of discontinuity and convergence. Georg Cantor developed in a few years (1874–97) a full-fledged theory of finite and infinite sets, which, after the expected adverse reactions, was already acceptable to most mathematicians by 1900.

Based on the Bourbaki reconstruction of mathematics, the defenders of the logical and the anti-historical sequence dogmas could make bold proposals of curriculum reform. Learning a few intuitive concepts of set theory and logic in kindergarten and the first grades, children would have at their disposal all the tools needed to learn and understand every branch of mathematics, from the most elementary arithmetic to the most advanced modern disciplines. The "New Math" was here. The old would quickly fall into disrepute. Or so they thought (see Cooper, 1985; Moon, 1986).

Learning from Errors

The reaction did not take long. Already in the late fifties, Morris Kline voiced his protest, which crystallized later in the fateful question: "Why can't Johnny add?" (Kline, 1973). Johnny could indeed recite the truth tables of logical connectives, the definitions and properties of unions and intersections of two arbitrary sets, even the definition of cardinality via bijective correspondences. If small enough, he might indeed be able to find the "cardinal numbers" of two given sets, but couldn't add'em carryin'.

Japanese teachers rejected the New Math proposals after a few month's trial, and British teachers after a few years. The battle cry became: "Back to basics!" The trouble is that everybody had a different idea of what was basic, or basic for what. After all, sets and logic are basic, no doubt. Nevertheless, the idea was rather: "Back to the thirties!" But history is not defied in vain. You never simply go back to the old after the new arrives.

Simply going back to basics as reverting to the good old days would be to refuse learning from the errors of math education in the last forty years.

It might well be true that the dogma of historical sequence errs in forgetting the very errors of history, as seen from today's historical perspective. But the dogma of logical sequence also errs in projecting the mathematician's neatly organized mental world onto the road maps of the child's mind, and the dogma of historical anti-sequence errs in absolutizing today's historical perspective as neatly organized by an expert, be it Klein or Bourbaki, onto the road maps to get there.

My attempt to synthesis is the following: Both the logical and the anti-historical viewpoints help install road signs at dangerous curves and at the entrance of dead-end roads; from those vantage points, one can find short-cuts and compress distances. But the main direction of travel, to which compressing and subverting, shortcutting, and road signaling help, is to be found in a careful use of the historical viewpoint. A careful use.

Historical Sequences as Heuristics

Logic has been often chided for lack of creativity. Hegel once sentenced that Minerva's owl always flies in the evening; too late, that is. Bertrand Russell remarked that the only time somebody learned something from a syllogism was the day when a German professor was reading a humor magazine and was struck by some of the ads. Then he thought: Everything in this magazine is a spoof. These ads are in this magazine, ergo. . . .

Indeed, the task of logic is the organization of a road once traveled. To make it shorter, neater, safer. To be sure every leg of the road connects with the former. To make sure it starts from where it should, and leads where it claims. But logic gives no indication on how to travel the first time around. Or how to cut a new path through the thicket. That is the purpose of heuristics.

"Eureka!" screamed Archimedes, jumping out of the tub. A better trans-literation would be "Heureka!": "I found it!" Too late for heuristics. They should come before the findings. They are not results; they are clever tricks to beat elusive results out of the bushes. They are not scientific methods; they are artful ploys to find scientific methods, among other things. Why not curricular sequences?

Very little is known about heuristics, and none of them works for sure. George Pólya started the exponentially growing literature on probem solv-ing with a few heuristics (Pólya, 1945, 1954; see Schoenfeld, 1983, for a sample of the literature up to ten years ago. It took 65 pages of titles then; now it might take 650; compare with Schoenfeld, 1992).

Pólya's heuristics are still quite useful. And it has been exceedingly difficult to find new ones. Any heuristic on how to find heuristics would be wonderful. The main point of this chapter is that both the historical and the anti-historical logical perspectives provide such macroheuristics for educational research.

Let us switch gears and move away from our historical discussion to the main emphasis of my pedagogical argument.

Forward and Backward Heuristics

In the conclusion of his lecture at the 1983 International Congress of Mathematicians at Warsaw, Hans Freudenthal said:

> If mathematics teaching proves to be a failure, the reason is often, if not
> always, that we do not realize that young people have to start somewhere
> in the past of mankind and somehow repeat the learning process of

mankind. This is the lesson historians and educators can learn from each other. (Freudenthal, 1984).

That sounds pretty much like the pure dogma of historical sequencing. But Freudenthal carefully temperates the dogma with a "somewhere" and a "somehow." And, at the beginning of the lecture, he makes a careful precision. The young learner ought to recapitulate history "not as it actually happened but as it would have happened if people in the past had known something like what we do know now." (Freudenthal, 1984). Isn't he calling for a careful use of both the historical and the anti-historical logical sequences?

The main idea is to design two types of heuristics to help us find the optimal pedagogical sequencing for math curricula. One type, which I call "forward heuristics," should come from the historical sequence dogma and propose efficient ways of reviewing the phylogenesis of the particular mathematical subject, in order to optimize the ontogenetic mastery of that conceptual field. The other type, which I call "backward heuristics," should come from the logical and the anti-historical sequence dogmas and propose ways to trim, compress, and even alter the sequences found through forward heuristics. Forward heuristics lay out the rough draft of the roads on the mathematical map; backward heuristics do the redesigning, the shortcutting, and the road signaling.

Forward heuristics take the state-of-the-art picture of the historical development of the subject, whose optimal teaching sequence is to be researched.

The task is not easy. Concepts must be recaptured at the stage of formation they had reached at the time studied; even what today would count as an error or a dead-end street can be revalued relatively to the context in which it appears. Different sequences can be arranged according to the historical events, and the known information from cognitive science, psychological and educational research, will help trim them down to workable hypotheses.

Backward heuristics take the same state-of-the-art picture of the historical development of the subject, but look at it from the current stage of concept formation and logical structuring of that subject. From that vantage point, the same additional information helps detect the implicit aspects of children's mathematical activity, which correspond to the deeper layers that have only lately been made explicit by mathematical development. Different sequences can be arranged, which try to exploit those powerful restructurings, explicitly mentioning the historical sequences and the reasons to alter them.

According to forward and backward heuristics, to understand a mathematical concept means to reconstruct it, articulated with, and in contrast to, the former more naive views of it, and to be able to recapture and exploit the relations to those former views; last but not least, it means to take the current construction also as relative, provisional, and open to further de- and re-constructions.

But heuristics are not to be taken dogmatically. They are only strategies to generate educational research hypotheses. Let us try to develop some of them in the fields of arithmetic, algebra, and geometry.

Numerical Systems and Numbering Systems

Back to the initial question: Where do natural numbers start from? As we saw in the Introduction, the Greeks said "two." Two thousand years later, a widespread Spanish arithmetic of 1777 still defined number as "a multitude composed of units," and stated that the unit "neither has any division, nor is a number, but the principle and foundation of all number" (Taboada, 1777).

Forward heuristics tell you to stop and look for contemporary traces of this privilege of the dyad over the monad, which might help children gain access to a more personal and secure construction of number.

If you read the purported "definitions" of sets in most textbooks, they say a set is a collection of elements or objects. Just that plural, signaled by the final "s," tells you that collections (or sets, or classes) should start from two. Would you say you have a coin collection if you have only one coin? Children can handle collection games easily, as long as collections have at least two elements. In this sense, for them number starts from two.

According to these heuristics, multiplication should start from doubling, and fractions from halving. Powers should also start from the second (i.e., the square) but not proceed beyond squares and cubes until much later. "Nature does not permit any further," would still say Cardano in the most important book on algebra in the sixteenth century (Cardano, 1968. See Vasco, 1985). Roots would come next, starting also from the square root. Two again.

Now you can try to convince children that just one isolated object can make a collection. Even a genius like Peano would not accept that statement a hundred years ago. He did not distinguish an isolated object from the singleton to which it belongs.

When you succeed in having children reconstruct singleton sets, you can challenge them to include the number "one" in the system of natural numbers. If you go upwards in multiplication from doubling an amount n to three times n, four times n, and so on, why can't you go backwards and define "one times n"? (By the way, shouldn't it be "one time n"?). If you go forward from one-half to one-third and one-fourth, why can't you go backwards and introduce a one in the denominator? (Should we call it "one-oneth"?). If you go upwards in powers, from the square to the cube to the fourth power, why can't you go backwards and define the first power? (Behind the cube and the square, is it a line?). If you go forward from the square root to the cube root to the fourth root, why can't you go backwards and introduce a first root? (Is it a "line root"?).

If you don't think about the natural numbers as a dead set, but as a lively relational and operational system (Vasco, 1986), even that number one does not look so natural, after all. What about zero?

When you are sure children are able to construct the empty set, you can also challenge them to incorporate the number "zero" into the system of natural numbers. In his first axiomatic reconstruction of arithmetic in 1889 (*Arithmetices Principia Nova Methodo Exposita*), Peano started from one, not from zero. In his second (*Sul Concetto di Numero*) in 1891, he did start from zero.

Can you add zero to something? Try deciding what it means to add zero, multiply by zero, or raise to the zeroth power. What about zero to the zeroth power? Is it zero, or one? What would you say? My Zen-style answer to teachers is: Why not one-half? (Average the two limits of x^y at the origin along the positive coordinate axes).

Ancient numbering systems provide cues to very modern number bases. Some Central and South American Indians counted "one, two, two-and-one, two-and-two, one hand." But they kept going to two hands, counted on their toes to two hands and a foot, and completed a man with two hands and two feet. (No known feminists yet.) It was not a fixed base system, like the Mayans did have. But backward heuristics suggest skipping many of the historical details, and trying to go as fast as possible to that feat of human ingenuity that was the invention of fixed-base numbering systems.

If you wish to use another base besides ten, you should try one hand as the more natural number base for a numbering system. I have tried all bases from two to sixteen, and indeed there is none like base five, using one hand as the basic higher-order unit. One child stands in front of the class and counts units lifting fingers in his left hand, and counts hands on fingers of his right hand. A second child counts persons as hands of hands on the fingers of her left hand, and hands of people on fingers of her right hand. At one hundred and twenty-five, they have to call a third child to raise a finger to their right. Try it.

From this viewpoint, understanding natural numbers would mean to be able to go upwards from one-two on, taking into account both order and cardinality; to form higher-order units out of basic packs; to recode counting into addition, addition into multiplication, and multiplication into powers; to go backwards to one and zero, to subtraction, division, and root extraction, and to incorporate one and zero into the system; to distinguish numbers from numerals, and to be able to translate from one numbering system to another, not by rote, but because you know what those symbol systems are talking about.

From Rhetorical to Symbolic Algebra

Babylonian, Egyptian, and Chinese problem sets are not too different from the "word problems" that cause so much havoc among beginners in high school algebra. The interesting part is not the wording of the problems, but the wording of the solutions. No unknowns, equations, or formal symbols appear at all. Only a little speech on how to proceed to find the answer. What is the area of a circle eighteen steps in diameter? You subtract one ninth of the diameter and square the result. You can learn many things from this little piece of rhetorical algebra; even that the approximation to our real number π used by the Egyptians was closer to 3.16 than to 3.14.

Forward heuristics immediately generate a proposal: Why not try simple enough word problems so that their solutions can also be given in words? Children are quite able to appreciate by themselves the need to keep track of numbers, to use symbols, boxes, or simply regions of a sheet of paper to keep records, and as the complexity of the problem grows, they will partially reinvent and fully appreciate the power of symbolic algebra. In research done by J. Walters (1985) at Harvard, second graders even reinvented matrix notation in order to be able to answer questions about the number of children and adults in a bus making several stops along the way.

The Greeks developed another algebraic method beyond rhetorical algebra. They thought of quantities as lengths of line segments, products of two factors as areas of rectangles and products of three factors as volumes. They reconverted them to lengths wherever needed, and knew many possible transformations of figures that would keep area or volume constant. Geometric algebra was the finest tool for demonstrations for two thousand years.

Forward heuristics suggest that children understand squares and cubes as areas and volumes, and that the association of mental arithmetic with lengths, areas, or volumes should improve children's understanding of the results, ways to check them, and sources of self-formulated problems and solutions.

The manuscripts of Regiomontanus and Luca Pacioli show the development of an abbreviated, stenographic form of rhetorical algebra from the thirteenth to the sixteenth century that reached maturity and power in the hands of Tartaglia, Cardano, Ferrari, del Ferro, Bombelli, and a host of Renaissance mathematicians. Armed with their "syncopated algebra," they could hunt for solutions to previously unsolvable problems. The solution of the cubic and the quartic are their most dazzling trophies.

Forward heuristics provide a clue to multiple representations in algebra: Say what you have to say in words, write them down, use shorthand, abbreviations, initials, and private symbols, until you realize that other powerful symbols have already been invented. Compare them with yours, contrast their advantages and shortcomings, and learn to appreciate the mathematicians' Esperanto.

Backward heuristics help control the overabundance of possible sequences pursuable from the forward heuristics viewpoint. The latest developments in the history of mathematics—abstract algebra, category theory, logic or functional analysis—help detect and discard (with care) many historical offshoots that turned out to be sterile and misleading.

From the standpoint of logic, algebraic expressions that do not involve equalities, inequalities, or other relation symbols are called "terms". Terms represent both active transformations and their passive results. This double view of a term, active and passive, escapes the eyes of those who do not look backwards from the latest developments. From the passive viewpoint, terms represent static results of active operations. So it was in the early symbolic algebra. Standard algebra textbooks see only the passive aspect of terms. From the active viewpoint, every term is a short program that is efficiently coded in algebraic form. Backward heuristics suggest another multiple representation scenario: A term should be translated as a program or algorithm—a list of instructions to calculate output values from inputs. Hence, it can also be represented as a flowchart, or, better still, as a tree-like arrangement of machines or "number grinders." The computer or the pocket calculator help materialize the triple representation term-algorithm-number grinder.

For a striking example of the potential use of historical heuristics to improve the teaching of algebra, see the study by Eon Harper (1987) about letters as "unknowns" in Diophantus and as "givens" in Vieta. Understanding algebra from this viewpoint is knowing what conceptual systems lie under the different symbolic systems used to handle operators and relations on the real and complex numbers. (See Vasco, 1986).

From Geo-metrics to Geometry

Land measuring and surveying can be regained as a starting point for geometry. Large figures drawn on gym floors, big enough to stand inside them and to run around them, may teach more geometry than small figures drawn on blackboards and notebooks. Area-preserving transformations might be more easily found and checked with figures large enough to simulate vacant lots and farm fields. Active exploration of space together with small-scale plane representations of the results of exploring might be a better general objective for sixth-grade geometry than premature intro-ductions of geometric theorems and proofs. Microcomputers can provide playgrounds for such space explorations and drawing boards for those plane representations, but nothing can substitute for real-life exploration of the familiar space around us.

The absence of demonstrations (for lack of an axiom system) from the times of Pythagoras to Euclid's Elements need not be a problem. Forward heuristics suggest dealing with proto-theorems through verifications, without demonstrations, slowly building up connections among related propositions in order to retrace the steps that led to the Euclidean synthe-sis.

Forward heuristics suggest attending to the historical appearance of changes in focus from the static to the transformational approach to geom-etry. But backward heuristics suggest attending to those unconscious transformations that might be at the basis of apparently static observa-tions. For instance, the static approach to symmetry in most elementary textbooks, where "symmetry" is interpreted as a property of a figure, should come from a type of brain activity already identified by the "Gestalt" psychologists: mental rotations and reflections that leave the figure invariant. In this interpretation, "symmetry" is an active operator that transforms figures, not a static property of some of them. (See other related suggestions for learning sequences in geometry in Vasco, 1986; Clements and Battista, 1992).

Understanding geometry from this viewpoint means being able to explore outer and inner space in an active way, modeling internally the external world through dynamic mappings that allow for mental systems of transformations and relations, progressively freeing those systems from their concrete outer-space counterparts.

Heuristics from the Past and Schools for the Future

In spite of almost 40 years since the beginnings of cognitive science in 1956 (Gardner, 1985), cognitive research on the construction of mathematical concepts is still immature. Perhaps the new thrust it needs might come from historically inspired conjectures: forward and backward heuristics. But the recent *Handbook of Research on Mathematics Teaching and Learning* (Grouws, 1992) still shows no trace of this line of research in its almost 800 pages. But one must remember that this handbook was six years in the making.

In Germany there is a strong historically inspired line of research in the Society for the Didactics of Mathematics (Gesellschaft für Didaktik der Mathematik, GDM), and in particular at the Institute for the Didactics of Mathematics (Institut für Didaktik der Mathematik, IDM) of the University of Bielefeld. Several meetings on the relations between the history of science, the history of education, and research in mathematics education have been held in Germany since 1984. Literature on the meetings, research proposals, and results can be obtained from IDM, Universität Bielefeld, Bielefeld, Federal Republic of Germany.

In France, the University of Paris-North holds periodic research seminars on the relations between history and pedagogoy of mathematics under the direction of Professor Christian Houzel.

In North America, after almost a decade of pioneering work and humble bulletins of the International History, Philosophy, and Science Teaching Group IHPST, two international conferences on History, Philosophy, and Science Teaching have taken place, the first in Tallahasseee, Florida, in 1988 (see Herget, 1989), and the second in Kingston, Ontario, in 1992. There is a new journal at Kluwer Academic Publishers, called *Science & Education*, now in its second volume, where these topics are directly dealt with.

This chapter collects the social learning that occurred in the last two decades and presents an overview of one of the many sources of fruitful research hypotheses on the mental processes each child goes through in order to construct his or her own version of number, fraction, rectangle, meter, or polynomial; forward and backward heuristics are also a source of testable conjectures on the optimal sequencing of learning activities that help children build models, test conjectures, guide inquiry, and create and relate mental, gestural, graphical, verbal, and symbolic representations of those temporary constructs.

Small-scale research on pilot sequences arranged according to the historically motivated heuristic must be complemented by large-scale collaborative research on the success of those sequences with large class sizes and teachers without special training.

The first chapters of this book's Part I draw up a definite role for the history of science and mathematics in teacher training and in the formative years of psychologists and educational researchers. History teaches teachers to expect the occurrence of primitive stages, to appreciate their value as launch platforms, to expect roundabout routes, to appreciate the value of errors; above all, history teaches them to wait with patience. History teaches researchers to distrust their present mental models and conceptual definitions, to dig under them to find archaic strata and preliminary constructs, to retrace the steps of humankind in each child's development; history ultimately teaches them to be prepared for wonder. But by history, I mean here history learned not just as a curiosity for yesterday's events, but as a source of heuristics to plan the learning events in tomorrow's schools.

References

Bourbaki, N. 1950. The architecture of mathematics. *American Mathematical Monthly* 57: 221–32.

———. 1968. *Elements of mathematics: Theory of sets*. Reading, MA: Addison-Wesley.

Cardano, G. 1968. *The Great Art or the rules of algebra*, trans. and ed by T. Richard Witmer. Cambridge, MA: MIT Press.

Carpenter, T. P., J. M. Moser, and T. A. Romberg, eds. 1982. *Addition and subtraction: A cognitive perspective*. Hillsdale, NJ: Erlbaum.

Clements, D. H., and M. T. Battista. 1992. Geometry and spatial reasoning. In D. A. Grouws, ed., pp. 420–64. *Handbook of research on mathematics teaching and learning*. New York: Macmillan.

Cooper, B. 1985. *Renegotiating secondary school mathematics: A study of curriculum change and stability*. London: Falmer.

Freudenthal, H. 1984. The implicit philosophy of mathematics history and education. *Proceedings of the ICM*, August 16–24, 1983. Vol. 2, pp. 1695–1709. Warszawa/Amsterdam: PWN/North Holland.

Fuson, K. C. 1992. Research on whole number addition and subtraction. In D. A. Grouws, ed., pp. 243–75. *Handbook of research on mathematics teaching and learning*. New York: Macmillan.

Gardner, H. 1985. *The mind's new science*. New York: Basic Books.

Gelman, R., and C. R. Gallistel. 1978. *The child's understanding of number*. Cambridge, MA: Harvard University Press.

Grouws, D. A., ed. 1992. *Handbook of research on mathematics teaching and learning*. New York: Macmillan.

Harper, E. 1987. Ghosts of Diophantus. *Educational Studies in Mathematics* 18: 75–90.

Herget, D. E., ed. 1989. The history and philosophy of science in science teaching. *Proceedings of the 1st International Conference*, Tallahasee: Florida State University.

Kline, M. 1973. *Why Johnny can't add. The failure of the New Math*. New York: Vantage Books.

Kneale, W., and M. Kneale. 1961. *The development of logic*. Oxford: Clarendon Press.

Mandler, J. M. 1983. Representation. In *Handbook of child psychology*, 4th ed., edited by P. H. Mussen. Vol. 3, pp. 420–94. New York: John Wiley.

Moon, B. 1986. *The 'New Math's' curriculum controversy: An international story*. London: Falmer.

Piaget, J., and R. Garcia. 1982. *Psicogénesis e Historia de la Ciencia*. México: Siglo XXI Editores. French trans.: *Psychogenese et histoire des sciences*. Paris: Flammarion, 1983. English trans.: *Psychogenesis and the history of science*. New York: Columbia University Press, 1989.

Piaget, J., and B. Inhelder. 1948. *La représentation de l'espace chez l'enfant*. Paris: P.U.F. English trans.: *The child's conception of space*. London: Routledge & Kegan Paul, 1956.

Pólya, G. 1945. *How to solve it*. Princeton, NJ: Princeton University Press.

———. 1954. *Mathematics and plausible reasoning*. 2 vols. Princeton, NJ: Princeton University Press.

Schoenfeld, A. H. 1983. Problem solving in the mathematics curriculum *MAA Notes,* n. 1. Washington, DC: MAA.

———. 1992. Learning to think mathematically: Problem solving, metacognition, and sense making in mathematics. In D. A. Grouws, ed., pp. 334–70. *Handbook of research on mathematics teaching and learning*. New York: Macmillan.

Secada, W. G., K. C. Fuson, and J. W. Hall. 1983. The transition from counting-all to counting-on in addition. *Journal for Research in Mathematics Education* 14: 47–57.

Steffe, L. P., E. von Glasersfeld, J. Richards, and P. Cobb. 1984. *Children's counting types: Philosophy, theory and applications*. New York: Praeger.

Taboada y Ulloa, J. A. 1777. *Aritmética práctica*. Madrid: Antonio de Sancha. [Rare book, Widener Library, Harvard University.]

Vasco, C. E. 1985. *El algebra renacentista*, 2a. edición. Bogotá: Universidad Nacional de Colombia.

———. 1986. Learning elementary school mathematics as a culturally conditioned process. In *The cultural transition,* edited by M. I. White and S. Pollak. Boston/London: Routledge & Kegan Paul, pp. 141–75. [Available also as ERIC document ED 259 910, Columbus, OH: ERIC-CSMEE.]

Walters, J. 1985. Organizing a notation. ETC-Project Zero Preliminary Report. Unpublished manuscript.

5

Inside Understanding

DAVID N. PERKINS, DAVID CRISMOND,
REBECCA SIMMONS, and CHRIS UNGER

We cherish understanding, try to attain understanding, try to teach for understanding, and yet do not understand understanding very well.

To appreciate this point, it is only necessary to compare what we expect of remembering with what we expect of understanding. Suppose, for example, that a student who has been studying Darwin's theory of natural selection says, "I remember the three key principles pretty well." We would expect this student to be able to name the principles—variation, selection, and inheritance—and perhaps to repeat their definitions. Now suppose that this same student says, "I *understand* the three principles pretty well." Then what sort of a performance would we look for, to test the matter? Paraphrase? Well, but paraphrase made up only of straightforward substitutions for words in the textbook would not prove much. Explanation? Perhaps that comes closer, but repetitions of textbook explanations should not persuade us either. If such tests seem too rote, how about truly novel creative applications of the concepts? To be sure, this would give evidence of understanding. But it seems to demand too much of what might be only a routine or modest understanding. The moral should be clear: At first thought, we have only a vague idea of how a person might demonstrate understanding, much less what the psychological mechanisms of understanding are.

The question might be summed up this way: "What do people have when they have an understanding of something?" One reason to investigate this mystery is simple curiosity about the nature of understanding, so central a function of human cognition. Another reason is that understanding often comes hard. Darwin's theory, for example, baffles many students (Brumby, 1979, 1984; Jungworth, 1975), as does Newton's theory of dynamics (Brown and Clement, 1987; Clement, 1982; McDermott, 1984; White, 1983, 1993). In numerous other areas of science and mathematics, recent research has shown that students harbor deep misconceptions about what they have supposedly learned. Misconceptions have been well documented in algebra (Matz, 1982), physics (Chi, Feltovich, and Glaser, 1981; Chi, Glaser, and Rees, 1982; Larkin, McDermott, Simon, and Simon, 1980; McDermott, 1984; White, 1983, 1993), computer programming (Kurland, Pea, Clement, and Mawby, 1986; Linn, 1985; Perkins, Schwartz, and Simmons, 1988), and biology (Deadman and Kelly, 1978; Hackling and Treagust, 1984; Mintzes, 1984). If we had a better understanding of understanding, perhaps we could fathom the difficulties students have and find ways to help.

In exploring what it means to understand, we offer a fictional case of three students who are studying natural selection. We consider first the "outside" of understanding, the ways that understanding appears in overt behavior. What do people do and say that tells us that, yes, they understand?

Understanding on the Outside

Bonnie and Cal have been studying Darwin's theory of evolution. Cal doesn't quite get it, so he asks Bonnie to explain.

"Take seals' flippers, for example," Bonnie says. "Let's say a prehistoric seal happens to be born with longer flippers. That's *variation*. So the longer flippers help him to swim better, to get away from sharks, say. That's *selection*—he's more likely to survive. Then, when he gets to be a father, his offspring are likely to have longer flippers because he does. That's called *inheritance*. So flippers get longer and longer, generation by generation."

"I see what you mean," Cal says. "But the flippers can't get longer and longer forever, generation after generation."

Bonnie pauses, visions of seals with absurdly long flippers in her head. "Oh yeah," she says slowly. "I never thought about that. Now why doesn't that happen?" Bonnie falls silent again. "Oh, I see. It's this way. If the flippers are too long, they get in the way. So if the seal happens to have very long flippers, it's a disadvantage, so he's less likely to survive. So flippers stop getting longer."

"Well, let's see if I have this straight. Say I'm a prehistoric horse and I run a lot. I grow big leg muscles running away from mountain lions, so I'm even more likely to get away from mountain lions or whatever. And so my kids are born with big leg muscles. Is that how it works?"

"No, not quite," says Bonnie. "You yourself, the original horse, have to be *born* with the big leg muscles, or at least the tendency to grow big muscles when you grow up. What you develop during your life, just because there are more mountain lions to run from, doesn't count. You can't pass that on to your offspring."

"No? How come?" asks Cal. "It would really make sense. Say I'm a horse and I grow up in an area with a lot of mountain lions. So I do a lot of running. It would really be useful to pass those muscles along to my kids. That's the way it should work, sort of like passing along your hard-won earnings to your kids."

"Well," says Bonnie, "maybe that would be neat. But that isn't the way it works. There's a catch. What gets passed on is determined by your genes. But your genes are fixed when you're born, in fact when you're conceived. So, if you happen to work hard later and grow big muscles, your genes don't know that. Conception is like rolling dice; maybe you'll get stronger leg muscles and maybe you won't. If you do get stronger legs, and that's what you happen to need to escape from mountain lions, and so you survive, then you'll pass on that trait."

With this dialogue in mind, let us return to the question posed earlier: What do people do and say that tells us that they understand something? Bonnie certainly seems to understand natural selection well. Her overt behavior illustrates what might be called an "understanding performance" (Gardner, 1991; Perkins, 1992) with at least the following three key characteristics.

Offering Explanations

First, people display their understandings of things by offering explanations. For instance, Bonnie explains natural selection by giving examples, such as the inheritance of longer flippers. She highlights critical features such as selection and inheritance. Moreover, she responds to the new puzzle Cal raises about seals' flippers getting longer and longer forever. In contrast, if Bonnie simply described seals and listed terms without being able to explain anything, that would be an inadequate performance—she would seem to lack understanding.

Articulating Richly Relational Knowledge

Second, people express their understanding in explanations constructed of richly relational knowledge. For example, Bonnie's discussion relates genetic variation to morphological variation, genetic and morphological variation to survival advantages, and survival advantages to preservation of the trait. This is a complex web of cause and effect that Bonnie can not only articulate but also illustrate with her knowledge about seals and horses. If Bonnie's explanation were sparse, only involving one simple rule for instance, that would suggest a sketchy understanding.

Displaying a Revisable and Extensible Web of Explanation

Third, people demonstrate their understanding by revising and extending their explanations. For example, Bonnie's account of natural selection falls far from a canned recital. She revises and extends her knowledge about variation and selection. To be sure, her original seal example could be straight out of the textbook. But Bonnie revises her explanation in response to Cal's challenge about the ever-longer flippers, which is obviously not from a textbook. Moreover, in her critique of Cal's own example of the horse, she extends her web of explanation from the seal to the horse. Thus her web of explanation is both highly *extensible* and *revisable* in fundamental ways. If it were not, we would see her as just parroting, not understanding.

While these characteristics mark the kind of performance we expect from someone who understands, it's also worth underscoring that this performance is frequently *fragile*—partial, halting, flawed, and evanescent. For example, Cal tries to construct his own illustrative example, the account of the horse strengthening his legs. While including selection and inheritance, Cal's example misses the crucial role of inborn variation, even though this appeared in Bonnie's account of the seal. So Bonnie has to try to correct Cal's conception. Maybe Cal grasps Bonnie's explanation and maybe not, but, if he does, Cal's improved conception may well backslide in a few seconds, tomorrow, or next week.

At this point, we can look back to our original question and record some progress. "What do people have when they have an understanding of something?" The rough answer is that people have an ability to display a certain range of generative performances involving explanation.

While the present analysis emphasizes the importance of explanation to understanding, it's worth remarking that people might be said to "understand" in certain senses of the word without being able to explain. For instance, an able jazz pianist could be said to understand how to play jazz, yet might not be able to explain how in words, or even in gestures or by systematic demonstration. Such meanings of "understand" certainly are important and deserve analysis. Nonetheless, for present purposes, we focus on meanings of understand that highlight explanation, noting that such meanings have special prominence in a wide range of academic as well as nonacademic contexts.

Understanding on the Inside

Bonnie's understanding performance is a clue to what her understanding is like on the inside. On the outside, we hear Bonnie offering a rich verbal explanation as she copes with Cal's challenge about seals' flippers. Mentally, she explores a rich conceptual network that we will call an *explanation structure*.

What is an explanation structure? It is a rich network of explanatory relationships that are encoded mentally in any of the many ways the mind has available—through words, images, cases in point, anecdotes, formal principles, and so on. This explanation structure is more than a memorized explanation: It is *extensible* and *revisable*. For example, we know that Bonnie has a flexible explanation structure about natural selection because, in response to Cal's challenge, she extends it to the puzzling case of seals' flippers getting longer and longer.

Parts of Bonnie's explanation structure for natural selection are well rehearsed. For example, as mentioned earlier, the account of the seal that Bonnie offers Cal may well be straight out of the textbook Bonnie has thoroughly studied. These well-learned components are the *substrate* on which Bonnie builds during her conversation with Cal. But other parts of the explanation structure are novel, created on the spot to extend this substrate—Bonnie's responses to Cal's challenge about ever-longer flippers and to his mistaken example of the horse. Some of these *extensions* may get consolidated into Bonnie's initial substrate, expanding it and giving her a greater repertoire to work from later. Other momentary extensions may simply be forgotten. Bonnie may reconstruct them later, on another occasion, or never recover them at all.

This temporary character of extensions helps to account for a characteristic of understandings noted earlier: their fragility (Perkins, 1992; Perkins and Martin, 1986). An explanation structure is, in part, a momentary construction. It is sustained by the current context—the ongoing conversation, illustrations lying on the table, scratch work on a blackboard. Explanation structures should not be seen as static but as expanding as we engage the topic and contracting as we set the topic aside, with new associations left in the substrate that make later reconstructions and extensions easier.

All this marks some progress on the opening question: "What do people have when they have understandings?" They have explanation structures, rich extensible revisable networks of relationships that explain relevant aspects of the topic. Any explanation structure includes a stable substrate and momentary extensions, many of which will be forgotten but others that will get consolidated into the substrate. An explanation structure only counts as an understanding because it is extensible and revisable. If not, it would just be a rigid template.

The Access Framework of Understanding

How do explanation structures get built, extended, and revised? What makes them hard to construct? Why are they so often fragile and flawed? To answer these questions, we offer what we call the *Access Framework* of understanding (Perkins, 1993). The name comes from the guiding premise of the framework: To display understandings—that is, to build, extend, and revise explanation structures—you need to be able to call on several resources. In particular, you need:

1. *Knowledge* Access to certain kinds of knowledge (for instance, knowledge about Darwin's three principles, about seals, or about the importance of testing a theory against puzzling cases).
2. *Representation* Access to the knowledge facilitated by well-chosen representations (for instance, prototypical cases, clarifying metaphors, lucid diagrams).
3. *Retrieval mechanisms* Access made possible by retrieval mechanisms that recover relevant information from memory or an external source (e.g., recollections of what the textbook said or what seals are like).
4. *Construction mechanisms* Access to new implications, elaborations, applications, and so on, mediated by effective construction mechanisms for building new explanation structures (e.g., when Bonnie explained the case of seals' flippers).

We call *knowledge, representation, retrieval mechanisms*, and *construction mechanisms* the four dimensions of the Access Framework. They are not so much separate categories as they are somewhat separately analyzable aspects of the information processing required for "understanding performances." In the remainder of this chapter, we explore some aspects of each dimension in turn, at the end sketching broadly the import for education.

The Knowledge Dimension: Above and Beyond Content Knowledge

It should come as no surprise that achieving understanding depends on content knowledge. An understanding of algebra, for example, calls for knowledge of such central concepts as variable, equation, solution, and expression. In Bonnie's case, an understanding of the theory of natural selection required knowledge of the three principles of Darwin's theory: variation, selection, and inheritance. However, understanding depends not only on these central concepts but on other supporting knowledge that assists in the process of building explanation structures. General content-level knowledge is one such type of supporting information. When Bonnie grapples with Cal's puzzle about the seals, for example, she must draw not only on Darwin's principles but on her general knowledge about what seals are like and why very long flippers might get in their way. Equally relevant, however, are systems of knowledge more abstract than typical content (Collins and Ferguson, 1993; Ohlsson, 1993; Perkins, 1992; Perkins and Simmons, 1988). Two of these classes of higher-order knowledge—problem solving and epistemic—will serve as good examples for our discussion.

Problem-solving Knowledge

Learners need access to a wide range of knowledge about how to solve problems in order to make sense of incoming information and apply it appropriately (cf. Brown, Bransford, Ferrara, and Campione, 1983; Campione et al., 1991). They frequently need to engage in extended problem solving in a domain in order to assimilate new facts and ideas. Unfortunately, learners' knowledge of problem solving is often limited or even counterproductive. Reductive strategies such as trial and error, perseveration and quitting, proceeding on a guess, and equation cranking often dominate (Perkins and Simmons, 1988). Instead of actively engaging in problem solving, students commonly develop stock answers and respond in stereotyped ways.

A particularly striking instance of such formulaic thinking comes from work with elementary students in arithmetic (Lester, 1985). When asked to figure out how many chickens and how many pigs were on a farm that included 18 animals with 52 legs in all, many students solved the problem by adding 18 and 52. When asked why they added, they said that since the problem asked, "How many in all," the correct strategy was to add the two numbers together.

Some strategies for problem solving are specific to a discipline, while others cut across several disciplines or have general utility, regardless of the subject. Metacognitive strategies, for instance, help students to monitor progress and stay on task (Brown, 1978). General heuristics such as breaking problems down into manageable parts and seeking alternative solution paths also help regulate the problem-solving process (Brown, Bransford, Ferrara, and Campione, 1983; Campione et al., 1991; Polya, 1954; Scardamalia and Bereiter, 1985; Schoenfeld, 1980, 1985). Finally, supportive beliefs and attitudes about problem solving foster progressing on problems rather than perseverating on an unfruitful path or stopping altogether (Dweck and Bempechat, 1980; Dweck and Licht, 1980; Perkins, Hancock, Hobbs, Martin & Simmons, 1986; Perkins et al., 1993).

In sum, inflexible and limited problem-solving heuristics may result in explanation structures that are rigidly bound and relationally impoverished. Conversely, rich problem-solving knowledge empowers students to go beyond formulaic or trial-and-error strategies, to think about and reflect on problems in a domain. Bonnie revealed her readiness to solve problems when she responded to Cal's challenge of the seal flippers. Ideally, any student's repertoire incorporates a wide range of problem-solving attitudes and strategies from general attention and progress monitoring to domain-specific strategic knowledge.

Epistemic Knowledge

Students also need "epistemic knowledge" to help build cohesive and flexible explanation structures. By "epistemic" we mean knowledge of the "rules of the game" for justification and explanation in a domain. For example, any domain—biology, algebra, physics, literature, history—depends on one or another kind of evidence to justify claims. Knowledge of what sort of evidence to use acts as a watchdog for incoming content knowledge, discouraging superficial, passive reception of content and provoking episodes of problem solving that revise old understandings and build new ones (Collins and Ferguson, 1993).

The notion of "epistemic knowledge" may at first seem erudite and philosophical, but Bonnie and Cal both make vigorous, albeit tacit, use of such knowledge in their discussion of the seals. Cal, after hearing Bonnie explain that flippers get longer generation by generation, detects a potential anomaly in the theory. His epistemic watchdog is on guard, encouraging him to test limits in the theory. He challenges Bonnie, arguing that flippers can't get longer and longer forever.

Bonnie, too, displays an epistemic insight into the problem. She understands that scientific theories must hang together. She knows that laws or axioms must be consistent with the evidence of what happens in the world. Although Bonnie does not immediately know the answer to Cal's question, she recognizes that the theory of natural selection must certainly take into account such obvious outcomes. As she sorts out this puzzle, Bonnie grounds her thinking in the precepts of the theory, arriving at a response that maintains the internal coherency with the core concepts of the theory.

In summary, the development of rich and valid explanation structures requires not only considerable content knowledge but other equally important types of knowledge as well. Substantial higher-order thinking, employing problem-solving knowledge, epistemic knowledge, and more, is necessary for deep understanding.

The Representation Dimension: Complementary Conceptual Anchors

A few days later, between classes, Bonnie overhears Cal attempting to explain natural selection to Alexander. She listens in, hoping to find that Cal indeed "has it."

> "So, you see," Cal says, "just because the horse grew big leg muscles doesn't mean that his kids will be born with big leg muscles." Bonnie smiles. "It depends, like throwing dice. You know how you get a six sometimes and sometimes you don't. Well, sometimes his kids will inherit his big leg muscles and sometimes they won't."
>
> Bonnie frowns. "Now what happened?," she asks herself.
>
> Bonnie thinks back. "Oh, I remember," she says to herself. "I used to think that you could pass on acquired traits. How did I get it straight?" "Oh yes," she thinks. "I remember now how Mr. Holly explained it. I asked whether if I practiced to become a really fast runner, I could pass those genes on to my kids so that they could be fast runners. 'No,' he said. 'It's not quite like that, Bonnie. For example, if you dyed your hair

orange, do you think that your kids would be born with orange hair?' I certainly didn't think that! But how did it all work? 'Okay,' he continued. 'Do you think that because you're learning geometry right now that your kids will automatically know geometry when they are born?'"

"Oh, I see what you mean," she had said. "Just because I learn geometry, or dye my hair orange, or even practice running fast, doesn't mean my genes change. It doesn't work like that. I can't change my genes by what I do. My genes are just the way they are." "Right," Mr. Holly had agreed, with enthusiasm. That makes sense, Bonnie thought to herself. "And I don't think that I would want my kids to have orange hair anyway."

So why didn't Cal "get it"? After all, Cal heard from Bonnie what would seem to be a sufficient explanation, including specific mention of the matters Cal became confused about. While there could be many reasons for Cal's muddle, it is important to recognize that the necessary information in a bare-bones sense often is not enough for understanding. Particularly worth attention are the kinds of *representations* Mr. Holly offered Bonnie in direct contrast with those that Bonnie offered Cal.

The theory of natural selection might be explained through many representations, for example, verbal definitions, a "story," a cartoon strip, paradigmatic cases, the juxtapositioning of contrasting cases, and analogies. Mr. Holly provided Bonnie with a set of highly contrasting *examples*—one kind of representation—that made extremely salient the conceptual point. In contrast, Cal picked up on Bonnie's single analogy of the dice that chance is involved, failing to see—perhaps as a result of having only one analogy—*when* the dice are rolled: at conception.

We will call representations that effectively "hook into" one's current understanding to make a point *conceptual anchors*. Such representations help the learner to build explanation structures by being particularly clear, memorable, and to the point (Perkins and Unger, in press). Johsua and Dupin (1988), for example, have found that students offered the representation of a continuous train being pushed about a continuous track have been greatly aided in their differentiation of "energetical" and "material" aspects of electrical flow. Likewise, Clement (1987) and Minstrell (1982) have found that building on students' intuitions about springs and bendy surfaces can greatly facilitate their appreciation of Newton's Third Law.

But why sometimes use more than *one* representation, as Mr. Holly did? It is often the case that several complementary representations are needed to build a complex explanation structure (Perkins and Unger, in press). For example, Mr. Holly's set of examples from dying hair orange to practicing running provided Bonnie with (1) some examples where genetic modification seemed totally implausible (orange hair) coupled with (2) other examples that were closer to natural performances (running), where genetic modification might at first seem plausible. The combination clarified the point that not even natural performances yielded genetic modifications, according to Darwin's theory.

A number of sources in the literature suggest that multiple representations are often advantageous. For example, in experiments asking subjects to generalize the problem-solving principles used in sample problems, Gick and Holyoak (1983) discovered that two examples informed subjects much better than one example. Investigators in science instruction have found the use of multiple complementary representations to be equally helpful. The *ThinkerTools* environment developed by White and Horwitz (White, 1993) offers two complementary representations of velocity and acceleration to cultivate sixth graders' understanding of Newtonian mechanics. The heat and temperature curriculum developed by Wiser (Wiser, Grosslight, and Unger, 1989; Wiser & Kipman, 1988) relies heavily on complementary models of heat and temperature not only at the macrolevel but on the molecular level as well.

In sum, complementary conceptual anchors can help to relate new knowledge to old knowledge, or even restructure old knowledge (see again Perkins and Unger, in press). As the tale of Bonnie, Cal, and Alexander illustrates, it isn't enough for the information just to "be there"; the representations must function as complementary conceptual anchors, too. Then, and only then, might understanding take hold, grow, and prosper.

The Retrieval Dimension: Avoiding Inert Knowledge

While knowledge and representation play evident roles in Bonnie's, Cal's, and Alexander's efforts to understand the theory of natural selection, another dimension of cognition could easily be overlooked: *retrieval* of knowledge. For example, when Bonnie encountered Cal and Alexander conversing, she need not have wondered about their getting Darwin straight; she might well have thought about weekend dates or the school basketball game that night. Later in the day, Bonnie found herself ruminating about her own understanding of acquired characteristics, but she might well never have reviewed her thinking on the matter.

The moral is simple: In order to function as tools of understanding, knowledge and representations have to be retrieved from long-term memory. It is useful to distinguish "pop up" and "dig out" retrieval of information. In "pop up" retrieval, the task context reminds one of relevant knowledge structures, which simply come to mind. This is in keeping with spreading activation notions of information retrieval, whereby information structures become primed for retrieval through links to related information structures (e.g., Anderson, 1983). In "dig out" retrieval, the individual makes a calculated effort to recover relevant information. "Dig out" retrieval efforts can range from simple verbal cueing of oneself (e.g., asking "Now what do I know about natural selection?") to vigorous efforts to piece together half-forgotten information. Here again, spreading activation is implicated, but in a more metacognitive way, through the individual's self-cueing rather than through simple contact with the task context.

Investigations have shown that considerable knowledge which people possess is "inert": It is present in memory but neither pops up nor gets dug out on appropriate occasions. For example, in studies of students' programming skills conducted at the Educational Technology Center, we found that novice programmers had much more information about commands than they seemed to. Often, they did not retrieve appropriate commands while trying to program. However, if these commands were mentioned, they recognized them and could proceed to use them effectively. Also, in a series of studies conducted by John Bransford and his colleagues, students and others commonly failed to retrieve in problem-solving contexts information that they were known to possess (Bransford, Franks, Vye, and Sherwood, 1989).

Other studies conducted by Bransford and his co-workers have disclosed some of the conditions for acquisition of "pop up" knowledge (Brown, Bransford, Ferrara, and Campione, 1983). When learners master knowledge through "problem-based learning," acquiring the knowledge as they work through problems, they tend to retrieve and apply it in similar problem-solving contexts later. Presumably this is because the knowledge has become associated with contextual cues for its use; the spreading activation from these cues primes the target knowledge structures. In contrast to problem-based learning, conventional schooling often leads students to associate knowledge structures only with direct questioning cues ("When did Columbus discover America?") rather than cues that signal opportunities to apply the knowledge.

In a similar spirit, Perkins and colleagues (Perkins, Schwartz, and Simmons, 1988; Schwartz, Perkins, Estey, Kruideneir, and Simmons, 1989; Schwartz and Perkins, Chapter 14, this volume) included in supplementary materials designed to enhance students' learning of computer programming (1) a learning strategy designed to help students associate programming commands with their practical applications and (2) programming strategies designed to encourage students to interrogate their knowledge bases for relevant information. The first of these encouraged "pop up" retrieval while the second encouraged "dig out" retrieval. Although there is no way of isolating the impact of these strategies among several others taught, the overall intervention was quite successful in enhancing students' mastery of programming.

The concepts of "pop up" and "dig out" retrieval help to explain Bonnie's alertness to Cal's and Alexander's conversation and her later ruminations, too. Her earlier conversation with Mr. Holly had engaged her in active examination of her ideas about inheritance of acquired characteristics, a kind of problem-based learning fostering "pop up" retrieval. Moreover, Bonnie's behavior throughout these episodes suggests that she is an aggressive thinker, probing others—and herself—for information: She "digs out" information. In general, instruction that cultivates active learning and fosters active self-interrogation is far less likely to leave learners with bodies of inert knowledge.

Other phenomena associated with the retrieval dimension include transfer of learning to remote contexts (Salomon and Perkins, 1989), the role of conceptual models (Mayer, 1989), the role of mnemonics (Paivio, 1971), and more. In general, the retrieval of information involves phenomena and pitfalls considerably more subtle than those of traditional rote learning with regurgitation on command.

The Construction Dimension: Catching On Versus Working Through

Bonnie spies Alexander alone in the hall the day after hearing his and Cal's conversation about horses. Cal sure had it fouled up, she thought to herself. How about Al?

> "You know the business about the horses, Darwin and all?" she begins out of the blue. Al looks bewildered. "The stuff Cal was talking about yesterday?" she asks. "So what's *your* idea about how the horses get stronger legs?"
>
> Al looks even more bewildered. "Well, ah . . . ." Then he remembers a point. "Well, for sure, not by exercising. You can't pass on exercise. It just doesn't work that way."
>
> "Yeah, okay, so how does it work?"
>
> "Well, it happens when you're born—you're born with stronger legs."
>
> "But did you think about the fact that colts are tiny little things," Bonnie says. "They don't have strong legs."
>
> "Yeah," Al says and squints. "Yeah. Well . . . ." He shrugs. "You know, I really don't get it. That's the way things are with these ideas. You either get 'em or you don't."

Faced with making sense of new ideas or explaining old ideas from a new angle, most people act as if they are drawing from some tacit theory of learning. Bonnie's questions and Alexander's response suggest that the two hold different theories of learning. Al thinks that understandings get built by "catching on." Understanding comes quickly, almost intuitively, if it comes at all. In contrast, Bonnie (as well as Cal) build understandings by "working through." Over a period of time, she has been elaborating on a concept, applying it to new cases, testing its limits.

The cognitive enterprise of building a new understanding is inevitably complex, and involves detecting similarities, symmetries, and hierarchies among the facts of a domain that get drawn together into a structural whole. Although extensive analysis along these lines would be fruitful, some important points emerge simply from contrasting the approaches of *catching on* versus *working through*.

Catching on is the bread and butter of constructing everyday understandings. You do it when you laugh at a joke, orient yourself to an unfamiliar kitchen, or catch up on the life of a long-absent friend. From a psychological standpoint, catching on reflects the rapid marshaling, adaptation, and coordination of remembered facts, explanations, scenarios, even relevant conversations, in order to build an understanding for new situations.

Catching on serves us perfectly well, but there are drawbacks when catching on is the sole tool for building new understandings. Often, when learning a new topic, you do not have relevant cognitive structures on-hand to permit the rapid encoding characteristic of catching on. In particular, since Alexander is not familiar with anything like the complex notions of natural selection, his expectation to catch on to a whole new domain is unreasonable.

Moreover, a catching on approach often yields simplistic explanation structures that overly reduce complicated matters to stereotypes. People who rely on catching on rarely test their prior assumptions, and end up incorporating superficial features to their naive concepts. Alex needs to work through these challenges, but he instead affirms his catch on philosophy: You either get it or you don't.

Working through begins where catching on leaves off. While most of us would grant that Darwin himself undertook protracted and extensive working through to construct his new theory of natural selection (Gruber, 1974), far fewer acknowledge that the rest of us must do much working through to build a similar explanation structure, even with Darwin's guidance.

From a cognitive standpoint, working through involves what is called *elaborative processing*—where reflecting on, extending, and testing ideas improves the retrievability and depth of a cognitive structure. Building understandings from the ground up involves putting ideas into categories, and creating new categories when old ones no longer are doing the job. It entails referencing varied examples, puzzling out confusions, and managing an audit trail of failed early prototypes, chance guesses, and miscued conclusions. The conversations between Bonnie and Cal involve persistent *working through* some of the puzzling aspects of evolution. Bonnie even pursues the audit trails of others by hounding her friends. The understanding she builds is less fragile because elaboration has helped establish the substrate and relational links between new concepts and established knowledge.

So what are we to make of Bonnie, Cal, and Alex's deep-rooted attitudes toward building understandings? A key insight may come from Carol Dweck's distinction between "incremental" and "entity" learners (Dweck and Bempechat, 1980; Dweck and Licht, 1980). She discovered that many youngsters consistently behaved as though something to be learned were one single entity that they had to grasp whole—"you either get it or you don't." Other youngsters recognized the importance of incremental learning, nibbling away at puzzling concepts bit by bit, doing what we have called *working through*.

Dweck discovered that some quite intelligent students could be entity learners, ready to quit if they did not catch on, whereas some not-so-bright students could be incremental learners, ready to grind away and make some progress. In our scenario, Bonnie seems sharper than Cal. But Dweck would describe both Bonnie and Cal as incremental learners. It's nice to be naturally "sharp," but, however sharp Alexander may or may not be, as an entity learner he will surely construct fewer and less elaborate understandings, and will not fulfill his potential as a learner.

Education Access

It is commonplace to note that learning depends on access—to adequate facilities, informed teachers, illuminating materials, and so on. Unquestionably, many disadvantaged populations have suffered from lack of access to substantive educational opportunities.

In this sketch of the *Access Framework,* we make an analogous point about the inner world of the mind. Just as students need physical access to good teachers, facilities, and materials, they also need mental access to a wide repertoire of higher-order knowledge, accessible representations, and rich contexts that facilitate activation of relevant knowledge. Just as unfortunate social practices often deprive students of physical access, unfortunate educational practices often deprive students of the mental access they need.

Access Depends on Knowledge

Too often, education simply does not offer access to areas of knowledge crucial to building explanation structures. While most texts and teachers reliably provide "the facts," constructing understandings often calls for considerably more: problem-solving strategies and epistemic principles not addressed at all in typical instruction. Those students who manage to understand anyway do so by picking up these matters on the side or by "reading between the lines," special avenues of access not discovered by many other students.

Access Depends on Representations

There is more to good access than the availability of knowledge in principle. Whether knowledge is genuinely and usefully accessible depends on whether the representations that carry the knowledge offer effective "conceptual anchors," disclosing important networks of relationships in a vivid and memorable way. While a number of effective conceptual anchors have figured in recent educational experiments, the textbooks, wall charts, exercise sheets, and other paraphernalia of typical education represent knowledge in ways too didactic to provide good conceptual anchoring.

Access Depends on Retrieval

The right knowledge well represented cannot help learners with understanding if they do not retrieve it from memory or from external sources at moments when they are trying to build understandings. Knowledge acquired in the course of working through problems or otherwise explicitly linked to applications contexts is more likely to "pop up" on later occasions of relevance than knowledge learned by rote. Moreover, relevant knowledge is more likely to be retrieved when people engage in active, aggressive efforts to "dig out" information from memory. Unfortunately, typical schooling encourages neither of these paths.

Access Depends on Effective Construction Mechanisms

Sometimes, access to a good range of relevant knowledge mediated by apt representations suffices for understanding. Certainly learners often catch on: relatively automatic mechanisms assemble an explanation structure, working from a collection of prefabricated structures. However, the catching on approach is not effective when students are faced with novel and complex conceptual systems, especially in areas where they may already harbor contrary intuitions. In these circumstances, building an adequate explanation structure requires a much more self-conscious and protracted process of working through. Unfortunately, typical education neither makes room for nor supports the challenging process of working through the complexities of difficult conceptual systems.

To sum up, it is a curious fact that instruction rarely creates conditions conducive to "understanding performances," even though virtually all instruction aspires to understanding. In particular, typical schooling fares poorly on a report card that scores for dealing with full-spectrum knowledge, the use of powerful representations that provide conceptual anchors, the cultivating of "pop up" and "dig out" retrieval, and the fostering of habits of learning by working through difficult ideas. Moreover, other shortfalls besides those elaborated here could be mentioned within the compass of the Access Framework. For example, under *construction mechanisms,* we have not discussed the need to manage complexity during construction to avoid cognitive load bottlenecks (Case, 1985, 1992); under *retrieval mechanisms,* we have not discussed ways of teaching for "far transfer," so that understandings acquired in one context inform the learner in other, very different contexts (Perkins and Solomon, 1988).

Accordingly, the Access Framework and other integrative efforts in like spirit point toward what might be called "a pedagogy of understanding." As we come to appreciate more clearly the conditions under which understanding thrives, a pedagogy of understanding that can speak to most students seems within reach.

References

Anderson, J. R. 1983. *The architecture of cognition.* Cambridge, MA: Harvard University Press.

Bransford, J. D., J. J. Franks, N. J. Vye, and R. D. Sherwood. (1989.) *New approaches to instruction: Because wisdom can't be told.* In S. Vosniadou and

A. Ortony (Eds.), *Similarity and analogical reasoning*, pp. 470–497. New York: Cambridge University Press.

Brown, A. L. 1978. Knowing when, where, and how to remember: A problem of metacognition. In *Advances in Instructional Psychology*, edited by R. Glaser. Vol. 1. Hillsdale, NJ: Erlbaum.

———, J. D. Bransford, R. A. Ferrara, and J. C. Campione. 1983. Learning, remembering, and understanding. In *Cognitive development*. Vol. 3 of *Handbook of child psychology*. 4th ed., edited by J. H. Flavell and E. M. Markman, pp. 77–166. New York: Wiley.

Brown, D., and J. Clement. 1987. Misconceptions concerning Newton's law of action and reaction. *Proceedings of the second international seminar on misconceptions and educational strategies in science and mathematics*. Ithaca, NY: Cornell University.

Brumby, M. N. 1979. Problems in learning the concept of natural selection. *Journal of Biological Education* 13(2): 119–22.

———. 1984. Misconceptions about the concept of natural selection by medical biology students. *Science Education* 68(4): 493–503.

Campione, J. C., A. L. Brown, R. A. Reeve, R. A. Ferrara, and A. S. Palincsar. 1991. Interactive learning and individual understanding: The case of reading and mathematics. In *Culture, schooling, and psychological development*, edited by L.T. Landsmann, pp. 136–70. Norwood, NJ: Ablex.

Case, R. 1985. *Intellectual development: Birth to adulthood*. New York: Academic Press.

———. 1992. *The mind's staircase: Exploring the conceptual underpinnings of children's thought and knowledge*. Hillsdale, NJ: Erlbaum.

Chi, M., P. Feltovich, and R. Glaser. 1981. Categorization and representation of physics problems by experts and novices. *Cognitive Science* 5: 121–52.

———, R. Glaser, and R. Rees. 1982. Expertise in problem solving. In *Advances in psychology of human intelligence*, edited by R. Sternberg, pp. 7–75. Hillsdale, NJ: Erlbaum.

Clement, J. 1982. Students' preconceptions in introductory mechanics. *American Journal of Physics* 50, 66–71.

———. 1987a. Overcoming students' misconceptions in physics: The role of anchoring intuitions and analogical validity. *Proceedings of the second international seminar on misconceptions and educational strategies in science and mathematics* 3: 84–97. Ithaca, NY: Cornell University.

———. 1987b. *The use of analogies and anchoring intuitions to remediate misconceptions in mechanics*. Paper presented at the annual meeting of the American Educational Research Association, Washington, D.C., April 1987.

Collins, A., and W. Ferguson. 1993. Epistemic forms and epistemic games. *Educational Psychologist* 28(1): 25–42.

Deadman, J. A., and P. J. Kelly, 1978. What do secondary school boys understand about evolution and heredity before they are taught the topics? *Journal of Biological Education* 12(1): 7–15.

Dweck, C. S., and J. Bempechat. 1980. Children's theories of intelligence: Consequences for learning. In *Learning and motivation in the classroom*, edited by S. G. Paris, G. M. Olson, and H. W. Stevenson, pp. 239–56. Hillsdale, NJ: Erlbaum.

Dweck, C. S., and B. G. Licht. 1980. Learned helplessness and intellectual achievement. In J. Garbar and M. Seligman (Eds.), *Human helplessness*. New York: Academic Press.

Gardner, H. 1991. *The unschooled mind: How children think and how schools should teach*. New York: Basic Books.

Gick, M. L., and K. J. Holyoak. 1983. Schema induction and analogical transfer. *Cognitive Psychology* 15: 1–38.

Gruber, H. E. 1974. *Darwin on man: A psychological study of scientific creativity*. New York: Dutton.

Hackling, M. W., and D. Treagust. 1984. Research data necessary for meaningful review of grade 10 high school genetics curricula. *Journal of Research in Science Teaching* 21(2): 197–209.

Johsua, S., and J. J. Dupin. 1987. Taking into account student conceptions in a didactic strategy: An example in physics. *Cognition and Instruction* 4(2): 117–35.

Jungworth, E. 1975. Preconceived adaptation and inverted evolution, a case of distorted concept formation in high-school biology. *The Australian Science Teachers Journal* 212: 95–100.

Kurland, M. D., R. D. Pea, C. Clement, and R. Mawby. 1986. *A study of the development of programming ability and thinking skills in high school students*. New York: Bank Street College of Education, Center for Children and Technology.

Larkin, J. H., J. McDermott, D. P. Simon, and H. A. Simon. 1980. Scientific reasoning: Garden paths and blind alleys. In *Research in science education: New questions new directions*, edited by J. Robons. Colorado Springs, CO: Biological Science Curriculum Study.

Lester, F. 1985. Methodological considerations in research on mathematical problem-solving instruction. In *Teaching and learning mathematical problem solving: Multiple research perspectives*, edited by E. A. Silver, pp. 41–69. Hillsdale, NJ: Erlbaum.

Linn, M. C. 1985. The cognitive consequences of programming instruction in classrooms. *Educational Researcher* 14: 14–29.

Matz, M. 1982. Towards a process model of high school algebra errors, in *Intelligent tutoring systems*, edited by D. Sleeman and J. S. Brown, pp. 25–50. New York: Academic Press.

Mayer, R. E. 1989. Models for understanding. *Review of Educational Research* 59(1): 43–64.

McDermott, L. C. 1984. Research on conceptual understanding in mechanics. *Physics Today* 37: 24–32.

Minstrell, J. 1982. Explaining the "at rest" condition of an object. *Physics Teacher* 20(1): 10–14

Mintzes, E. 1984. Understanding and misunderstandings of biology concepts. *School Science and Mathematics* 84(7): 548–55.

Ohlsson, S. (1993). Abstract schemas. *Educational Psychologist* 28(1): 51–66.

Paivio, A. 1971. *Imagery and verbal processes*. New York: Holt, Rinehart, & Winston.

Perkins, D. N. 1992. *Smart schools: From training memories to educating minds*. New York: The Free Press.

———. 1993. Person plus: A distributed view of thinking and learning. In *Distributed cognitions*, pp. 88–110, edited by G. Salomon. New York: Cambridge University Press.

———, and F. Martin, F. 1986. Fragile knowledge and neglected strategies in novice programmers. In *Empirical studies of programmers*, edited by E. Soloway and S. Iyengar, pp. 213–29. Norwood, NJ: Ablex.

————, and G. Salomon. 1988. Teaching for transfer. *Educational Leadership* 46(1): 22–32.

————, and R. Simmons. 1988. Patterns of misunderstanding: An integrative model of misconceptions in science, mathematics, and programming. *Review of Educational Research* 58(3): 303–26.

————, and C. Unger. In press. A new look in representations for mathematics and science learning. *Instructional Science*.

————, E. Jay, and S. Tishman. 1993. Beyond abilities: A dispositional theory of thinking. *The Merrill-Palmer Quarterly* 39(1): 1–21.

————, Schwartz, S., and R. Simmons. 1988. Instructional strategies for the problems of novice programmers. In *Teaching and learning computer programming: Multiple research perspectives*, edited by R. Mayer, pp. 153–78. Hillsdale, NJ: Erlbaum.

Perkins, D. N., C. Hancock, R. Hobbs, F. Martin, and R. Simmons. 1986. Conditions of learning in novice programmers. *Journal of Educational Computing Research* 2(1): 37–56.

Polya, G. 1954. *Mathematics and plausible reasoning*, 2 vols. Princeton, NJ: Princeton University Press.

Salomon, G., and D. N. Perkins. 1989. Rocky roads to transfer: Rethinking mechanism of a neglected phenomenon. *Educational Psychologist* 24(2): 113–42.

Scardamalia, M., and C. Bereiter. 1985. Fostering the development of self-regulation in children's knowledge processing. In *Thinking and learning skills: Research and open questions,* edited by S. F. Chipman, J. W. Segal, and R. Glaser. Vol. 2, pp. 563–77. Hillsdale, NJ: Erlbaum.

Schoenfeld, A. H. 1980. Teaching problem-solving skills. *American Mathematical Monthly* 87: 794–805.

————. 1985. *Mathematical problem solving*. Orlando, Fl: Academic Press.

Schwartz, S., D. N. Perkins, G. Estey, J. Krudeneir, and R. Simmons. 1989. A "metacourse" for BASIC: Assessing a new model for enhancing instruction. *Journal of Educational Computing Research* 5(3): 263–97.

White, B. 1983. Sources of difficulty in understanding Newtonian dynamics. *Cognitive Science* 7: 41–65.

————. 1993. *ThinkerTools*: Causal models, conceptual change, and science education. *Cognition and Instruction* 10(1): 1–100.

Wiser, M., and D. Kipman. 1988. *The differentiation of heat and temperature: An evaluation of the effect of microcomputer models on students' misconceptions*. Educational Technology Center draft article, July 1988.

————, L. Grosslight, and C. M. Unger. 1989. *Can conceptual computer models aid ninth graders' differentiation of heat and temperature?* Tech. Report TR89–6. Cambridge, MA: Harvard Graduate School of Education, Educational Technology Center.

II

Using Technology to Make a Distinctive Contribution

In Part II of this book, we explore the ways in which technology can make a distinctive contribution to the learning and teaching of mathematics and science. To give "distinctive" more than a casual meaning, a strict standard is observed, including only those uses of technology that foster changes in the nature of teaching and learning, not uses that only improve the efficiency of what was done in the past. Thus the reader will not find here any discussion of the many ways computers and other technologies have entered the school to ease the lives of teachers and students in doing what they have always done.

There is no implication that we regard such applications of technology as unwelcome or undesirable. They are both welcome and desirable. However, given our sorry record of teaching mathematics and science, it is clear that changes in kind are needed. Changes in degree, helpful though they may be, simply are not sufficient.

"Shuttling Between the Particular and the General," Chapter 6 by Judah Schwartz, opens Part II. In this chapter, Schwartz describes the potential of computer technology in terms of a major pedagogical need—for environments in which students can build general knowledge by exploring its manifestations in particular cases. The next two chapters each offer an example of such use. Chapter 9 describes how such environments allow the researcher insights into students' thinking that are not available otherwise. The final chapter of the section describes principles of software design that follow from the pedagogy in the earlier chapters.

Schwartz begins by showing how both mathematical and scientific in-

89

quiry can be thought of as fugues that alternatively focus on particularities and generalities. Helping a student to develop some agility in traversing the path between the particular and the general becomes the core of the task of mathematics and science education.

Just how does one cultivate this kind of agility in students? The central point of Schwartz's argument echoes the position taken by many others in this volume—the learner must play an active role in constructing his or her knowledge. In mathematics and science, this active role is characterized by the posing and exploring of conjectures or hypotheses that build on what is already known and point to the unraveling of what is not yet known.

Schwartz goes on to describe a genre of software environments that he calls "Intellectual Mirrors." For the case of mathematics, he discusses the ways in which such software environments can offer students the opportunity to formulate and explore their own hypotheses and conjectures in particularly productive ways. In science, such software environments allow student and teacher to position themselves appropriately between the particularities of the perceptions of the world around them and the generalities of the abstractions that are used to fashion scientific models and theories.

In Chapter 7, "Conceptually Enhanced Simulations," Joseph Snir, Carol Smith, and Lorraine Grosslight discuss an example of the design philosophy described by Schwartz. They begin by identifying three levels of student understanding in science, emphasizing that many students can and do experience phenomena without understanding these phenomena in terms of any scientific theory or concept. The authors use the term "conceptually enhanced computer simulations" for the same kind of software environment that Schwartz refers to as "Intellectual Mirrors." The primary feature of this software is its ability to help students bridge the discouraging gap between the phenomena they perceive and experience and the concepts that are the stuff of theory.

The chapter goes on to present a case study of work done with sixth- and seventh-grade students on the understanding of the concepts of weight and density, examining how the distinction between these concepts was used in teaching about properties of matter as well as flotation and thermal expansion.

The theme of bridging the gap between the particular and the general is played out in the domain of mathematics in Chapter 9, "Creating Cybernetic and Psychological Ramps from the Concrete to the Abstract." The author, James Kaput, and his colleagues at the Educational Technology Center have been investigating how youngsters come to grasp the concept of intensive quantity and learn to work with it. The ubiquity of this concept cannot be overstated, given that it appears, among other places, in the guise of density or velocity or temperature in science class and in the guise of rate, ratio, or proportion in mathematics.

The software environments that Kaput and his colleagues have built, like those discussed in earlier chapters, help to bridge the gap between the particularity of perception and the generality of the abstract concepts out of which theories are built. In particular, the environments Kaput discusses draw heavily on the unique capability of the computer to represent the same general situation simultaneously in different ways, offering different representational "windows" on it. Users of the software can choose to manipulate some feature of the situation in any of the presented representations and the software environment can show the consequences of that action, not only on the representation that was manipulated directly, but also on each of the other representations simultaneously displayed. This use of multiple representations, made possible and feasible on a wide scale by the advent of the microcomputer, constitutes a new vehicle for developing understanding. We will need to explore it much more fully in years to come.

Multiple linked representations can do more for education than enhancing understanding, as we are told by the title of E. Paul Goldenberg's Chapter 9: "Multiple Representations: A Vehicle for Understanding Understanding." In this chapter, Goldenberg introduces us to the power of multiple representation software as a tool for gaining insight into the way people learn. Focused on the domain of algebra, his discussion and provocative conclusions suggest that the issues he raises will find applicability in other domains as well. Observing students manipulating multiple representations, Goldenberg argues, offers a glimpse of the rich internal models that they construct in their attempt to understand. In so doing, *we* come to understand more.

Part II concludes with Chapter 10, "The Right Size Byte," a second chapter by Judah Schwartz, which draws from his and others' experience some major principles of design for the kinds of software highlighted in this book. He discusses the issues involved in choosing a topic and a pedagogical approach, as well as the question of how much and what sort of control and responsibility should reside within the software in contrast to control and responsibility residing with the students and teachers using the software. Schwartz closes with a discussion of problems and opportunities offered by both simplicity and complexity in software design.

6

Shuttling Between the Particular and the General: Reflections on the Role of Conjecture and Hypothesis in the Generation of Knowledge in Science and Mathematics

JUDAH L. SCHWARTZ

Introduction—A Pair of Contrapuntal Pairs

Although counterpoint between the particular and the general is a universal theme in education, it has special pertinence in science and mathematics. In this chapter I will describe how this theme has traditionally played out in both science and mathematics education. I will then describe what I believe to be the vastly expanded opportunity that microcomputer technology and carefully crafted software provide for engaging this theme in these subject areas.

One way to characterize the problem of science education is that it must focus both on the *perceptions* of natural phenomena and on the generation of an explanatory tapestry of *conceptions* of those phenomena. We perceive the phenomena of nature directly through our anatomical sensory apparatus. Beyond direct sensory perception, we rely on instruments: our eyes are augmented by telescopes and microscopes, our ears by microphones and amplifiers. Our sense of touch is extended by thermometers and strain gauges, our sense of smell by chemical detectors of all sorts, and our proprioceptive sense by accelerometers and gyroscopes. Other instruments extend our perception beyond visible wavelengths of light, audible frequencies of sound, and the molecules our olfactory sense cannot detect.

Indeed, all the measurements of science are quantifications of such extended perceptions of the phenomena of nature.

The sea of perceptions in which we are continually and inevitably embedded is extraordinarily rich in nuance, subtlety, and complexity. This richness almost always stands in the way of understanding. I say this because we normally hold understanding of nature to mean some ability to predict how nature will behave under a set of circumstances that we specify. The myriad interactions that give rise to the phenomena we perceive, either with unaided or augmented senses, block the building of parsimonious predictive models of nature. As necessary and as wonderful as they are, full and elaborated descriptions are no substitute for explanation and prediction.

Building explanations and theories of the way nature behaves requires us to abstract mercilessly from the complexity of our perceptions those aspects of nature's behavior that we believe to be central, relevant, and focal to the phenomenon we are trying to explain. We must express these elements and their interrelationships formally in order to define concepts that form the building blocks of our scientific models. These models and the concepts of which they are composed, in turn, must be consistent with the data that served as the basis for the definition of our concepts. Moreover, they must also predict the results of previously unperformed experiments.

In short, while we apprehend nature via our perceptions, we understand nature via our conceptions and the explanatory models we build with them. Perceptions are, of necessity, specific and particular. If we perceive a cat feeding, it is a particular cat with a particular shape, color, size of tail, and size of whiskers that we see feeding on a particular kind of food at a particular temperature and having eaten at a particular time in the past. If we hear a note played on a violin, we hear a particular mixture of sound frequencies with a particular attack and decay made by a string of a certain length and composition and subject to a particular degree of tension. In building a theory of feline behavior or of the oscillatory motion of stretched strings we must decide which of these and other particularities to incorporate and which to omit. The omitted particularities determine the possible degree of generality of our explanation.

Once we have formulated concepts and built theories with them, we must explore the validity of the theories by matching the entailments and predictions of the theory with the outcome of new experiments on nature. The enterprise of learning, teaching, and making science is thus a continuing odyssey, to and fro, between percepts with their confusing wealth of nuance and detail and concepts with their sparse, often lifeless, abstractions that lend themselves to the formulation of explanations. The odyssey is never-ending, for close examination of the percepts always seems to yield hitherto unobserved subtlety of behavior, while careful study of the entailments of the concepts always seems to suggest new ways of observing nature's phenomena and their subtleties.

Unfortunately, science as we teach it in our schools conveys little of this odyssey to students. Under the best of circumstances we tend in the elementary grades to emphasize the richness and diversity of nature's phenomena with almost no attention to the importance of theory in understanding and explaining nature. In our woefully underpopulated secondary school science classes, we emphasize the ceremonial learning of the names of scientific constructs. We teach and test as if knowing names is an adequate substitute for understanding a densely woven tapestry of ideas that can link our explanations of nature to the ways nature behaves.

I believe the theme of the particular and the general is also central to the learning, teaching, and making of mathematics. The situation is different in that mathematics, as an intellectual discipline, is under no obligation to explain the behavior of any external world. Nonetheless, I believe this theme has dominated the evolution of new mathematics over the centuries and is intimately linked to the notion of conjecture. Unfortunately, the dominance of the theme and the role of conjecture in the making of new mathematics has had little to do with the way the subject is taught and learned in schools. Let me try to make the case.

For the most part, the mathematics we teach in primary and secondary schools is the mathematics already made by other people. Were we to teach language the same way, we would ask students to learn a play by Shakespeare, an essay by Emerson, a short story by Hemingway, but we would never ask them to write prose of their own. Given the difficulty teachers have in teaching mathematics and students have in learning mathematics, asking students to make mathematics might seem a hopelessly quixotic goal—one that stands little chance of being realized. Before rejecting this goal, however, it is worth exploring for a moment or two what the essence of creativity in mathematics might be and whether its realization is so utterly unreasonable.

I submit that the essence of mathematical creativity lies in the making and exploring of mathematical conjectures. A mathematical conjecture is a proposition about a previously unsuspected relationship thought to hold among mathematical objects. What is a mathematical object? A mathematical object is a formally defined construct such as a number, a shape, a vector, a matrix, or a function. In general, for each mathematical object there will be one or more defined mathematical operations that can be carried out on the object and that can transform it in some way.

Mathematical objects tend to be structured hierarchically, that is, all whole numbers are integers, all integers are rational numbers, all rational numbers are real numbers, all real numbers are complex numbers, and so on. Because of the proclivity of mathematical inventors to generalize mathematical constructs in this way, mathematical conjectures often take the form of inductive generalizations made from particular cases.

Thus, both science and mathematics as intellectual activities engage the theme of the particular and the general in ways that reflect the main purpose of the discipline. For the most part, however, the teaching and learning of these subjects in schools does not reflect the centrality of this theme in these disciplines. I believe the reasons for the absence of this theme in science instruction are different from the reasons for its absence in mathematics instruction. In the next sections of this chapter I will explore these reasons and in each instance explain why I believe that the microcomputer, with appropriately crafted software, offers the hope that we stand on the threshold of a revolution in the way these subjects can be taught and learned.

Percept and Concept in Science Education

We derive our naive intuitions about the way nature behaves from the totality of our sensory experience. We know a great deal about falling bodies, the rising and setting sun, and the seasons because of what we see, hear, smell, taste, and feel. Often, however, phenomena of nature that we seek to explain impinge "indirectly" on our perceptual apparatus. For example, the temporal scales of geological phenomena, and even many biological phenomena, are such that we cannot observe these events and processes as they occur but must infer their nature from the record left in layers of rock or from extant biological forms and the behavior of species. At the other extreme, we frequently encounter temporal scales so short that the very notion of process is unintuitive. Many is the youngster (and adult) who regards light as traveling with infinite velocity and thus requiring no time for transmission over arbitrarily large distances.

Similarly, the spatial scales that characterize many of the phenomena we seek to explain are dramatically removed from the spatial scales that our sensory apparatus can apprehend. The particulate theory of matter, on which all contemporary science depends, is based on an understanding of the composition of matter on a scale far too small to be seen without the intervention of a chain of sense-extending instruments.

When we teach students about scientific phenomena for which they lack a sensory and therefore intuitive repertoire of experience, we often delude ourselves. By teaching our youngsters, as we do, to recite a catechism of scientific terms such as molecule, atom, electron, nucleus, proton, neutron, and isotope, we are tempted to believe that we are solving the problem of science education. But why should they believe these words to be anything but names for a series of fictions we have invented to keep them occupied in science class? And if they believe simply because we tell them to believe, have we not defeated, in a fundamental way, the purpose of teaching science?

It seems to me that adopting two linked strategies can lead to progress on this problem. First, we must devise ways to extend students' intuitions about nature's behavior. Second, we must create new instructional way stations to put along the all-too-often too wide gap between percept and concept. Neither of these strategies is new. However, I think the appropriate use of microcomputer technology offers us a qualitatively new kind of opportunity to pursue pedagogic directions we have always known were worth pursuing but which have been logistically impractical until now.

Let me illustrate the point with some examples concerning the confusions many people have about the relationships among position, velocity, acceleration, force, and momentum. At the simplest level, there is ample evidence that many students are unable to distinguish a graph of position versus time from a graph of velocity versus time for a motion they have just observed with their own eyes. This is true even for many students who have successfully completed a course in introductory physics. If, however, the students have access to Microcomputer-Based Laboratory (MBL) equipment, they can use position and motion detectors connected to a microcomputer to generate graphs of their own motion as they move. The immediacy of the connection between the motion, perceived kinesthetically, and the graphic record of the temporal process of moving goes a very long way toward clarifying the confusion.

Building workable theories of motion is a subtle undertaking that took the human species a long time to accomplish. For centuries, Aristotle's notions about the way things moved held sway in people's minds. Even today, most people hold the Aristotelian view that a force is a necessary concomitant of motion, rather than the Newtonian view that a force is a necessary concomitant of a *change* in motion. This seemingly trivial difference has extraordinary consequences when the entailments of the two formulations are played out.

I believe the primary reason this seemingly inconsequential difference was overlooked for centuries is that our terrestrial surround is filled with frictional forces. As a result of these dissipative forces, most motion seems to stop of its own accord. Actually, the motion stops because of the frictional forces acting on the moving body. In an environment in which there are no forces present, frictional or otherwise, a moving body continues to move with constant velocity. It took a genius of the stature of Newton to understand the utility of the abstraction of a force-free environment as a setting for the building of a theory of motion. If one idealizes in this fashion, the relationship between force and acceleration, or change in velocity, is much more evident.

Imagine now a software environment in which it is possible to control the amount of frictional force present. In a sense, this is equivalent to controlling the degree of abstraction of the environment. In such an environment, it becomes possible not only to simulate the sorts of friction-governed motion we perceive daily, but to simulate motion in friction-free environments where the dynamic behavior of the moving bodies lends itself much more readily to devising concepts necessary for powerful theories of motion. Moreover, it is possible within such an environment to move smoothly and gradually from a percept-like simulation of the frictionful world to the conceptually clean simulation of the friction-free world.

Sir Isaac Newton's Games (Schwartz, 1985) and *ThinkerTools* (White,

1993) are just such microcomputer software environments. In *Sir Isaac Newton's Games*, the user can control the motion of a "puck" by administering to it a series of impulses of fixed magnitude but varying direction. The user can also choose to have the puck acted on by friction or by the attraction of a gravity-like central force field. In the case of motion with friction, if the frictional force is sufficiently large, the motion of the puck under the series of administered impulses resembles the motion of a soccer ball kicked about a playing field. As the amount of friction is reduced, the motion of the kicked puck more and more nearly approximates the idealized state described in Newton's First Law, which asserts that a body in motion subject to no forces will continue to move with a constant velocity. A special feature of this environment is that the user affects the motion of the puck via a series of impulses. After the puck responds to the administered impulse, the action freezes. A trail of markers at the previous positions of the puck serve as an implicit record of its velocity. This way of representing time repeatedly presents the user with the implicit question, "What will happen next?" and, because the action has frozen, offers time to ponder the next move.

In *ThinkerTools*, users again control the motion of a puck by exerting forces on it. As an environment for learning about simple dynamics, *ThinkerTools* has many features that are similar to those of *Sir Isaac Newton's Games* and some important differences. In *ThinkerTools,* time varies continuously, a more realistic mode of representation than the series of frozen instants used in *Sir Isaac Newton's Games*. Another feature of *ThinkerTools* is its explicit mode of representing velocity by plotting its Cartesian components. Clearly, there is no resolution, nor should there be, of the problem of which way of representing time or velocity is better. Each representation has its merits and each is appropriate for particular pedagogic situations. Experience with both of these software environments has shown that students, of widely varying ages and degrees of formal science education, gain insight into such matters as the relationship between force and acceleration, the reason orbiting bodies stay in orbit, and the problem of how to turn when there is "nothing to push against."

Particular and General in Mathematics Education

In mathematics, the counterpoint between the particular and the general parallels the percept-concept counterpoint in science. Indeed, the percept-concept counterpoint is, in some sense, a special case of the particular and the general.

I have written elsewhere (Schwartz, 1989) about "intellectual mirrors," a genre of software environments that allows its users to explore their own understanding of a mathematical domain. One feature of such software environments is that while the user explores a particular question, the environment can display a logical universe of inquiries to which the user's particular inquiry belongs. Here are some examples of such environments.

The first example is the series of programs with the collective name *The Geometric Supposer* (Schwartz and Yerushalmy, 1983–92; Schwartz and Yerushalmy, 1993; Schwartz, Yerushalmy, and Wilson, 1993). Perhaps the best way to introduce the *Supposer*s is to explain the cognitive conundrum that we encounter when we set out to teach geometry.

It seems evident that the human cognitive apparatus needs the external aid of drawings and diagrams in order to think about spatial and visual matters. Yet as soon as one moves to answer that need by making or providing diagrams to be used in the learning of geometry, one runs the risk of defeating one's own purposes.

Here is the heart of the matter. Consider, for example, the class of shapes we call regular polygons. We can construct a regular 3-gon, a regular 17-gon, a regular (any *particular* number)-gon, but we cannot construct a regular N-gon. Similarly, we can construct any particular triangle, but we cannot construct a triangle that is *any* triangle. If we produce a diagram of a triangle, then, aside from the size of the triangle, there is only one such triangle. This contrasts sharply with the situation in algebra where we have a notation system that allows us to write expressions that can denote *any* linear function, for example.

The geometry we wish to learn, teach, and make does not deal with the properties of particular shapes but rather with the properties of classes of shapes. How are we to resolve this seeming conflict, between the cognitive need for diagrams and images on the one hand and the necessarily particular and specific nature of those diagrams on the other?

Suppose that starting with a particular triangle we make some geometric construction and discover some interesting property of our figure. Clearly, we would like to know whether this interesting property is true for other triangles as well. One can view the construction made on the original triangle ABC as a procedure that takes the three points in the plane A, B, and C as its argument. Imagine that as the procedure is executed we record the steps of the procedure. The recorded procedure can then be repeated on any other triplet of points in the plane. While this repetition of the procedure clearly cannot prove anything, it can lead to added or lessened conviction that the property observed to be true in the original particular case is indeed generally true. The psychological and logistical costs of making and exploring the conjecture are thus dramatically reduced.

The ability of the *Supposer*s to capture users' procedures allows them to explore the effect on these procedures on other members of the same class of shapes. This process directly confronts them with the question: "What is this construction a case of?" The *Supposer* is thus a tool for exploring particularity with an eye toward the problem of generality. The *Supposer* does not necessarily induce users to greater degrees of generalization, but it does provide the setting and the occasion.

These notions about intellectual mirrors are also instantiated in a series of software environments about algebra that include the *Function Analyzer*

(Schwartz et al., 1988), the *Function Supposer; Explorations in Algebra* (Schwartz et al., 1990) and the *Function Supposer; Symbols and Graphs* (Schwartz and Yerushalmy, 1992). They are designed to help students and teachers with learning and teaching algebra using visual and well as symbolic representational tools.

The design of these software environments is predicated on the pedagogic conviction that the proper algebraic primitive is the function. The function has a variety of powerful representations, among them the symbolic and the graphical. The capability of even relatively modest microcomputer hardware equipment makes it possible to build formal algebra environments in which a function is always represented by both its symbolic and its graphical representations. Moreover, it is possible in such environments to manipulate the symbolic representation of the function and see the consequences of that manipulation on the function's graphical representation. Similarly, it is possible to manipulate the graph of the function, using suitable graphical manipulations, and to see the consequences of those manipulations on the symbolic representation of the function.

If these environments were simply facile ones for exploring the symbolic and graphical representations of a function, they would be useful, but not revolutionary. They have the potential, however, to support a revolutionary pedagogic approach to algebra, one that evokes the theme of the particular and the general much as the *Geometric Supposer* does.

Any function one chooses to explore in the *Function Analyzer* or one of the *Function Supposer*s is, of necessity, a particular function, and both its graph and its symbolic expression are peculiar to it. Let us consider, however, the set of symbolic and graphical manipulations of the function that are available to the user of these environments.

Users can manipulate the symbolic representation of the function by positioning a cursor on any numerical parameter in the expression and sequentially incrementing that parameter with an increment of any size. Each variation of the symbolic representation of the function is plotted and a family of graphs representing the series of modified symbolic expressions is displayed. Clearly each such modified expression is a different particular function, although each belongs to a common family of functions.

Users of these environments can also manipulate the graphical representation of functions by horizontal and vertical translations, horizontal and vertical stretching and squeezing, and reflections in the horizontal and vertical axes. Each variation of the graphical representation of the function is plotted and the corresponding symbolic representation of the modified function displayed. It is similarly clear that each such graph represents a different particular member of a family of functions.

In each case, a modification of the function creates a new function that belongs to the same family, provided that that family of functions is suitably defined. Consider the following examples.

We depict a particular quadratic function symbolically by

$$3x^2 - 2x - 5$$

and graphically by

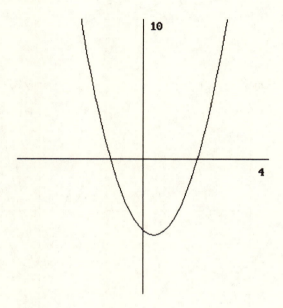

If we modify the symbolic expression of the function we can readily see how it can be said to belong to each of the following families.

Here are the graphical representations of Families A, B, and C.

Family A: $3x^2 - 2x - 5$, $x^2 - 2x - 5$, $-x^2 - 2x - 5$, $-3x^2 - 2x - 5$ ...
Family B: $3x^2 - 2x - 5$, $3x^2 + 1x - 5$, $3x^2 + 4x - 5$, $3x^2 + 7x - 5$ ...
Family C: $3x^2 - 2x - 5$, $3x^2 - 2x - 1$, $3x^2 - 2x + 3$, $3x^2 - 2x + 7$ ...

Similarly, if we modify the function graphically we can display our function's membership in a different set of families.

Here are the symbolic representations of Families D, E, and F.

$$\text{Family D: } 3(x - 2)^2 - 2(x - 2) - 5$$
$$3x^2 - 2x - 5$$
$$3(x + 2)^2 - 2(x + 2) - 5$$
$$\cdots$$

Family E: $3(x/2)^2 - 2(x/2) - 5$
$3x^2 - 2x - 5$
$3(2x)^2 - 2(2x) - 5$
. . .

Family F: $3(-x)^2 - 2(-x) - 5$
$3x^2 - 2x - 5$
$-[3x^2 - 2x - 5]$
. . .

Family A;

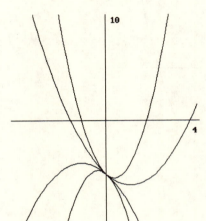

Family B;

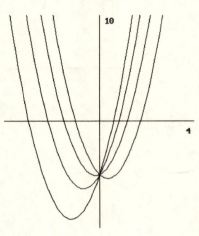

Family C;

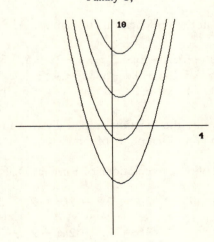

Family D;   Family E;

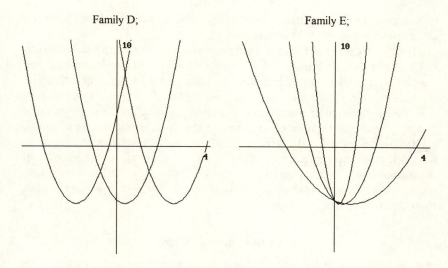

Family F;

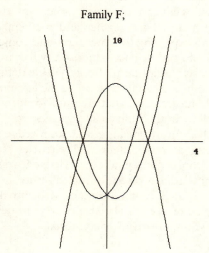

Starting from these observations, we may pursue a different pedagogic approach to the learning and teaching of algebra as a formal mathematical system. Instead of beginning, as we normally do, with particular functions expressed symbolically, and then, almost as an afterthought, turning to the graphs of those functions, we turn from the outset to particular functions expressed both symbolically and graphically. Because we have independent ways of manipulating both the symbolic representation and the graphical representation of a function, and because the manipulations that we perform of necessity generate other functions that belong to the same families of functions as the original, it becomes feasible to ask questions about the invariant properties of those families.

The investigation of the invariant properties of a family of mathematical objects, in this case families of functions, is a far more sophisticated and potentially far more rewarding activity for algebra students and teachers than many of the activities one now observes in the algebra classroom.

Exploring particular functions as a way of allowing students to generate conjectures about families of functions turns the learning and teaching of algebra into a *Supposer*-like activity. As in the case of the *Geometric Supposer*, no amount of exploration of particular cases is a substitute for proof. On the other hand, we expect that as in geometry, the ability to explore particular cases will lead students to demand "ways of knowing" other than demonstration.

Going Beyond the Known

If these instances of the counterpoint of the particular and the general in science and mathematics education are not anomalous, then it ought to be possible to envision a future for science and mathematics education in which the making and exploring of hypotheses and conjectures will play a central role. In such a future, science education will cease to be an endless catalog of unrelated facts or a litany of polysyllabic definitions. In such a future, mathematics education will cease to be the learning of calculational ceremonies. In such a future, ideas that are put forward will be explored in environments that allow both students and teachers to see the entailments of the ideas. In such a future, making new knowledge will be added to learning and teaching as core intellectual activities. In such a future, schools will be not simply places where knowledge is transmitted but also places where new knowledge is made. In such a future, intellectual ferment rather than intellectual docility will become the hallmark of students and teachers. Such people are likely to be skeptical and questioning, just the sort of people a growing, creative society needs.

References

Schwartz, J. L. 1985. *Sir Isaac Newton's games*. Pleasantville, NY: Sunburst Communications.

———. 1989. Intellectual mirrors; A step in the direction of making schools into knowledge-making places. *Harvard Educational Review* (February) 59(1): 51–61.

Schwartz, J. L., and M. Yerushalmy. 1983–92. *The Geometric Supposer series*. Pleasantville, NY: Sunburst Communications.

———. 1992. *The Function Supposer; symbols and graphs*. Pleasantville, NY: Sunburst Communications.

———. 1993. *The Geometric superSupposer*. Pleasantville, NY: Sunburst Communications.

Schwartz, J. L., M. Yerushalmy, and W. Harvey. 1988. *The Function Analyzer*, Pleasantville, NY: Sunburst Communications.

————. 1990. *The Function Supposer; explorations in algebra*. Pleasantville, NY: Sunburst Communications.

Schwartz, J. L., M. Yerushalmy, and B. Wilson. 1993. *The Geometric Supposer: What Is It a Case Of?* Hillsdale, NJ: Lawrence Erlbaum Associates.

White, B. Y. 1993. *ThinkerTools*: Causal models, conceptual change and science education. *Cognition and Instruction* 10 (1): 1–100.

7

Conceptually Enhanced Simulations: A Computer Tool for Science Teaching

JOSEPH SNIR, CAROL SMITH,
and LORRAINE GROSSLIGHT

The use of computer simulations for science teaching is increasing steadily (Gallagher, 1987). To date, among the primary arguments for using computer simulations has been the fact that they give students the opportunity to witness or "perform" experiments that might otherwise be too expensive, time consuming, or too dangerous for them to do in the laboratory. Using simulation software, for example, a student can "send" a rocket to the moon, detect radiation from a radioactive material, or slide an object on an air track. Typically, such computer simulations represent real world events on the computer screen as closely as possible to the way they appear in reality. Typically, too, they are well suited for letting students observe novel phenomena and for allowing them to perform various manipulations that affect the on-screen events.

Science education, however, also involves introducing students to new ideas that they cannot observe directly—that is, the theories that scientists have developed to understand and explain observed phenomena. There is now considerable evidence that students have great difficulty in understanding and internalizing these theories, in part because they come to science class with their own ideas, which are different from the ideas of scientists in many respects. A central challenge for science educators is to develop ways of helping students understand the ideas of scientists. Often this means that students must be helped to make fundamental changes in their own conceptual frameworks. Simply providing students with laboratory experiences or computer simulations that replace or represent laboratories does not suffice; students typically try to understand these situations

106

(either in the laboratory or on the computer screen) in terms of their pre-existing ideas.

In this chapter, we consider one way computer simulations can be used to address the problem of teaching for conceptual change and understanding. In particular, we argue that a new kind of computer simulation is called for, one that allows students to perceive what cannot be directly observed in laboratory experiments. We believe the concepts and ideas used for interpreting the experiments should also be made accessible to the student. We will call such simulations "conceptually enhanced simulations" because they are based on models that provide explicit representations for sets of interrelated concepts. Students can perform experiments using these simulations, enabling them to conceptualize the experiments they perform with real-world materials in terms of the scientist's concepts and theories.

This chapter is organized into four main parts. The first part identifies three levels of learning about a natural phenomenon that should be addressed in school science. In this part, we define the problem the computer simulation should help us solve, by showing how students can observe or experience a phenomenon but not understand it in terms of the scientist's theories and concepts.

The second part classifies model systems and simulations more generally and identifies the kinds of model systems that can play an important role in helping students understand the theoretical frameworks of scientists. We argue that computer simulations that build mathematical laws into a code can be helpful in this respect. Further, computer simulations that give visual representations for a set of interrelated (normally unobservable) concepts guide students in thinking about phenomena at a more theoretical level.

The third part shows how we applied these ideas in developing computer simulations for a particular set of purposes, that is, to help students grasp the distinction between mass and density and to understand the phenomenon of flotation. These topics are notoriously difficult for middle school students, in part because many students come to class with a conceptual framework that unites distinct senses of heaviness (including heavy and heavy for size) into one concept of weight. Thus, this is a clear case where science teaching needs to help students make conceptual changes (in this example, differentiate the concepts of mass and density) and restructure their understanding of these new conceptual entities. And it is a good case to show how "conceptually enhanced simulations" integrated with other more standard science education tools can provide special assistance in the process.

In the fourth and last part we reflect on the kinds of activities such conceptually enhanced simulations allow, and, in turn, the ways planned activities may affect the overall design of simulations. We refer to several studies we have conducted showing that these simulations, when embedded in a larger curriculum unit, are effective in bringing about conceptual change. An exciting challenge for future research is to examine the role of the conceptual models themselves in bringing about this change and whether the effectiveness of conceptually enhanced simulations depends on the ways in which they are used, in addition to their basic structure and design.

Three Levels of Learning About Natural Phenomena

Science education should enrich students' understanding of natural phenomena at three different levels. At the first level, students need to learn some directly observable facts about natural phenomena, and form some simple generalizations based on these facts. For example, students can directly observe a particular object's color and size, or that it is hot to the touch, heavy, or made of wood. Students can also directly observe simple relations between objects (e.g., one object is ahead of another, one object is heavier than another, one object floats in a given liquid). Based on such observations, students might form simple generalizations like: "Wooden objects float on water" or "Metal objects expand when heated." We call this a "concrete" or "object" level, because it is grounded in everyday observation of concrete objects.

At the second level, students need to learn the current scientific theories by which the facts observed at the first level can be conceptualized and explained. Theories make use of sets of interrelated concepts, many of which are mutually interdefined and cannot be simply or directly observed. For example, the concept of density is defined as mass per unit volume. As such, it cannot be directly observed, but must be inferred by relating other observations and measurements. Further, concepts such as density emerge in explanations of facts such as why some objects float and others sink in certain liquids. We call this a "theoretical" or "conceptual" level because it is concerned with relations among a set of theoretical (conceptual) entities rather than the relations among the objects themselves.

At the third level, students need to learn about the purposes and methods of science. For example, they must learn what a model or theory is, and that scientists develop models and theories to help them understand phenomena. Students also need to become aware of some of the principles scientists use in deciding what is good science (e.g., criteria used in judging how good a law or model is). We call this third level a "metatheoretical" or "metaconceptual" level, because it involves reflection about the epistemological basis of the conceptual level.

We believe that students have preexisting ideas at all three levels. No one disputes that children work with basic object level descriptions (the first level). Larkin's work (1983), for example, clearly shows that novice physics students exploit such object level descriptions in solving certain kinds of physics problems. Further, a number of researchers have argued that children organize their basic knowledge of how objects behave by using intuitive theories (Carey, 1985; Driver and Erikson, 1983). These intuitive theories, frequently different from the accepted scientific theory, govern how students make inferences from specific experiences. Finally, recent work suggests that children have some metaconceptual ideas about how knowledge is generated in everyday life and in science (Carey et al., 1989; Wellman, 1990). However, students typically believe scientists learn simply by making observations and do not understand the deep role that hypotheses and hypothesis testing play in knowledge generation.

If we are right in assuming that students have existing ideas at all three levels, then successful science instruction involves modifying students' existing conceptual and metaconceptual organization while linking it to their factual observations. Unfortunately, given current educational practice, we believe students rarely make changes at more than the first level. There is extensive evidence that students have difficulties with regard to the second level (frequently trying to assimilate the new facts they are learning in science class to their old conceptual frameworks). And they are seldom explicitly introduced to a constructivist epistemology at the third level.

In this chapter, we argue that properly designed computer simulations can be used to help students make changes at all three levels. To explain more completely how simulations may help in these ways, however, we first need to consider more precisely what we mean by models and simulations.

Model Systems and Simulations for Science Teaching

On the Structure of Model Systems in General

Gentner (1983) has developed a framework for thinking about how analogies work in science. This framework describes analogies in terms of a structure mapping between two domains. She views any domain as an organized system of objects, object attributes (predicates that take only one argument), and relations between objects (predicates that take two or more arguments). Thus, in making a structure mapping between two domains, one can ask what elements of the two systems are mapped: objects, object attributes, or object relations.

Using Gentner's basic framework, we can distinguish between two different types of model systems: (1) object-attribute models, in which it is important that the model resembles the referent object with regard to basic attributes (typically aspects of the object's appearance); and (2) relational models, in which it is important that the same systematic pattern of relations between predicates holds in both the model system and the system modeled.

Pictures and some scale models are examples of object attribute model systems. In such model systems, more attention is paid to mapping object attributes than object relations, and there is no attempt to map higher-order relations among predicates.

In contrast, the power of a scientific model lies in its ability to sustain a network of relations that was abstracted through an analysis of the real system. In making scientific models, a set of relational predicates rather than the attributes of objects are mapped from one domain to another.

For example, scientists have used the waves in a ripple tank as a model system for sound waves. Clearly, the two systems are not alike in physical appearance. However, if one thinks about the underlying causes of wave-like motion in the two domains, and analyzes the system in terms of the abstract relations of force and energy, one can see that there is a common process at work. The formulas that describe the behavior of the two systems can be obtained by solving the same basic wave equation. Thus, the two systems are isomorphic.

Scientists have used model systems not only to help them understand new phenomena and to explain these phenomena to others, but also to do simulations of actual experiments. Given that the same mathematical description underlies the behavior of both systems, scientists can do experiments with the relevant variables of the model system to learn about the behavior of the modeled system. In simulations, the performance of the model system is examined when some process takes place within it. The simulation is, then, defined as the dynamic execution or manipulation of the model system (Barton, 1970). Continuing with our example, one can use the ripple tank to understand the phenomenon of wave interference, and to study how wave interference is affected by parameters such as the wavelength of the interfering wave, in a domain that is easier to work with and in which the interference is observable. By doing these experiments in the ripple tank, one can make predictions about and understand the interference phenomenon for sound waves (or even light waves).

In searching for analogous physical systems, one is looking for two systems: a familiar or well-understood system that can be used as a model for a less familiar or well-understood system. For students to understand one system as a relational model for another, students must be able to (1) identify the relevant set of relations in the familiar system and (2) figure out how those same relations apply to different elements in the less familiar system.

Significantly, Gentner and Toupin (1986) have found that at least by age 8 children are able to understand such relational models in a nonscientific context. This finding suggests that students may be ready to understand appropriate relational models in science and that such models can be used as an important tool in science education.

Computer technology offers new possibilities for designing model systems for science teaching. In the next section we will build on the distinctions previously discussed concerning levels of understanding natural phenomena and kinds of mapping to explore some of the options and advantages that computer-based model systems afford.

Computer-Based Model Systems and Simulations for Science Teaching

In building a computer model and simulation, the program designer makes choices about: (1) which objects, object attributes, and relations of the referent domain should be represented on the screen (i.e., in the visual model); (2) the way(s) in which those objects, attributes, and relations will actually be represented on the screen; and (3) the way the screen visuals will be controlled by the computer and the user when running the simulations (i.e., the nature of the program code). We propose that the power of models and simulations created for the purpose of facilitating conceptual change is linked to choices made along these three dimensions.

Selecting what to represent

It is common in computer simulations to represent selected visual attributes of the objects and to show the observable interactions of objects. In this respect, the computer screen corresponds to what students can visually observe in the laboratory and directly mimics some of the visual aspects of the laboratory experience. We have called such models "pictorial models" because they represent visual attributes. The pictorial computer simulation can be used to extend the range of the students' experience, performing more experiments or those that would be difficult for them to do. For example, in *Operation: Frog* (Goldhammer and Isenberg, 1984), the student can gain experience in performing dissections, and in *Measurements: Length, Mass, and Volume* (Blake and Grenetz, 1984) the student can gain experience with obtaining basic measurements of objects on the computer screen.

We also mention here that the core idea behind the pictorial model could be generalized such that the pictorial model would be one in a class of models that attempt to provide imitations of what might be directly perceivable in the real world. Thus, a particular program might offer a hearable model of a cricket's "chirps" so that the student could explore how these sounds or rhythms change under different conditions.

While such a class of models can provide a rich array of experiences, we believe that more experience is not necessarily enough to ensure conceptual change. We believe that the student often needs something different, something that will put the student into direct contact, not only with the observable aspects of objects, but with representations of intrinsically unobservable attributes and relations that are relevant to understanding a particular phenomenon in the manner of an expert. Computers offer great flexibility as providers of modeled systems; the program designer can choose to create dynamic visuals that make "observable" what is in nature "unobservable."

One important kind of "unobservable" is a set of interrelated concepts. We believe that certain "directly unobservable" concepts and relations can be visually accessed by students, if students are presented with intuitive visual analogs for the set of concepts. We have termed models and simulations that use visuals in this way "conceptually enhanced models and simulations."[1] In a conceptually enhanced model, the program designer adds visual representations of the concepts used in explaining a specific phenomenon (the theoretical level) to the representation of the observable features of the objects (the concrete level). This enables students to observe, simultaneously on the same screen, two levels of thinking about the same phenomenon and to live in (or experience) the conceptual space in which the expert thinks.

Consider, for example, the concept of momentum. While one can observe that when a pool cue strikes a ball the ball's speed and direction change, the theoretical concept of the ball's momentum (a vector quantity) is not directly observable. In a computer simulation, however, one could choose to add visual representations not only for the moving object itself, but for its momentum. (See White and Horwitz, 1987, for a description of the *ThinkerTools* software, which explicitly represents momentum.)

The arrow representation for momentum used in *ThinkerTools* is not presented to the students as the formal vector defined in physics, but rather as a means by which students can manipulate the object and subsequently reflect on the object's movement in the pictorial part of the screen. As shown by White and Horwitz (1987), the addition of this visual representation for the conceptual entity brought about dramatic changes in the students' understanding of physical motion.

Synchronization of these two kinds of visual representations on the same screen gives students direct access to a model for abstract concepts that they could not see or manipulate in either the laboratory or in pictorial simulations alone. Thus the students gain not only more experience with a specific phenomenon, but have the opportunity to restructure their conceptual understanding of it.

Selecting representational conventions

Once program designers decide on what objects and object attributes to represent, they face choices in the way to represent them on the screen. The designer can use iconic or abstract representations. Iconic symbols are readily interpretable, because they generally resemble reality as closely as possible. For example, in the *Operation: Frog* software, the frog on the screen looks like a real frog. With more abstract symbols, the conventions used may not be immediately obvious from the visual itself. For example, in *Fall Guy: Investigation of Falling Objects* (1988), students can explore the movement of different objects under the influence of the earth's gravitational field. The objects are simply represented as dots of differing sizes. Similarly, nonvisual attributes, such as mass, may be represented iconically with pictures of brass weights, or abstractly with dots or numbers.

One advantage of using more iconic representations is the ease of initial interpretation by the program user. However, an advantage of abstract codes is that they may help a student abstract away from extraneous visual attributes in a situation and see the fundamental similarity among different situations. For example, in *Fall Guy: Investigation of Falling Objects*, the abstract representational format conveys the idea that falling objects behave similarly and follow similar movement patterns regardless of whether they are a ball, an apple, or a chair.

Because each type of representation has advantages, the program designer may choose to link the two: having one model with iconic representations and another with more abstract representations. The iconic model may help students immediately understand the situation. The abstract model may help the student abstract away irrelevant details and generalize the model appropriately. And the fact that students work with multiple models for the same phenomenon with different kinds of representations may help students to understand an important metaconceptual point about modeling—that it is important for models to represent attributes in clear and consistent ways, but that there is more than one way to do this.

Running the simulation

A final important dimension of a computer model system concerns the nature of the underlying program code. The program code is itself not directly visible, but it determines how the computer actually models the situation.

Some simulations are based on a discrete set of predetermined screens that the user will see later. When users run these programs, they are essentially signaling the computer to display these predetermined screens in response to a particular student action. Although this kind of program can be very instructive, the software can never produce an unexpected situation because all the screens are predetermined (e.g., *Operation: Frog*, 1984; *Measurements: Length, Mass, & Volume*, 1984). In essence, such a simulation is only attribute mapped: The correspondence between the model and reality is captured only in screen visuals, not in the behavior of the program code.

In contrast, there can be simulations in which the program code embodies relevant physical laws as a set of mathematical formulas. The behavior of objects on the screen is a direct result of the program's rules for their behavior in accordance with the physical laws. Usually this is done by representing the system in the initial screen in one of its equilibrium states. As students interact with the program, they perturb this initial state. When this occurs, the program reacts by searching for a new state of equilibrium that is governed by the proper physical laws embedded in the program. Such simulations can be said to be structure mapped in that the laws governing the behavior of objects are built into the code. Thus, new discoveries are possible using these simulations.

Comparing the Power of Different Kinds of Models and Simulations

We believe the weakest type of model and simulation is one that involves the representation of only visual attributes and the use of predetermined screens. While the student can use this kind of simulation in place of a laboratory experience (and avoid some of the mess, or do experiments that are hard to do), the simulation itself will always be less powerful than the laboratory experience.

When the programmer embeds the mathematical laws into the underlying program code and represents only visual attributes of the situation, the computer simulation can resemble the laboratory situation in two respects: (1) the same kinds of visual events are observable in both systems and (2) both kinds of models capture mathematical regularities and relations that allow for new discoveries. A possible advantage of such computer simulations over laboratory experience is that they permit students to perform a wider range of experiments more easily, with a larger range of parameters than would be possible in traditional laboratories. This use of computer simulations in turn increases the chances of truly novel discoveries.

However, one limitation of both structure-mapped pictorial computer simulations and laboratory models is that they do not provide visual representations for the set of concepts used in the explanation of phenomena. Thus, in cases where students bring alternative conceptions or frameworks to bear on understanding the phenomena, the model system itself does not provide direct guidance about how the students' concepts need to be restructured. An advantage of structure-mapped, conceptually enhanced computer simulations is that they do provide such guidance; hence they may be more effective model systems to use when the goal is promoting conceptual change. In the next section, we will develop an extended example of such a conceptually enhanced model and simulation.

Teaching About the Phenomenon of Flotation and the Concept of Density Using Conceptually Enhanced Models

In this section we describe the conceptually enhanced models we have developed for teaching about the concrete phenomenon of flotation and the concept of density used to explain it. The teaching is at once on two levels—the concrete and the conceptual. Furthermore, the software allows students to change the model by which materials are represented, giving us the opportunity to have classroom discussion about metaconceptual issues as well.

In the past, several attempts to teach about the phenomenon of flotation were based solely on laboratory experimentation. (See, e.g., the Elementary Science Study curriculum unit *Clay Boats* (1969) and the curriculum unit on density and flotation developed by Rowell and Dawson (1977)).

Laboratory experimentation provides an excellent opportunity for students to experience and explore natural phenomena and even to induce some general rules about those phenomena, but it does not provide explicit guidance toward or reference to the concepts scientists have used in formulating the relevant laws. We believe it would be helpful, in such a case, to use a conceptually enhanced computer simulation in conjunction with laboratory experimentation when teaching these concepts and laws.

In presenting our example, we will describe some of the main decisions we made as program designers, in accordance with the principles stated in the first part of the chapter.

Defining the Set of Concepts to Be Mapped in the Model

A first decision concerns the aspects of a phenomenon the model should account for. Choosing these aspects depends, in part, upon the age and background of the students. Our density curriculum was intended for sixth-, seventh-, and eighth-grade students, and our decisions about what to include in the model were guided by didactic as well as scientific considerations. There were four concepts that we decided to represent explicitly: the mass of objects, their volume, their density (mass per unit volume), and their material kind. The concept of mass was defined as the amount of material in an object and the procedure to find the mass of an object involved putting the object on a balance and counting the number of small mass units needed to balance the object. In this way we used a procedure similar to weighing the object that is known to students this age and avoided a discussion of differentiating between mass and weight.

Previous research has shown that even elementary age children have distinct concepts of size, weight, and material kind, which they are beginning to interrelate (Smith, Carey, and Wiser, 1985). Although the core of their weight concept is felt-weight (i.e., how heavy something feels), they are beginning to think that weight is an inherent property of objects. (In this respect their concept of weight is more akin to the physicist's concept of mass than weight, and they do not clearly differentiate weight and mass.) They are also beginning to form crude generalizations linking size and weight and weight and material kind. For example, they believe that large objects tend to be heavy and they believe some materials (like steel) are heavier kinds of materials than others (like wood). However, they use two different senses of weight in these generalizations about materials (heavy and heavy for size), and in fact unite these two senses of weight into one weight concept. These difficulties with differentiating the concepts of weight (or mass) from density frequently persist into the middle school (Smith, Snir, and Grosslight, 1992), high school (Hewson, 1986), and adult (Duckworth, 1986) years.

In designing our curriculum, therefore, we decided to build on the strengths in students' initial understandings: for example, their understanding of the distinction between size and weight and their intuitive understanding of the intensive nature of material kinds. Through the conceptual models, we then pushed the students to see density as an intensive quantity associated with given material kinds. Thus, students were initially presented with situations where mass and density do not covary, but material kind and density do (temperature is held constant). Only later do students consider situations where the density of a given material varies with temperature changes.

We did not map the parameter of pressure in our visual models at any point. Because we were modeling only noncompressible solids and liquids, pressure is not a variable that affected the density of materials. (*Note*: Hydrostatic pressure was, however, an important variable in the program code for the flotation simulation—see *Embedding the Physical Laws in the Code*, below. This example shows how a concept represented in the program code need not be given visual expression.)

Creating Visual Representations Both for the Visual Attributes of a Phenomenon and for the Relevant Concepts

Representations for visual attributes

In the computer simulation of flotation, one has the option of performing experiments (moving objects in and out of liquids) while viewing only observable visual attributes of the objects, liquids, and events. In this mode, one sees an object and a container with liquid (Figure 7-1). There is no attempt to make the object or liquid look three-dimensional. The objects (corresponding to a chunk of homogeneous material in the real world) are shown as colored rectangles of varying size. There are five

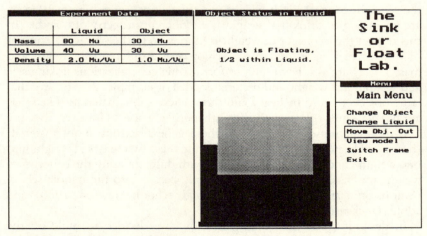

Figure 7-1 Screen from the Sink or Float Lab showing the pictorial representation of the experiments along with a data table.

possible colors for the rectangle, corresponding to five different materials with different densities. The container of liquid is shown as a cross-section of an open rectangular container. It is filled to a specified level with one of five different color liquids. Thus, the liquid is also represented as a colored rectangle. In this way qualitative information about the relative size of the object and liquid and the kind of material they are made of is directly presented, but not information about mass or density. In a later model we have lifted the restriction for homogeneity and as such the model also includes objects made from two materials.

In the measurement lab, objects are given a similar pictorial representation (i.e., colored rectangles of varying size). Again, corresponding to what they could do and observe in a lab, students can find the mass of the object by placing the object on one side of a balance scale (on the computer screen) and adding mass units on the other side until the balance is in equilibrium (Figure 7-2). In this way, visual icons corresponding to the total mass of the object are introduced in the context of a normal measurement procedure. Students can also make a formal measurement of the volume of the object, by tiling it with standard-size units, again introducing explicit visual icons for the volume. These representations do not provide much beyond what students can do in the laboratory. As in the laboratory, the density can then be found numerically, by dividing the number of mass units by the number of volume units. However, students have difficulties understanding why the resultant number should be viewed as a property of the material kind rather than the object. Further,

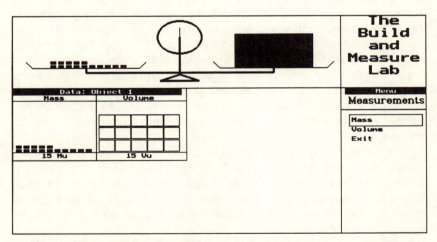

Figure 7-2   Screen of the Build and Measure Lab illustrating the pictorial representation of the object (top, right) on a balance scale with the number of mass units (top, left) needed to balance it. Data summary shows total number of mass units as well as icons resulting from a previous volume measurement.

the pictorial representations used in the simulation provide them with no guidance on this issue.

In summary, the computer representation introduces explicit icons to represent the two observable elements of volume and mass but does not yet provide a visual representation for the abstract concept of density. We suggest that it is important to add a visual representation for this abstract concept that shows how density is distinct from, yet inter-related with, mass and volume.

Visual representations for conceptual attributes

The computer simulation also has the option of allowing students to perform experiments while using models that give an integrated visual depiction for the set of concepts involved. In creating a visual depiction of density, we had two options. First, we could have moved to a microscopic level and created screen visuals (e.g., dots) to correspond to subatomic particles like protons and neutrons. With such visuals, students would be helped to understand density as a property of material kinds by associating it with the numbers of the atomic elements and the distance between atoms. Such a depiction would give real meaning to the numbers. However, because we felt that the entities themselves (protons) would be unfamiliar to the student, we chose not to take this approach.

Instead, we decided to create visual representations of conceptual attributes of objects (volume, mass, density, material kind), which are accessible to students on a macroscopic level. In our program, once the student has found the mass and volume of an object (which introduces separate icons for mass and volume), the student can ask the computer to find the density visually. The computer then visually distributes the mass icons into the volume icons, creating a conceptual model for the object which simultaneously shows its total volume, mass and density (Figure 7-3). Thus, the abstract mathematical procedure of division that is problematic for students is replaced by the simulated procedure of dividing the mass among the volume units. In the resulting conceptual model, a square corresponds to a size unit, a filled black rectangle corresponds to a mass unit, and the number of black rectangles per square corresponds to the density and the material kind.

Like the microscopic model, this conceptual model helps the student see density as a property of material kind. Different materials of different density look more or less crowded according to the number of filled rectangles in the square size units. In this way, the model exploits the visual spatial relation "in each" to portray directly the abstract relation "per" (i.e., mass per size unit).

In the measurement lab, students have the option of changing the object (making it bigger or smaller) while it is represented in conceptually enhanced form. In this way they can see that adding material to an object changes the volume and mass of the object, while the density of the material remains the same. Similarly, in the flotation lab, students can view

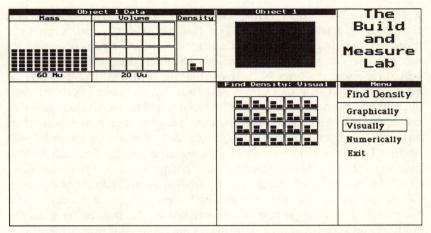

Figure 7-3 Screen of the Build and Measure Lab showing the result of finding the density visually. In the visual mode of finding density, boxes are moved one at a time from the "Volume" window to the "Find Density" window. Then the mass icons are distributed one at a time to each box until the distribution is complete. When the distribution is complete, the mass units icons and volume units icons return to their separate windows so students can compare how information is displayed in the "Find Density" window (an integrated conceptual model) with how information about each variable is separately displayed visually.

the density of the object or liquid while performing the experiments. This makes the variable of density more salient to students and helps them discover that it is the relation between the density of the object and liquid that is crucial to predicting not only whether an object sinks or floats, but also its level of submergence.

One advantage of making density "visible" using a conceptual model rather than a microscopic model is that the attributes of mass and volume are better known to students in this age range than the notion of atoms and protons. Indeed, historically, Archimedes and Galileo were able to distinguish weight and density, although they did not have an atomistic framework for understanding these concepts (Snir, 1991).

The scope of the conceptual model

As we have explained, our conceptually enhanced simulation of flotation incorporates a visual model for the concept of density. In this core model, density is visually conveyed by analogy to spatial "crowding." That is, density is represented via the spatial configuration of a specified number of small elements, (e.g., icons that stand for mass units) and their distribution within a specified area. Although we incorporated this visual analogy in order to teach about the concept of density, it could be adapted to serve as a representation for the relation between any two extensive quantities and the resulting intensive quantity. For example, a dot might represent a monetary unit (e.g., a dollar or a cent), a box might represent a piece of merchandise (an apple or a television) and the dots per box, therefore, would represent the price of the particular item. More relevant to science education, Wiser, Kipman, and Halkiadakis (1988) have adapted the visual crowding model to teach about thermal phenomena. In their series of conceptually enhanced simulations, they use an area unit to represent an amount of a given material (mass) and a dot to represent a unit of heat energy. Thus, the crowdedness of dots within a given area stands for the intensive quantity of temperature (heat energy/mass) for that material.[2]

While the crowding analogy can be applied to any number of contexts, the mapping must be clear and intelligible to students. A model will be successful only if this is true. Consider, briefly, the translation from the students' undifferentiated weight-mass concept to the representation of mass units as little black rectangles. While a qualitative estimate of an object's mass is directly obtainable by holding the object in one's hand, it is certainly not visible. Once it is put on a balance, however, students can see how many gram masses are needed to balance it. Students can make the translation between kinesthetic information and visually observable information because of prior experience with balance scales and because of their organizing concepts. Thus, their concept of mass can be meaningfully represented visually on the screen with mass icons (and numerically with digits) because their conceptual framework is robust enough to support the translation. Once this initial mapping is made, we can then use the representation of mass within a simulation to explore its role in various phenomena and its relation to other variables.

Multiple Representations

As mentioned earlier, a special advantage of computer-based model systems is that they permit the linking of multiple representations. Thus, one can interconnect different kinds of representations—for example, the verbal, numerical, pictorial, conceptual, and graphical. One can also shift the kinds of symbols used in a particular kind of representation (e.g., using different icons in the same basic conceptual models).

Linking different kinds of representations

In working with the pictorial simulation, the student gets practice linking verbal and pictorial representations. The student can build one or more objects of different sizes and materials in windows on the computer screen. The building process is carried out by choices in verbal representation—that is, children are presented with a given set of terms with which they can describe the activities they wish to carry out (e.g., "Change Volume" or "Change Material"). In this way, students are introduced to specific terms that they can use to think about the concepts and thereby to command screen events. Students can choose materials from which to build the blocks, and they can change their size and perform measurements and experiments with the objects they have built.

In working with the pictorial simulation, students can also use a third form of representation: numerical representation. Students can collect data about the objects and display the data numerically in a specific window. This allows students to get quantitative data about the specific volumes, masses, and densities of the objects created. Thus, the numerical representation gives quantitative information about volume, mass and density that was not present in the pictorial representation.

If the student is working only with data gathered while in the pictorial mode, the mass and density relations between objects can be seen only in their numerical values. The pictorial representation does not show these relations. However, the student can also choose to see the data collected about the volume and mass by placing it on the axes of a graphical representation. The density will be then represented by the slope of the appropriate line (Figure 7-4).

Finally, the program is designed so that the student can link pictorial, verbal, numerical, and graphical representations with conceptually enhanced visual models. In this way, the computer provides three distinct ways of finding the density of objects: numerically by dividing the numbers for mass and volume, visually by evenly distributing the mass unit icons into the squares representing the total volume, and graphically by drawing the line that represents the ratio. Thus, any understanding that the student has of the concept from one mode of representation can be used in consideration of the other mode.

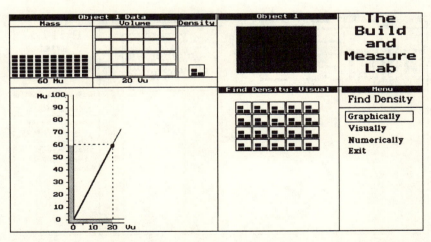

Figure 7-4 Screen of the Build and Measure Lab showing two ways students can find density: graphically and visually.

Multiple ways to visualize materials
(the "Change model" menu option)

In all the simulations built from the model previously described, we have the option "Change model" on the program menu. Using this option, the student can change the conceptual model from the filled little rectangles in an open square box to other models (Figure 7-5). When students choose to do so, the program offers them one of six ways by which to represent the density or the material kind of the objects (Figure 7-6). While all the representations are valid as representations for intensive quantities, some (such as the cross-hatching model) are more qualitative. (The more dense the material, the more dense are the crosses in the object) Some are more quantitative. (In the "Digits model," the digit in each box represents the amount of mass in this unit volume.) This option was designed to serve two purposes: (a) to show that the particular visuals for a concept are arbitrary; and (b) to show that there can be both qualitative and quantitative models for the same concept. As we discuss later, this menu option can be used to serve as the basis for integrating the third (metaconceptual) level in the teaching.

Embedding the Physical Laws in the Code—Structure Mapping

In the initial screen of the sink and float simulation the system is depicted in a state of equilibrium. For example, an object made of some low-density material is shown floating in a high-density liquid. When the user perturbs the equilibrium (e.g., by changing the liquid in the container to one with a lower density), the program reacts by searching for a new equilibrium according to selected physical laws that we describe below. The screen

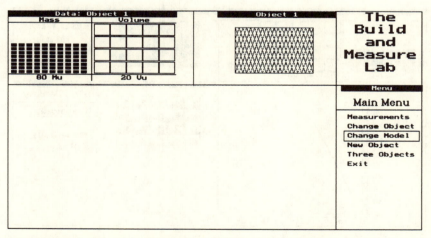

Figure 7-5 Screen of the "Change Model" option in the Build and Measure Lab. There is a similar "View Model" option in the Sink or Float Lab.

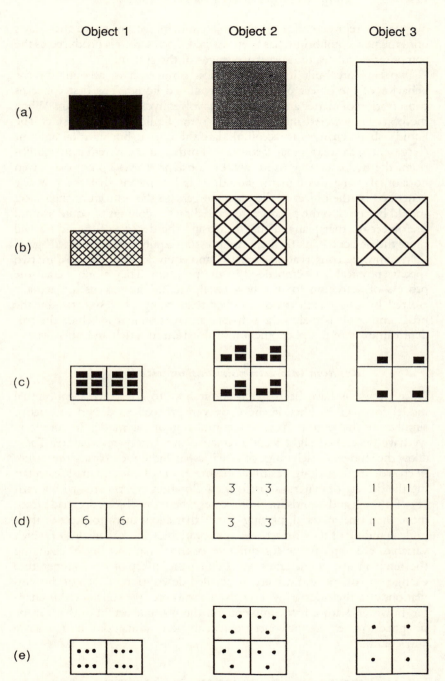

Figure 7-6 Representations of the same three objects using different conceptual models available in the computer program.

output is a representation of the object moving according to these laws until the new equilibrium has been reached. Each screen is produced as the computer calculates the successive stages of the system.

Two laws are built into the flotation simulation to account for the behavior of the object placed in the confined liquid. The first concerns conservation of matter and the second involves hydrostatic pressure. When the object is lowered into the liquid, some liquid is pushed aside. The liquid's shape changes to accommodate the object, but its total amount (represented as area) remains constant. Further, if the system is in equilibrium, the hydrostatic pressure will be constant at every point of a given horizontal plane through the liquid. This law means that the pressure generated by the object at the plane tangent to the bottom of the object should be equal to the pressure generated by the column of liquid around the object on that plane. Thus, decreasing the density of the liquid will cause the object to sink further until pressure equilibrium is reached again.

In summary, conservation of matter and equivalence of pressure are two specific physical laws embedded in the program. They alone dictate the process of searching for the new equilibrium. The screens are actually created by this search process rather than being predesignated by the programmer. This makes the software an environment in which the student can explore the phenomenon of flotation in a rich and open way.

Building Interactive Simulations with the Model

Once decisions have been made about how to construct a conceptual model for a given phenomenon, we can proceed to design interactive simulations that permit dynamic manipulation of that model. In our work, we have developed eight such interactive simulations and games. These allow the students a rich range of activities, including: exploring the nature of crowdedness, making basic measurements of volume and mass, calculating the density of materials, performing flotation experiments with a variety of objects and liquids including cases where the objects are made from more than one material, playing games that allow them to practice their understanding of the distinction among variables and knowledge of which variables are appropriate for different phenomena, and finally changing the temperature of materials to examine the effect of this temperature change on volume and density. A detailed description of each of the simulations and their design will be given elsewhere. We conclude this chapter, however, with a few comments on the possible activities that can be designed to integrate the conceptually enhanced simulations in the science curriculum.

On Designing Activities to Increase the Educational Value of Conceptually Enhanced Simulations

The purpose of this chapter has been to analyze the types of model systems typically used in science education and to argue for increased development and use of a new type of educational model system: a computer-based analytic model that provides explicit representations for the concepts scientists use to understand phenomena. In the preceding sections we have discussed the structure of such a model system and how it can be implemented to let students directly manipulate conceptual entities. There, we also proposed that the conceptually enhanced simulation should provide multiple modes of representation (especially pictorial, conceptual, verbal, and numerical) that should be synchronized so that the simulation's effectiveness in facilitating the process of conceptual change will be maximized. Indeed, we believe one of the unique advantages of building computer-based simulations is their ability to provide multiply linked representations that can help students create links among different representations of a phenomenon in their own minds.

To date we have designed and tested curriculum units using portions of this software with sixth-, seventh-, and eighth-grade students. (*Note*: In these curricula, we used the synchronized pictorial and conceptual models, but not the graphical models.) In each of our studies, we have found consistent improvement in student's understanding of density after working with our curricula. (See Smith, Snir, and Grosslight, 1992, for a description of the studies done with the sixth and seventh graders.) Further, in our latest study, done with eighth graders, we have found students made more progress in understanding density when they worked with our model-based curricula than when they worked with a curriculum based solely on laboratory experimentation (the standard Introductory Physical Sciences (IPS) curriculum on these topics). Taken together, these studies suggest that the software is not only accessible to many sixth to eighth graders, but is also important in helping students in this age range differentiate mass and density.

However, we believe simply making conceptually enhanced models or multiply linked representations available as tools for science teaching does not guarantee their effectiveness or proper use by students. In fact, a crucial aspect of the design of such tools concerns detailed thinking about the ways students will use (or potentially misuse) such simulations in classroom activities. Each of our curricula was, in fact, multifaceted and complex, involving a number of features we think are important in curricula designed to produce conceptual change. In concluding, therefore, we would like to highlight three aspects of curricular design that we believe will prove crucial to ensuring the effectiveness of such simulations as tools for facilitating conceptual change, consolidation, and elaboration. Further research will be needed to test the importance of these curriculum features.

A first crucial factor in designing activities concerns integrating computer models with laboratory experiences. As previously mentioned, the different computer models facilitate student investigations of phenomena in at least two ways: by allowing students to manipulate variables easily and by providing explicit representations for the concepts involved. For the computer investigations to lead students to restructure their understanding of natural phenomena, students need activities using the computer to model real-life laboratory situations and activities in which students construct laboratory situations to match what they have observed on the computer screen. For example, students might experiment with making a real object float in a given liquid and then create an analogous situation on the screen by choosing the right combination of materials for the liquid and the object so that the object will float. Or, students might examine the effects of changing an object's volume, first in the lab and then using the computer's "Change Volume" option in a simulation. Conversely, beginning with the computer simulation, students can be introduced to a situation in which an object floats even though its total mass is greater than the total mass of the liquid in which it floats. The students' challenge is then to create a situation in the real world where this happens, finding the special combination of materials and container size and shape necessary for this to occur. In these ways, the student may come to understand more deeply the importance of density rather than mass or volume alone in flotation.

A second important consideration is planning activities to emphasize the interplay among verbal, pictorial, and conceptual representations on the screen.

Students first manipulate the simulated events through the verbal dimension. Since all the user options offered by the software are displayed through written verbal commands, students need to relate to the terminology in order to control the program. By itself, this will not make them understand the concepts involved, but we believe that developing a precise and more differentiated vocabulary supports the process of making conceptual change. For example, in a simple activity, students are asked to build objects and then change their *volume* or *density* by using the right verbal menus. In a more complicated task, they are asked to make an object that is less *dense* than a given object presented on the screen but with more *mass*.

Another set of activities that exploit the multiply linked representations concerns the interplay between the pictorial and the conceptual representations on the screen. Although we have designed our software so that students can switch back and forth between conceptual and pictorial representations of the same phenomenon, we have found that students (if left to their own devices) may not use the software in this way. Rather, they may stay simply in the pictorial representation (perhaps because it is pretty and has nice colors). Thus, we think it is critical to design activities in which students need to coordinate the different representations in order to be successful.

For example, they need to be given tasks in which they must predict the behavior of the pictorial object based on seeing only the conceptual representation. In this way the student must constantly translate between conceptual and pictorial representations of a phenomenon. In our own sink/float software, for example, students can be given the task of making objects that will float in a liquid. They may first design the objects (using the conceptually enhanced representation of object and liquid) and then experiment to test whether their object really floats. Another nice example of such an activity is found in the *ThinkerTools* software (White and Horwitz, 1987) where students have to move an object from one place to another by using only the information given in the "data cross." (The data cross provides a conceptual representation of the number and direction of momentum units that have been applied to an object.) Significantly, White and Horwitz have found that their simulation was effective in bringing about conceptual change only when students were forced to link representations in this way. Simply providing them with multiple representations was not enough, since students frequently did not use them.

A final crucial factor in activity design concerns the need to discuss explicitly with students how one goes about building and interpreting models, and the choices one makes in model design. The models we chose, like any model, are arbitrary in certain respects and highly constrained in others. The models are designed to capture relational rather than surface similarities. One danger in using such relational models is that the learner may take the elements of the model at face value and think that they provide a direct "picture" of reality.

This problem is fundamental to any use of models, especially those portraying theoretical entities or conceptual relations. For example, in the case of our conceptually enhanced simulation, students might erroneously believe that steel is a material kind made up of three fundamental particles (because we represent steel as the "three icons per box" material) while aluminum is a material kind made up of one basic particle (because we represent aluminum as a "one icon per box" material). Thus, any serious science teaching that implements the tools of models and analogies must include discussion of the very nature of models as an integral part of the subject matter. In science classes, students should be expected to examine the questions: What is a model? Is the model the truth? What kinds of entities is the model designed to represent? What makes something a useful or valid model?

In other words, in presenting models, we are telling only part of the truth, and we have an obligation to tell the truth about that. We must make it clear that a model is not the whole truth. The fact that one can build computer simulations that are based on different, equally valid models provides an excellent opportunity for teaching students about the constructive nature of scientific inquiry and highlighting how different models and frameworks can be used to guide inquiry.

Notes

1. An important feature of conceptually enhanced models and simulations is that they use visuals that themselves are well understood by students; hence students can use these visuals to bootstrap their understanding of an unfamiliar or not well-understood concept. We distinguish providing students with synchronized

pictorial and conceptual models (used in our software and some of the software developed by White and Horwitz, 1987, and Wiser, Kipman, and Halkiadakis, 1988) and other synchronizations that have been provided between pictorial representations and graphical representations (Trowbridge, 1988a and b) or between tabular and graphical representations for measurements obtained using the MBL apparatus (Thornton, 1987). Because students may have difficulty interpreting graphical representations, especially in the middle school years, we believe graphical visual representations cannot play the role conceptually enhanced models do.

2. It should be noted that Wiser has found that both ninth- and eleventh-grade students make more progress differentiating heat and temperature when they have been taught using conceptually enhanced simulations than when they have been taught with a parallel curriculum without models (Wiser, Grosslight, and Unger, 1989; Wiser and Kipman, 1988). This result parallels the finding of White regarding momentum: students who played the same game without the conceptual representation for momentum did not make as much progress in conceptual understanding as those who did (White, 1981; White and Horwitz, 1987).

References

Barton, R. F. 1970. *Simulation and gaming*, p. 6. Englewood Cliffs, NJ: Prentice-Hall.

Blake, J., and C. S. Grenetz. 1984. *Measurements: Length, mass, and volume* [Educational software]. Garden City, NY: Focus Media Inc.

Carey, S. 1985. *Conceptual change in childhood*. Cambridge, MA: MIT Press.

Carey, S., R. Evans, M. Honda, E. Jay, and C. Unger. 1989. 'An experiment is when you try it and see if it works': A study of grade 7 students' understanding of the construction of scientific knowledge. *International Journal of Science Education* 11: 514–29.

Clay Boats unit: Teachers guide for Clay Boats. 1986. Reprint. Nashua, NH: Delta Education, Inc. Original edition, Newton, MA: Education Development Center, Webster Division of McGraw-Hill Book Co., 1969.

Driver, R., and G. Erikson. 1983. Theories in action: Some theoretical and empirical issues in the study of students' conceptual frameworks in science. *Studies in Science Education* 10: 37–60.

Duckworth, E. 1986. *Inventing density*. Grand Forks: University of North Dakota, Center for Teaching and Learning, Group on Evaluation.

Fall Guy: Investigating falling objects. 1988. [Educational software]. Pleasantville, NY: H.R.M.

Gallagher, J. 1987. A summary of research in science education—1985. *Science Education* 71(3): 307–457.

Gentner, D. 1983. Structure-mapping: A theoretical framework for analogy. *Cognitive Science* 7: 155–70.

————, and C. Toupin. 1986. Systematicity and surface similarity in the development of analogy. *Cognitive Science* 10: 277–300.

Goldhammer, A., and S. Isenberg. 1984. *Operation: Frog* [Educational software]. New York: Scholastic, Inc.

Hewson, M. G. 1986. The acquisition of scientific knowledge: Analysis and representation of student conceptions concerning density. *Science Education* 70: 159–70.

Larkin, J. 1983. The role of problem representation in physics. In *Mental models*, edited by D. Gentner and A. L. Stevens, pp. 75–98. Hillsdale, NJ: Erlbaum.

Rowell J. A., and C. J. Dawson. 1977. Teaching about floating and sinking: An attempt to link cognitive psychology with classroom practice. *Science Education* 61(2): 243–51.

Smith, C., S. Carey, and M. Wiser. 1985. On differentiation: A case study of the development of the concepts of size, weight and density. *Cognition* 21: 177–237.

Smith, C., J. Snir,and L. Grosslight. 1992. Using conceptual models to facilitate conceptual change: The case of weight-density dfferentiation. *Cognition and Instruction* 9(3): 221–83.

Snir, J. 1991. Sink or float? What do the experts think? or: The historical development of explanation for flotation. *Science Education* 75: 595–609.

Thornton, R. K. 1987. Tools for scientific thinking: Microcomputer based laboratory for physics teaching, *Physics Education* 22: 230–38.

Trowbridge, D. E. 1988a. Graphs and tracks. In *The conference on computers in physics instruction, proceedings*, edited by E. D. Redish and J. S. Risley, pp. 115–16. Reading, MA.: Addison-Wesley.

———. 1988b. Applying research results to the development of computer-assisted instruction. In *The conference on computers in physics instruction, proceedings*, edited by E. D. Redish and J. S. Risley, pp. 282–89. Reading, MA.: Addison-Wesley.

Wellman, H. 1990. *Children's theories of mind*. Cambridge, MA: MIT Press.

White, B. 1981. *Designing computer games to facilitate learning*. Tech. Report AI-TR-619. Cambridge: MIT Artificial Intelligence Laboratory.

White, B. Y., and P. Horwitz. 1987. *ThinkerTools: Enabling children to understand physical laws*. BBN Report 6470. Cambridge, MA: Bolt, Beranek & Newman.

Wiser, M., and D. Kipman. 1988. *The differentiation of heat and temperature: An evaluation of the effect of microcomputer models on students' misconceptions*. Tech. Report TR88-20. Cambridge, MA: Harvard Graduate School of Education, Educational Technology Center.

Wiser, M., D. Kipman, and L. Halkiadakis. 1988. *Can models foster conceptual change? The case of heat and temperature*. Tech. Report TR88-7. Cambridge, MA: Harvard Graduate School of Education, Educational Technology Center.

Wiser, M., L. Grosslight, and C. Unger. 1989. *Can conceptual computer models aid ninth graders' differentiation of heat and temperature?* Tech. Report TR89-6. Cambridge, MA: Harvard Graduate School of Education, Educational Technology Center.

8

Creating Cybernetic and Psychological Ramps from the Concrete to the Abstract: Examples from Multiplicative Structures

JAMES J. KAPUT

This chapter will reflect on several years' work of the ETC Multiplicative Structures/Word Problems Project from a representational perspective. The plan of the chapter is (1) to recount enough history to situate the reflection, (2) to provide a touchstone illustrative example based on our work, (3) to offer a theoretical context in which to interpret the example, (4) to revisit the work in more detail using the framework, and (5) to reflect on the entire project in ways that may help others see a more general approach to using technology to attack other mathematical targets of difficulty. Details regarding results of empirical work and software development are available in a variety of publications listed in the References and mentioned, as appropriate, throughout the chapter.

Capsule Background on the Project

The Mathematics of Quantity Versus the Arithmetic of Pure Number

The history of our effort helps reveal the source of the Project's dual title. The group of mathematics teachers and researchers who were among those who defined ETC's targets of difficulty decided at the outset that student difficulty with word problems was to be their target. Given all the research that had been done in that area, it was decided to focus on problems involving multiplication, division, rates, ratio, and proportion, a web of ideas now known as the conceptual field of multiplicative structures

(Vergnaud, 1983, 1988). Further studies revealed the center of this web to be the complex and subtle idea of "intensive quantity," especially as used to model multiplicative relationships.

The reader can think of *intensive quantities* as those used to express comparative relationships involving the "per" word, such as 6 candies per child, 30 miles per hour, 3 feet per yard, 2 dollars per 3 hot dogs, 3 grams per 2 liters, and so on. These include ratios, densities, and rates as well as scale conversion factors. Intensive quantities are usually made up of *extensive quantities*, which measure the "number of" or "measure of." Examples include 6 hot dogs, 30 miles, 4½ hours, 1.7 liters, and so on. Our working mathematical theory of quantity is well expressed by Schwartz (1988). Of course, the psychological aspects of quantity are quite another matter (Kaput and West, 1993).

The group's research agenda began with initially identifying behavioral difficulties, mainly trouble with word problems involving intensive quantities, and turned to ascertaining the important underlying cognitive structures associated with both good as well as poor performance. We then focused on determining how students could be helped to build cognitive structures that would support this web of ideas and what role technology might play in this process.

Our Guiding Assumptions

Three early assumptions have marked our work. The first two are curricular, the third a software design assumption. I will list and discuss these briefly.

The early and middle school mathematical experience should center on the mathematics of quantity rather than the arithmetic of pure number. Simply put, we have assumed throughout that children's mathematics should be *about* something—all numbers refer to elements or relationships in the child's experience, so that we never ask a child to compute or otherwise reason with pure numbers (unless there is some purpose-giving context for the activity); for example, we would not ask the question "What number do you need to multiply 7 by to get 42?" We might, however, put the child in the position of needing to know how many candies would each of 7 classmates get if 42 candies were distributed evenly among them. Or, in a different situation, how many children could get 7 candies apiece if there were 42 candies to be distributed evenly among them. The reader will notice that the formal pure-number calculation normally used to solve both of these two very different problems is the same for each, namely the division of 42 by 7, 42/7. Of course, the reasoning that leads to the division procedure, and even the execution of the division procedure itself, depends on the conceptualization of the respective situations. Furthermore, the critical difference between the models for the situations is in the role of the associated intensive quantities. The first starts with the two (extensive) quantities 42 candies and 7 classmates and generates the intensive quantity 42 candies per 7 classmates, which reduces to the intensive quantity 6 candies per classmate. The second requires a division of the (extensive) quantity 42 candies by the intensive quantity 7 candies per child, with a resulting extensive quantity answer of 6 children. The arithmetic of pure number largely disacknowledges the difference between these two situations and the conceptualizations needed to model them. It is thus little surprise, but enormously important, that students whose experience has been limited to the arithmetic of number have difficulty with such modeling acts.

The multiplicative structures curriculum should be longitudinally coherent. We assert first that multiplication, division, and rate and ratio should fit together both mathematically, as relating to the several ways that intensive quantities are involved, and conceptually, in terms of the cognitive growth of interconnections among their associated conceptual structures. We assert second that the ideas of rate, ratio, and proportion (an equality-comparison of ratios or rates, i.e., of intensive quantities) should be treated as special cases of linear quantitative relationships, eventually expressible as linear functions. This means that we represent and deal with these ideas in ways that extend smoothly to the mathematics of more general functional relationships, which in turn means that we use tables of data, coordinate graphs, and algebraic equations to represent these ideas. Our curricular assumptions are described in more detail in our 1985 Technical Report (Kaput, 1985) and in Kaput and West (1993).

The goal of computer software should be to help students extend what they know from familiar, concrete contexts to less familiar, abstract contexts by cybernetically linking more familiar representations to less familiar ones.

Thus, our software-based learning environments were not designed to facilitate computation directly (as calculators do), or provide direct "right/wrong" feedback, as classic computer-assisted Instruction did. Instead, it engages the students in a series of representation systems, beginning at the concrete level and "ramping upward" in abstractness to more abstract representation systems. Furthermore, these representations are systematically linked, so that the student typically is in a situation where the results of an action or choice in one representation can be viewed in another. In this way, we employ the student's sense-making power to render judgment on the adequacy or appropriateness of actions or choices that they themselves make. The computer reports and the student evaluates, instead of the reverse, which has often been the case historically. Thus, the computer is a structured medium for reasoning. The concrete representations involve manipulating objects on the computer screen— icons representing the entities in the situation being modeled—to enact multiplication, division, and ratio reasoning. We will refer to these as "Icon Calculation Environments" (ICE). These are intended to capitalize on the rich physical experience students have had with objects, especially with grouping and counting them and with counting the groups they might be arranged into (Kaput, in press a).

A Touchstone Example

I will now offer an example of how a concrete representation used in one of the ICE programs may be used to solve a standard missing-values proportion problem by using only grouping and counting actions. I will follow with an illustration of how this representation system is linked to other more abstract ones. These examples will then serve as a reference for the theoretical framework that follows. We remind the reader that the software described was built for research purposes in the mid 1980s and hence was not refined, especially in terms of interface and screen design, for general use. Nonetheless, more recent teaching experiments involving four sixth-grade classes have shown the software to be quite serviceable in laboratory contexts (Kaput and West, 1993). A software development project underway in the early 1990s (Kaput, Upchurch, and Burke, 1993) embeds this notion of object-based reasoning environments in a fuller set of tools for elementary school mathematics.

A SAMPLE PROPORTIONAL REASONING PROBLEM SITUATION:

> **Suppose that Noah decides to give 3 umbrellas to each pair of animals coming onto his ark (assuming that each pair will eat one over the next 40 days and 40 nights). If he has 21 umbrellas left, how many more animals should he allow onto the ark?**

Using ICE-2 the student first picks two types of icons from a pictorial menu by pointing and clicking, one type to stand for the umbrellas and the other for the animals. Let us choose the triangle to stand for an umbrella and a dog to stand for an animal. We then must input the given quantitative information in the spaces indicated in the screen shown in Figure 8-1.

We will now "grab" the icons from the reservoirs at the bottom of the screen and distribute them into the rectangular array of cells reflecting the intensive quantity 3 umbrellas per 2 animals. We are free to do so any way we choose, but the way we suggest to that minority of students who do not eventually choose it, is to put 3 umbrellas (triangles) and 2 animals (dogs) into each cell until we exhaust 21 umbrellas. We are also free to do this in any order, putting 3 umbrellas and 2 animals into one cell before moving on to the next; or we can distribute 3 umbrellas per cell until we use up 21 umbrellas before going on to accompany each triplet with 2 animals; or we may use a mixed distribution strategy. We can also adjust our distribution by using the "fix" option. Icon-objects moved out of the reservoirs leave gray shadows of their former selves. At each step in the process, the computer reports how many icons of each type have been removed from the reservoirs. In Figure 8-2, we show the results of a successful set of actions, which includes the numerical results displayed in inverse video.

In our teaching experiments, we preceded this proportional reasoning

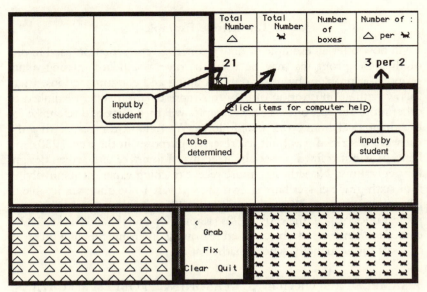

Figure 8-1 A starting-point screen.

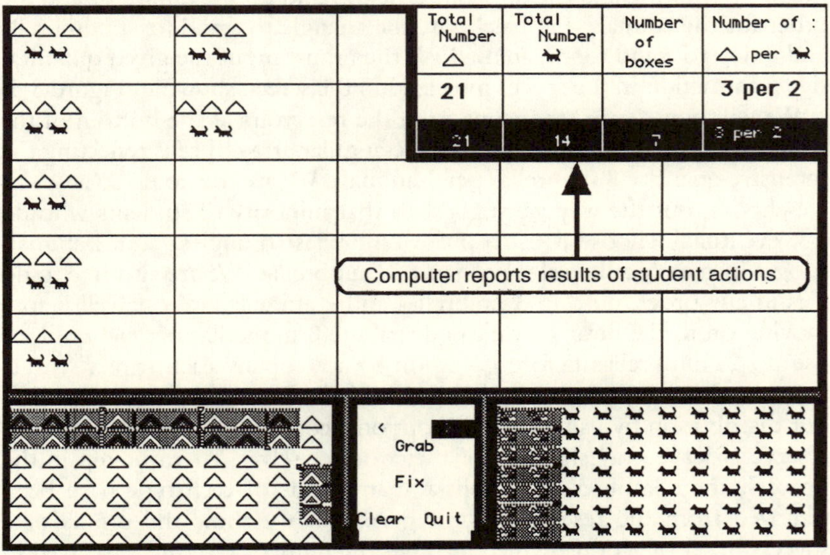

Figure 8-2 Screen illustrating a complete solution.

experience with concrete activities involving simpler multiplication and division with single sets of icons in a very similar environment we call ICE-1. Such problems might involve, for example, determining how many sets of 3 umbrellas could be formed from a set of 21 umbrellas. This can be regarded as a subprocedure of the larger procedure worked out concretely above.

The Boxes Strategy

The majority of sixth grade students with whom we have worked are able to abstract from the above activity a more general two-step strategy for solving such problems based on the cellular distribution of the icons. Indeed, we have seen this strategy appear spontaneously in significant numbers of students who have not been taught it explicitly (Kaput and West, 1993; West et al., 1989), even in considerably younger children. The "boxes strategy" (so named because the students are wont to refer to the rectangular cells as "boxes") consists of first dividing the given quantity by the number of items per box and then multiplying the resulting number of boxes by the number per box of the second (unknown) quantity. In the above problem this boils down to the following steps:

1. (21 umbrellas)/(3 umbrellas/box) = 7 boxes
2. (7 boxes)*(2 animals/box) = 14 animals

(Note that the computer reports the number of boxes used as the student progresses through the solution.) As discussed in Kaput and West (1993); West, et al., 1989, and below, this strategy is much more transparent than the standard school-taught strategy for missing value proportion problems, where one sets up and then solves an algebraic equation representing the proportion. That can be learned and applied on a mnemonic basis, and actually functions cognitively as a black box. Virtually no students can explain why they "cross multiply and divide" to solve a proportion equation.

Linking to More Abstract Representations

Actions on sets of objects intended to enact a proportional relationship can be linked to increasingly abstract representational forms: first, a table of data—which records the numerosity of the sets—second, a coordinate graph—which displays the the numerosities and the relationship between them in another way—and third, various forms of algebraic equations to display these in yet another way. Pictured in Figure 8-3 is a screen where all four representations are shown. The picture needs considerable explication, and a student would seldom actually be confronted with all four representations simultaneously. Indeed, the process of building familiarity

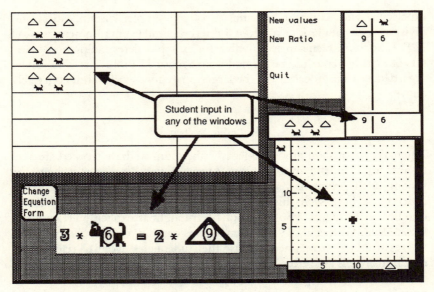

Figure 8-3   Screen illustrating all four representations.

with each of the representations involved requires months, if not years. (Note that by pointing and clicking the mouse button, the student can turn any window on or off as desired—once it has been introduced, of course).

The student is introduced to the new representations one at a time, beginning with the table of data—which is initially used as a way of accumulating an historical record of various iconically computed solutions to problems all sharing the same underlying ratio. Then, with the table familiar as a recipient of previously performed actions on objects, the student can then move to act directly on the table by inputting potential solutions as numbers in the table (actually, in the space below the table since the table itself is reserved for recording accurate solutions). With the actions at least partially abstracted and internalized, inputting numbers in the table amounts to an abbreviation of the previous activity on objects. The student can then view the proposed solution in the icon window if desired.

Similarly, the pattern of introduction is repeated for the coordinate graph, which is introduced as a means for displaying the data accumulated in a table and then can be used as a direct recipient of inputs itself, with the option of viewing the inputs in any of the other representations available. Not shown is an intermediate version of the coordinate graph that ties more closely to the icon representation by stacking sets of icons on the respective axes instead of using numbers.

The algebraic representation has not been fully tested. It is more complex than the others, in part because several equivalent forms of equations can be used, either singly or in pairs. The numbers in ovals are the variables and change in correspondence either with changes made elsewhere or as direct inputs, whereas the other numbers are fixed. For an unbalanced "equation" (corresponding to an asymmetric set of icons, a number pair that does not fit into the table, or a point "off the 2/3 line" in the graph), an appropriately directed inequality sign replaces the equality sign. It is perhaps apparent to the reader, as with many students, that the previously introduced representations act as stabilizing referents for the newer ones.

Two types of actions are supported in the various representations; one type is "natural" to that representation, for example, manipulating objects, typing numbers in the table, clicking on points in the coordinate graph, or typing numbers into the dynamic variables of equations. The other, not shown here, is simple incrementing from a command independent of the representations (we have used simple buttons labeled "MORE" and "FEWER"), where the variables, numbers of umbrellas and numbers of animals, can be incremented separately or simultaneously, with the result viewed in any of the representations as desired.

Theoretical Framework

We now turn to describing a larger view of mathematical representation systems in which the previous work can be interpreted.

A Representational Perspective on Technology and School Mathematics

We find it useful to posit two sources of structure in experience:

1. Mental conceptions, the organizing structures of mind that are used to select, parse and configure the ongoing flow of experience.
2. Materially realizable notation systems (a) that contribute to the structuring of experience by providing means for forming the conceptions, and (b) that support communication of conceptions among individuals.

Notation systems are instantiated within particular media, such as paper-pencil, computer screen, sound waves, and so on. Most school mathematics utilizes historically received, publicly shared notation systems, but notation systems can also consist of personal, idiosyncratic marks.

Mathematical notation systems are usually employed in combination with one another and with natural language. One important way of using notation systems in combination is to use one (A) to represent another (B), as when one uses a coordinate graph to represent a set of ordered pairs. When a notation system is used in this way, we refer to B as a *referent* of A and the ensemble A, B and the correspondence between them as a *representation system*. When the notation system (A) is used to represent some aspect of a nonmathematical situation (C), for example, the distribution of umbrellas on the deck of an ark, we refer to it as a (mathematical) *model* of that situation. Again, we refer to C as a *referent* of A. In both cases, A has (relative) semantic content provided by the referential relationship. Further explication of these ideas can be found in Kaput (1987, 1989, 1991, 1992).

One reason we pay close attention to the roles of notation systems is the almost infinite representational plasticity of electronic media. We can create notations of almost any variety, in some cases reflecting abstract structures or ephemeral and transient strategies, and in other cases, as with the icon-objects, capturing in the computer medium the very common experiences of manipulating objects. Furthermore, we can link these notations in almost any way we choose creating notational bridges or ramps from the students concrete experience to the ever more abstract objects and relationships of more advanced mathematics.

From our representational perspective, one can characterize three forms of school mathematical activities:

1. Syntactically constrained transformations within a particular notation system (without external referential semantic content).
2. Translations between notation systems, including the coordination of actions across notation systems.
3. Construction and testing of mathematical models.

Currently, the first type of activity strongly dominates at all levels. For example, learning the arithmetic of pure number amounts to learning the syntax of the usual base-ten Arabic numeration system; the bulk of standard secondary school algebra amounts to learning the syntax of transformations of the character strings of algebra. On the other hand, learning the mathematics of quantity amounts to type (3) activity. Quantities, which include numbers and their units, constitute a notation system combining pure numbers and natural language fragments that is an especially fruitful source of models of situations, which act as referents. Furthermore, ICE-2 can be regarded as a concrete representation of the discrete quantity notation system.

Furthermore, unlike syntactically constrained operations on numerals in some algorithm, operations on quantities can be thought of as *semantically* constrained, by students' understanding of their situational referents. In these terms, one can characterize our general approach as building referential meaning for mathematics—either across notation systems as we extend or translate from one to another, or with nonmathematical situations.

There is a fourth and very important kind of long-term learning deserving of mention here. It involves the consolidation or crystallization of relationships and processes into conceptual objects or "cognitive entities"

(Greeno, 1983) that can then be used in relationships or processes at a higher level of organization. Examples of this kind of "vertical" mathematical growth include the act of counting leading to (whole) numbers as objects (Steffe, Cobb, and von Glasersfeld, 1988), taking part-of leading to fraction numbers (Kieren, Nelson, and Smith, 1985), functions as rules for transforming numbers becoming objects that can then be further operated on, for example, added or differentiated (Harel and Kaput, 1991). As we will see, notation systems can facilitate this "entification" or "encapsulation" process.

Interactions Between Conceptions and Notations

An ongoing objective of our research has been to understand how notation systems interact with our mental apparatus to extend mathematical understanding and competence. But, as always, the devil is in the details. To help conquer the devil, we will elaborate the representational perspective outlined before to include the processes of interaction that seem to be at the heart of learning and using notation systems, as depicted in Figure 8-4.

I suggest that we build and elaborate our mental structures in cyclical processes that go in opposite directions. The upward arrow depicts two types of processes: (1) deliberate interpretation (or "reading"), and (2) the more passive, less consciously controlled and less serially organized processes of having mental phenomena *evoked* by the physical symbols. The arrow pointing downward also depicts two types of processes: (1) the act of projecting mental contents onto existing symbols, and (2) the act of producing new ones ("writing"), which includes the physical elaboration

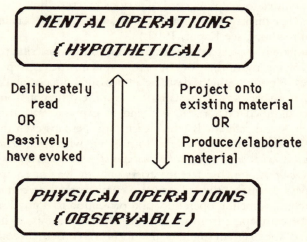

Figure 8-4   Relations between physical and mental structures.

of existing ones. One can also regard the vertical dimension of this diagram as depicting a form of reference, wherein the material notation at the bottom "represents" the conception. This is sometimes referred to, especially in the Piagetian literature, as the signifier-signified relationship (Vergnaud, 1987). It also matches the framework used by Saussure early in this century (Saussure, 1959).

Projections occur in reading and evoking as part of the underlying cyclical processes matching percepts and concepts (as described by Grossberg, 1980). I nonetheless distinguish downward-oriented projections from upward-oriented interpretive acts on the basis of the objective of the process, on where it gets its major impetus. In the downward-oriented case, one has cognitive contents that one seeks to externalize for purposes of communication or testing for viability. Upward-oriented processes are based on an intent to use some existing physical material to assist one's thinking.

Projections need not amount to writing in the usual sense, but include acting on virtually any kind of physical system or apparatus, where the syntax of the system itself (as well as the medium in which it is instantiated) determines the kind of "writing" that it can accept. In each of the computer-instantiated notation systems described earlier, we see different forms of writing, ranging from standard numerical input to the manipulation of screen objects. We also see here an illustration of a critical difference between a notation system that is computer instantiated versus one that is instantiated in the paper-pencil or physical objects media. By instantiating the syntax of the notation system directly in the computer medium, much more constraint can be built into acts of writing than usually appears in, say, physical manipulatives. A physical objects version of our icon-based notation system would require obedience to a substantially larger set of written rules to accomplish the same level of constraint, to say nothing of the abilities to keep a record of actions taken or link these to another system. (For further discussion of constraints and supports in the computational medium, see Kaput, 1992.)

We now wish to extend this framework to help describe representation acts involving more than one notation system, that is, type (2) and (3) activities. Figure 8-5 helps describe a horizontal dimension of reference—which, as a species of representation, is quite different from the vertical signifier-signified one. Here, I intend to express relationships between notation A and referent B where each (and perhaps even the correspondence) is expressible in material form—but where *the actual referential relationship exists only as mental operations of a person for whom the notations are interpretable*. Such reference exists only by way of composite actions that "pass through" the subjective mental world—as combined acts of interpretation, mental operation, and projection to a physical display—it does not exist apart from the actions of interpretants, although, as the bottom of the diagram suggests, members of a consensual community may

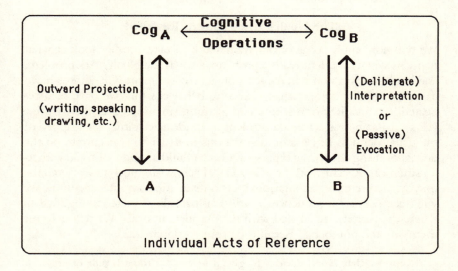

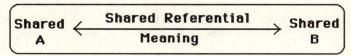

Figure 8-5 A horizontal dimension of reference.

share the referential relationship in the sense of being able to generate the interpretive acts as needed.

The items A and B depict physical observables—for example, an ordered pair in a table A that refers (in the sense just described) to a set of screen objects in a rectangular array of cells B as discussed previously. Of course the reference in this case is based on the numerosity of the two sets of icons involved, so the mental operations in this case include counting the respective sets of objects. Note that *the directionality of the reference in general depends on the cognitive operations involved,* which in turn depend on the context, and hence the direction is not fixed. At one time B may act as a referent for A (e.g., as above, the pair A acting to represent the numerosities of B), and at another the situation may be reversed. The numerals may be given or constructed in advance and one counts out a set of objects to represent the ordered pair of numerals. I suggest that experience with such two-way reference is at the heart of developing competence with multiple representations. I further wish to emphasize that the essence of our work is depicted in the upper levels of these diagrams, where cognitive operations and elaborations, that is, learning and thinking, take place. A fuller discussion of these matters can be found in Kaput, 1991.

The Noah's Ark Problem Revisited

We will now apply some of our framework to take another look at what happens when a student reads a problem, such as the Noah's Ark problem, and begins to work on it in the icon-object environment ICE-2 introduced earlier. This discussion, while reflecting behaviors that we have seen repeatedly in a variety of teaching and learning situations over the past few years, treats an abstract modal student in an idealized situation stripped of the usual richness of classroom situations in order to concentrate on the details of using the iconic representation to build a model of the (synthetic) situation. Recent work by Miera (1991) shows in much more detail the microstructure of representational acts outside the computer medium. We will trace a plausible sequence of actions as partially depicted in Figure 8-6, where the actions are labeled with the numbers in ovals. We will describe them "by the numbers." Recall the problem statement:

> **Suppose that Noah decides to give 3 umbrellas to each pair of animals coming onto his ark (assuming that each pair will eat one over the next 40 days and 40 nights). If he has 21 umbrellas left, how many more animals should he allow onto the ark?**

1. The student must read the text constituting the problem statement. As noted, the text C refers to a fictitious situation D.

2. As this process of parsing and interpreting takes place, producing the beginnings of Cog(C), almost simultaneously, Cog(D) begins to be constructed, based on an interaction between previously constructed knowledge about such a situation D, both particular and general, and Cog(C).

3. As the construction of Cog(D) fills out, the student begins the process of selecting information assumed to be relevant to the problem solution and abstracting quantitative relationships from among those relationships constructed in Cog(D). In this problem the information is not especially implicit so the main activity is construction of the intensive

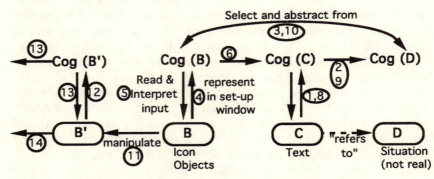

Figure 8-6   Actions used to solve the Noah's Ark problem.

quantity "3 umbrellas per 2 animals" from the statement that Noah gives 3 umbrellas to every pair of animals. Note that the initial statement refers to a "pair" of animals, which may draw on the student's knowledge of the biblical story, and requires translation to "2 animals."

4. Now the extracted information must be projected onto the computer representation, which takes the form of inputting values, the given information, into the upper right window in Figure 8-1. Crucial interactions take place between the student's conceptualization and the particular form that the data must take in that window for the projection of that conceptualization to "fit" the structure of the representation system.

5–10. This sequence constitutes a comparison between what the student reads as an input and the original problem statement, a kind of checking activity.

11–14 . . . Now the student begins a set of manipulations and elaborations of the iconic representation B leading to the result in Figure 8-2, which includes intermediate checks returning to Cog(C) and Cog(D) as in (5–10) above. Notice that the feedback provided within B (including the inverse video) helps facilitate this checking process by holding (the student's version of) the given information and translating the results of the manipulations into a numerical form by doing the counting after every step. Thus, the intermediate evaluative steps need not return to the text, but rather may take place with reference to the new iconic representation and the cognitive structures associated with it. Presumably, the last (ideal) step is a comparison with the original statement, however.

Reflections on the Ideal Steps and the Interaction Between Cognitions and Notational Forms

The Role of Prior Knowledge—Forming Cog(D)

The key initial steps in the modeling act for this example are the production of Cog(D) based on the reading of the text and then the mapping of aspects of this conception onto B. The conception Cog(D) is built out of one's prior knowledge in complex ways that, if well understood, would leave many cognitive psychologists looking for something new to do. In this case, knowledge of the biblical story surely plays a role in setting the "frame," building the "schema," generating the "script," and so on, that holds the details in place. Among the details are the two pieces of quantitative information, the 3 umbrellas and 2 animals, and the semantic relation between them, namely, that the two animals would be protected by, possess, or at least be associated with, the three umbrellas. This background knowledge would also help account for and set aside the irrelevant quantitative information about 40 days and 40 nights.

Furthermore, depending on the background knowledge available, the two animals may even be semantically linked as a male-female pair, the start of a "nuclear family." This semantic knowledge plays a role in helping conceptualize, respectively, the two (extensive) quantities as cognitive units. The prior knowledge about "pairs" is likely to contribute more to this unit formation than prior knowledge about three umbrellas, which presumably did not exist, and needs to be constructed de novo.

Similarly, building the cognitive structure that embodies the "per relation" between these units that constitutes the (intensive) quantity 3 umbrellas per 2 animals is affected by the semantic structure being assembled in Cog(D). Again, prior knowledge of Noah's ark may contribute to the assimilation of the umbrellas into the understanding of the text-based problem statement (the fact that it was raining), and the prior knowledge of the semantic relation between umbrellas and the "organisms" that use them likewise helps form a connection between the two units that yields a higher order cognitive unit made up of the two other cognitive units.

Role of the Features of B—The Rectangular Array of Cells

The "mapping" of the quantitative structure selected and abstracted from Cog(D) to a conceptualization Cog(B) based on the rectangular array of cells B amounts to an integration of cognitive structures. Somehow, the semantic links that help form both the lower order cognitive units, 2 animals and 3 umbrellas, as well as the higher order unit, 3 umbrellas per 2 animals, must be integrated with the structure of the array—assuming that the initial connection between icons and entities in the story has already been chosen (the lowest order entities).

We have seen instances when this integration, or mapping, was subverted by an inappropriate choice of icons, especially in the single icon environment ICE-1 used for posing and solving multiplication and division problems (Kaput, 1988). For example, this occurred most frequently when D involved one entity, say, newspapers, whose semantic relation with the other entity was containment, as with pages. Here in ICE-1, the appropriate choice would be for an icon to stand for a page and the cell to stand for the containing entity, namely, a newspaper. If the student chose an icon, say, a rectangle, to stand for the *containing* entity (newspaper), a breakdown of the solution process followed, and, in some cases, total confusion resulted that was difficult to recover from. This illustrates the strength and importance of the Cog(D) and Cog(B) linkages. We have also seen solution breakdown in ICE-2 when students made capricious choice of the two icons that inadvertently implied a link between the objects being represented that was not part of the given information and that came to influence student actions later in the process.

We have also observed cases of students whose Cog(D) is so poorly structured that they choose an icon to stand for the entity in the problem situation D that appears most prominent to them, for example, picking a person-icon to stand for Noah. In the case at hand, the icon-object relations are more straightforward, although the lack of an umbrella icon forces a choice of a more abstractly related icon. In response to the need for students to be clear about what is standing for what, a new version of the software (not shown) requires the student to state (in text) what each icon chosen stands for.

Let us now assume icons have been successfully chosen and turn our attention to the specific characteristics of the array and actions on icons within it that seem to be related to the cognitive processes involved in solving the problem. You will notice in Figure 8-1, the small caption "click items for computer help." This appears after the student has entered the given information and can, among other things, help with the icon grabbing and distributing process. In particular, one option assists with the grabbing process by automatically taking either 2 animals or 3 umbrellas when the user chooses one or the other to be moved upward from the reservoirs to the cells. This is a physical instantiation of the first-level cognitive entity formation.

A second and major feature is inherent in the role of the cells as containers for the two sets of icons. The semantic relations between the two types of objects being modeled can vary almost without bound: tight association (4 tires per car), containment (4 candies per bag), arbitrary association (4 ships per 5 antelopes), price (4 muffins per 3 dollars), and so on. The perceptual feature of the array that corresponds to any such relation between the two types of objects is mutual containment and contiguity within the same cell. We have not implemented, but could easily have, a feature that enhances the grabbing action so that a single "grabbing" action would result in isolating and joining both types of objects simultaneously, for example, 3 umbrellas and 2 animals would be moved to a cell simultaneously. This would supplant the separate grabbing actions that a student must now perform. With Piaget, we have assumed that "cognitive entification" occurs as the result of reflection of internalized actions to a new organizational level ("reflective abstraction"). Hence we require the student to perform actions, in this case grouping actions, to initiate the needed entifications.

Alternative organizations of intensive quantities are sometimes appropriate, for example, when one needs to keep the aggregate sets of objects separate, rather than mixing them homogeneously. For example, one can imagine that a store sells 3 medium-size sweatshirts for every 2 small-size ones. In buying an inventory of sweatshirts, one would order sets of each where the aggregate subtotals would maintain the 3:2 ratio, but with an assumption that the groups would remain separate. There is yet another organization of the quantities and the objects associated with an intensive quantity such as 3 umbrellas per 2 animals, a chunking of the whole set of 21 umbrellas with the whole set of 14 animals. This organization is only weakly reflected within the array of ICE-2 because the sets of icons remain in 3:2 subsets inside separate cells. A stronger feature would allow the objects to migrate together into subsets of 21 and 14 elements inside a larger containing set. However, this level of organization is necessarily embodied in the numerical representation of the total number of umbrellas and animals that have been moved up into the array. By counting the respective elements in the separate cells, one is treating them as subsets of a larger set, and the resulting numerosity of the respective two subsets likewise addresses this new level of organization. Thus this level of organization appears in the the window in inverse video—see Figure 8-2.

An interesting trade-off exists between the cellular organization and the larger subset organization, whereby the former emphasizes a homogeneity of the distribution of umbrellas and animals and the latter emphasizes their respective collectivities. There is an underlying homogeneity in the situation being modeled in the example at hand—Noah gives 3 umbrellas to each pair of animals appearing at dockside. Furthermore, the incrementing/distributing action in the situation parallels that of the ICE-2 model. In other situations, the underlying actions might not be as parallel and the homogeneity might be more problematic, as when one is modeling a neighborhood where, overall, there are 3 cars for every 2 houses. Here, homogeneity probably does not hold, yet it is customary to use an intensive quantity in this way to describe the "density" of cars in the neighborhood. We have developed another environment that supports a sampling activity (see Kaput and Pattison-Gordon, 1987) which addresses the issue of homogeneity even more directly (see also Schwartz, 1988, who discusses local vs. global application of intensive quantities). In yet another situation, the two types of objects might be "clumped together" separately—for example, when one is balancing sets of A-objects with sets of B-objects on a scale, where 3 A-objects weigh the same as 2 B-objects. Here, the model closest to the situation would involve maintaining the two types of objects as separate sets.

While the underlying mathematical model for these different types of situations may be the same, the appropriate intermediate concrete models might vary. The representational plasticity of the computer medium allows us to create different types of intermediate modeling environments with different types of features that require less initial abstraction from the situation being modeled, such as ICE-2 and its variants discussed previously. However, the number of these is not only limited, it should be quite small to avoid a Tower of Babel effect. Nonetheless, we have concluded that *no single system can capture all the essential aspects of such a complex idea-web as intensive quantity. And in each case there should be some link to the more abstract mathematical models traditionally used*, for example, coordinate graphs, tables, and equations, as in Figure 8-3.

Other Aspects of the Idea-Web of Intensive Quantity

Related to the matter of homogeneity of the objects or material that is to be modeled using intensive quantity is the role of the intensive quantity as a descriptor of an *intensive attribute* of the situation being modeled. Assuming homogeneity, a description of, say, the price per muffin in a bakery, tells nothing of the number of muffins sold or the total amount of money they cost their buyers. The price applies to all sets of muffins as well as it does to any one of them. Depending on the situation one is attempting to model, especially if some kind of homogeneity is assumed, this role of intensive quantities as global descriptors of intrinsic properties of situations may or may not be important. For example, if Noah were attempting to match many different-sized sets of animals with umbrellas, then his attention would be drawn to the fact that the 3 umbrellas per 2 animals is a general description that applies to all sets, and not merely to a particular one—he would be likely to think of the intensive quantity as a general rate rather than a particular ratio (Kaput and West, 1993; Thompson, 1992, 1993). On the other hand, when focusing on a situation involving only one value of the variables constituting the numbers of umbrellas and animals, this aspect of intensive quantity plays only a small role.

Before closing this discussion of relations between situations and potential models, we wish to emphasize the value of certain representations of intensive quantities in other reasoning processes not yet mentioned. One important example of such a process involves comparing magnitudes of intensive quantities with the same dimension.

Among the notations that we have discussed to date, the representation of an intensive quantity as the slope of a line in a coordinate graph offers the easiest comparison of intensive quantities, because a given intensive quantity, as the slope of a line consisting of an unbounded set of ordered pairs, is visually represented by a single conspicuous thing, the "tilt" of the line. Any other intensive quantity (with the same dimension, of course) can be compared with it by comparing the associated "tilt," because this tilt is a linearly ordered attribute of lines through their common point, the origin.

Consider the following two problems:

> **1. Which neighborhood has more cars per house, one where there are 3 cars for every 2 houses or one where there are 5 cars for every 3 houses?**

> **2. Which muffins are more expensive, those that cost 2 dollars for 3 muffins or those that cost 3 dollars for 5 muffins?**

Let us now compare the two problems regarding the structure of the prior knowledge involved in their solution (especially in building a Cog (D) as in the Noah's Ark problem—see Figure 8-6) and the structure of the representation B used in the reasoning process to solve them. In the muffin price comparison, we apply significant prior knowledge at the level of the initial scheme. In particular, most people already have available an intensive quantity to apply in such a situation, called "price," although it is likely to be in the unit-price form of dollars per item rather than in number of items per number of dollars. Depending on the solver's flexibility in transforming this prior knowledge into the form needed, this prior knowledge may help or hinder the mapping from Cog(D) to B. The mapping boils down to associating price with a line.

Just as important as the existence of this prior knowledge is the existence of *price-comparison* knowledge, whereby one interprets "more expensive." In other words, there exists a linear comparison scheme for price as well, which maps onto the tilt-slope comparison in B. Put differently, it helps interpret the differences in observed slope.

All this is meant to contrast with the cars-houses problem, where the prior knowledge is not likely to possess such structure. Number of cars per number of houses is not a quantity that we often deal with, and unlike "price," we do not have a ready-made word for it. And even less likely is knowledge about comparisons of such quantities, referred to as neighborhood "car density" (using an analogy with a very important type of application of intensive quantities in describing physical densities of various types).

Thus, we see important yet subtle differences in the existence of prior knowledge and its relation to a notation system.

Some Reflections on Computers and Notational Ramps and Bridges

Bridging Notations and Cognition

The Sapir-Whorf hypotheses regarding the influence of language on thought (Whorf, 1956), while contestable and difficult to operationalize in the context of natural language and everyday cognition, appear without question to have merit in the context of the special notations of mathematics. Different notation systems support dramatically different forms of reasoning, although the differences are strongly influenced by interactions between the knowledge structures associated with the notations and the prior knowledge brought to the reasoning. Given the immense complexity of human knowledge structures, such interactions are not easily accounted for. Nonetheless, we can be relatively explicit about the operant features and the knowledge associated with particular notations, both traditional and novel. Figure 8-7 is intended to help summarize our position.

We have been especially interested in using computers to support two forms of referential meaning-making, one involving reference relations between mathematical systems, for example, tables and graphs, and the other between mathematical and nonmathematical ones. The former are less problematic, and instantiating these in computer systems is a well-established use of modern computational power, for example, connecting equations and graphs. This appears in the lower left side of Figure 8-7. Nonetheless, they offer considerable promise by off-loading low level translation activity to the computer so that the student can focus on higher level relationships and action-consequences across representations. Another important contribution they offer is freeing the translation process from

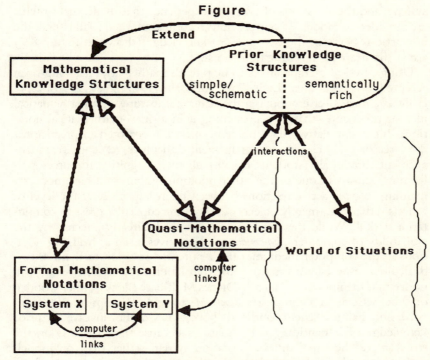

Figure 8-7 Overall framework.

serial, real-time constraints to virtually time-independent translation, so that results of actions across representations can be examined at will, in ways that optimize the development of understanding.

The other source of mathematical meanings is the rich reservoir of "natural" knowledge built from everyday experience, depicted in the upper right side of Figure 8-7. As indicated, we separate this knowledge into two general types, one being the rich, multilayered semantic knowledge of situations, as the knowledge of Noah's ark, for example. The other type is the somewhat simpler schematic knowledge by which the richer, more complex knowledge is often interpreted. An example includes our knowledge of discrete objects, their counting, grouping, and manipulating. We assume that the interpretation of complex, ambiguous situations proceeds through the use of this kind of simpler knowledge.

Our design of object-based reasoning environments such as ICE-1 and ICE-2 is intended to assist this interpretive process by reflecting this simpler knowledge in intermediate, quasi-mathematical notations, analogous to traditional manipulatives. These notations can then help bridge between the highly economical and efficient formal mathematical notation systems and the situations of everyday experience that the formal systems are intended to model. As our previous section attempted to illustrate, the interactions between the two types of knowledge (shown in Figure 8-7) are at the heart of the bridging process.

Using physical manipulatives to help teach mathematics has long been accepted as a good idea (Lesh, Post, and Behr, 1987; Post, 1980), especially as a means for embodying the structural features of a mathematical idea or procedure, that is, representing it in a quasi-mathematical notation. But manipulatives have never been widely accepted in practice for three reasons: (1) classroom management difficulties, (2) cognitive management difficulties (students exhaust all their cognitive resources performing actions in one or the other notation systems and have none remaining to track active relations between them, especially at the level of actions rather than merely objects), and (3) the curricular press to computational skill. While the third reason is only indirectly affected by the availability of computers, *cybernetic* manipulatives, used as bridging notations in the computer medium, offer a potential solution to the first two difficulties, especially by assisting the translation process. The reader will notice that manipulatives, such as Dienes Multibase Blocks, either wooden or cybernetic as in Thompson's *Blocks Microworld* (Thompson, 1992) involve only half the scheme outlined above—they do not involve the prior knowledge of semantically rich situations because their focus is on the structure of the usual number notation system rather than on modeling semantically rich situations. Incidentally, the results reported by Thompson (1992) in a careful comparison of traditional versus cybernetic multibase blocks showed significantly superior learning in the computer context except for the weakest students.

In Kaput (in press a) we offer yet another set of reasons for utilizing cybernetic manipulatives. When one acts on physical materials, each action overwrites the previous state, which can seldom be recovered, at least by the student. In a computer environment we can record significant prior states and student actions, and then represent the sequence of states that result—as a "filmstrip" of miniature screens, for example. Such a sequence might be replayed, offered in advance by a teacher to be "debugged," or otherwise changed. A student would be able to reopen any strip at any frame and resume the action, perhaps to repair or to alter a strategy to yield a branch off the original linear strip. Students could also compare one strip against another, in effect, comparing strategies as visible objects. In this way students' attention and action may be focused at a higher level. In (Kaput, in press a) we also discuss the option of recording the actions as a specialized script. In a sense, the filmstrips and scripts constitute complementary representations of a student's work—filmstrips describe the states while scripts describe the state-transitions. If specific scripts, based on particular actions on particular quantities, could have their particular values replaced by variables, then they also act as algorithms. A whole new option space opens up for building and testing algorithms by generalizing specific cases. Clearly, the world of cybernetic manipulatives merits serious exploration.

We Need a Theory to Inform Deliberate Construction of Notations by Designers and Students

Our design decisions for bridging notation systems have been mainly of the seat-of-the-pants type, driven by informal pedagogical knowledge. The new design space in mathematics as well as other domains is only newly opened, let alone explored (Norman, 1986). Its fruitful exploration will require better understanding of the structure of students' relevant prior knowledge and how to structure bridging notations so as to optimize the power of that prior knowledge without trapping students in the limitations associated with the very specificity from which it draws its strength. How closely should the notations match the semantic richness of situational knowledge?

The evolution of traditional notations, especially in mathematics (Cajori, 1929a,b), has yielded design decisions biased strongly on the side of generality and syntactical economy—from which they draw their enormous strength. That evolution, of course, took place within the constraints of static media and without any need to ensure learnability by the majority of the population—the notations were created by and for an intellectual elite (Kaput, in press b). *Both factors no longer obtain*. Now we have dynamic media of essentially unlimited plasticity, and we must make important ideas learnable by the large majority of the population. The key challenge seems to be to strike the right balance between abstractness and generality on one hand and concreteness and specificity on the other. Such balance is likely to vary from topic to topic and according to the needs of different learners.

Another set of questions even farther from being answered involves how to enable *students* to create and link their own notations. Building symbols is a major part of what it means to be human, both as a cultural phenomenon and as a matter of individual growth and cognitive function. On purely academic grounds, this skill in exploiting the representational plasticity of new media is of increasing importance and is likely to surpass skill in computation in importance, if it has not already done so. On a cultural level as designers, we are in a position somewhat analogous to the bioengineers relative to evolutionary change. We no longer need to wait for the Blind Watchmaker to fashion our notations. We can be more deliberate, more systematic, but we need more prior knowledge—of how notations function.

Note

The author wishes to thank Judah Schwartz for early and continuing support for and guidance in this work. The author also wishes to thank Clifton Luke, Laurie

Patterson-Gordon, Joel Poholsky, and especially Mary Maxwell West, for their important contributions to the work reported here—it would not have happened without their help. Some of the research reported on has been funded by NSF Grant MDR 885617.

References

Cajori, F. 1929a. *A history of mathematical notations*. Vol. 1. Notations in elementary mathematics. La Salle, IL: The Open Court Publishing Co.

————. 1929b. *A history of mathematical notations*. Vol. 2. Notations in elemantary mathematics. La Salle, IL: The Open Court Publishing Co.

Greeno, J. 1983. Conceptual entities. In *Mental models*, edited by A. Stevens and D. Gentner. Hillsdale, NJ: Erlbaum.

Grossberg, S. 1980. How does a brain build a cognitive code? *Psychological Review* 87: 1–51.

Harel, G., and J. Kaput. 1991. The influence of notation in the development of mathematical ideas. In *Advanced mathematical thinking*, edited by D. Tall and E. Dubinsky. Amsterdam and Boston: Reidel.

Kaput, J. 1985. *Multiplicative word problems and intensive quantities: An integrated software response*. Technical Report 85–19. Cambridge, MA: Harvard Graduate School of Education, Educational Technology Center.

————. 1987. Toward a theory of symbol use in mathematics. In *Problems of representation in mathematics learning and problem solving*, edited by C. Janvier. Hillsdale, NJ: Erlbaum.

————. 1988. Supporting concrete visual thinking in multiplicative reasoning. In *Focus on learning problems in mathematics*, edited by T. Eisenberg and T. Dreyfus. Special issue on Visualization and Mathematics Education, 35–48.

————. 1989. Linking representations in the symbol system of algebra. In *A research agenda for the teaching and learning of algebra*, edited by C. Kieran and S. Wagner. Reston, VA: National Council of Teachers of Mathematics; Hillsdale, NJ: Erlbaum.

————. 1991. Notations and representations as mediators of constructive processes. In *Constructivism and mathematics education*, edited by E. von Glasersfeld, pp. 53–74. Dordrecht, Netherlands: Kluwer Academic Publishers.

————. 1992. Technology and mathematics education. In *Handbook on research in mathematics teaching and learning*, edited by D. Grouws, pp. 515–56. New York: Macmillan.

————. 1994. The representational roles of technology in connecting mathematics with authentic experience. In *Mathematics as a didactic discipline: The state of the art*, edited by R. Bieler, R. W. Scholz, R. Strasser, and B. Winkelman. Dordrecht, Netherlands: Kluwer Academic Publishers.

————. In press a. Overcoming physicality and the eternal present: Cybernetic manipulatives. In *Visualization and technology in mathematics education*, edited by R. Sutherland and J. Mason. New York: Springer-Verlag.

————. In press b. Democratizing access to calculus: New routes using old roots. In *Mathematicical thinking and problem solving*, edited by A. Schoenfeld. Hillsdale, NJ: Erlbaum.

Kaput, J., and L. Pattison-Gordon. 1987. *A concrete-to abstract software ramp: Environments for learning multiplication, division, and intensive quantity.* Technical Report 87-8. Cambridge, MA: Harvard Graduate School of Education, Educational Technology Center.

Kaput, J., and M. West. 1993. Assessing proportion problem complexity. In *The development of multiplicative reasoning in the learning of mathematics,* edited by G. Harel and J. Confrey. Research in Mathematics Education Series. Albany: State University of New York Press.

Kaput, J., R. Upchurch, and M. Burke. 1993. Integrated tools for elementary mathematics. [Software]. No. Dartmouth: University of Massachusetts at Dartmouth, Department of Mathematics.

Kaput, J., M. M. Katz, C. Luke, and L. Pattison-Gordon. 1988. Concrete representations for ratio reasoning. In *Proceedings of the 10th Annual Meeting of the PME-NA,* edited by M. Behr, C. Lacampagne, and M. M. Wheeler. DeKalb, Illinois.

Kieren, T., D. Nelson, and G. Smith. 1985. Graphical algorithms in partitioning tasks. *Journal of Mathematical Behavior* 4: 25–36.

Lesh, R., T. Post, and M. Behr. 1987. Dienes revisited: Multiple embodiments in computer environments. In *Developments in school mathematics around the world,* edited by I. Wirzup and R. Streit, pp. 647–80. Reston, VA: National Council of Teachers of Mathematics.

Miera, L. 1991. Explorations of mathematical sense-making: An activity-oriented view of children's use and design of material displays. Ph.D. diss., University of California, Berkeley.

Norman, D. A. 1986. In Norman, D. & Draper S. (Eds.) *User-centered design.* Hillsdale, NJ: Erlbaum.

Saussure, F. de. 1959. *Course in general linguistics.* Glasgow: Fontana. Original edition in French, 1916.

Schwartz, J. 1988. Referent preserving and referent transforming quantities. In *Number Concepts and Operations in the Middle School,* edited by J. Hiebert and M. Behr. Reston, VA: National Council of Teachers of Mathematics; Hillsdale, NJ: Erlbaum.

Steffe, L.P., P. Cobb, and E. von Glasersfeld. 1988. *Construction of arithmetical meanings and strategies.* New York: Springer-Verlag.

Thompson, P. 1992. Notations, conventions and constraints: Contributions to effective uses of concrete materials in elementary mathematics. *Journal for Research in Mathematics Education* 23 (2): 123–47.

———. 1993. The development of the concept of speed and its relationship to concepts of rate. In *The development of multiplicative reasoning in the learning of mathematics,* edited by G. Harel and J. Confrey. Research in Mathematics Education Series. Albany: State University of New York Press.

Vergnaud, G. 1983. Multiplicative structures. In *Acquisition of mathematics concepts and processes,* edited by R. Lesh and M. Landau. New York: Academic Press.

———. 1987. Conclusion. In *Problems of representation in mathematics learning and problem solving,* edited by C. Janvier. Hillsdale, NJ: Erlbaum.

———. 1988. Multiplicative structures. In *Number concepts and operations in the middle grades,* edited by J. Hiebert and M. Behr. Reston, VA: National Council of Teachers of Mathematics.

West, M. M., C. Luke, J. Poholsky, L. Pattison-Gordon, S. Turner, and J. Kaput.

9

Multiple Representations: A Vehicle for Understanding Understanding

E. PAUL GOLDENBERG

A deep understanding in any field requires an ability to recognize common themes and underlying ideas regardless of the garb they wear. Consider linear functions: every one of them has a real root, a value for all x, and a slope; every one of them is uniquely determined by any two of infinitely many points, can be represented by infinitely many transformations from infinitely many other linear functions, and has uncountably many other features one might care to highlight. Within this multiplicity of features, there are a few that can be considered *representative* of the function: the symbolic form, of course, and the graph, but also statements like "linear, $\mathbf{R} \to \mathbf{R}$, passing through $(3,1)$ and $(5,0)$," or other lists of features that uniquely determine the function. Though most attention in classes tends to be devoted to symbolic expressions, students are generally taught a few of these representation forms. It is in the student's synthesis of the features that real Understanding lies. We cannot expect to understand that Understanding if we look only at the student's facility with one representation, or even the quality of a student's handling of each representation in isolation. But, as we observe students juggling the interaction among representations, we get a glimpse of the rich internal models they construct in their attempt to understand the bigger picture. And so *we* get a bigger picture.

The intent of this chapter is show how multiple representation aids the understanding of *Understanding*. For ease of exposition, I restrict my examples to a single domain—mathematical functions—and suggest that the arguments are readily transportable into other domains. I also vastly prefer thinking of all of us—researchers, professors, and novices—as students of

155

our own discipline rather than as subjects of some experiment. I will therefore refer to those individuals whose understanding we seek to understand as *students* without intending any suggestion about their standing in their field.

Introduction

Mathematics deals in abstractions—ideas like *function* or *ratio* or *point* that may have physical embodiments or exemplars, but are not physical objects themselves. Mathematical discourse, including teaching and testing, can only deal in representations of these abstractions. Functions, for example, may be represented through a string of symbols such as $f(x) = x^2 - 3x + 4$, or through tables, graphs, specialized icons, verbal descriptions, or even through physical objects that exhibit the right behavior. But each such representation is, in fact, only a partial picture capturing certain features of the underlying idea while ignoring or even slightly distorting others.

In current practice, the great bulk of mathematics teaching takes place within a single representational system. Much time and effort are spent in building students' skills in manipulating the formal symbolic language of traditional classroom mathematics, while relatively little time is devoted to other representations of the same ideas. The consequences for teachers and students of this narrow approach are discussed in this book and elsewhere. Here we concern ourselves primarily with the implications for researchers who try to understand Understanding.

Not surprisingly, research on process or outcome in the learning of mathematics is biased toward the prevailing learning methods. Many studies of "how students learn algebra" are really studies of how students learn the algebra that classes teach. At the least, this limits the kinds of questions that are asked. What are the characteristic algebra errors? How does this or that method reduce the number of students who make a particular error or class of errors? And so on. But there is a much more fundamental way in which the understanding of student understanding is limited when research is performed only in a single-representation environment. When only one representation is used, it is hard to tell whether a particular observation is or is not merely an artifact of that representation. By contrast, when we see students translate among representations, we can relatively easily discriminate between surface confusions about any *one representation* and true misconstructions of the *concept*.

An illustration is helpful. We[1] interviewed bright, mathematically successful precalculus students one by one as they worked with the *Function Analyzer* software (Schwartz, Yerushalmy, and Harvey, 1988) linking graphical, symbolic, and tabular representations of function. Our research focused on the effects of scale change on the appearance of a graph, but we needed to know in advance what expectations students had about various graphs. They all easily identified linear forms as linear. When we asked them to predict the shape of the graph of $x^2 + 7x + 1$, few could specify the graph precisely without plotting points, but they all readily said that it was a quadratic and that its graph would be an upward-opening parabola. One particularly strong student said that if the expression could be factored, he could say more about the graph, but in this case he would just have to "plug in points." After he made his prediction that this would be some kind of parabola, I showed him the unexpected graph in Figure 9-1. He was surprised at first, but quickly capitulated and said:[2]

> 69 S Well, because you add the new, other *x* term, it changes from a parabola to a line. So, what you're just——what you're doing is you're changing the whole equation, which changes the ultimate graph.

Because the student had expressed special expectations about a factorable case, I changed the function to $x^2 + 7x + 6$, but the student knew enough to see that the change of the constant term affected the graph in a quantitative but not qualitative way. Therefore, even before he saw the graph, he explained:

> 71 S Well it would be a different slope line, but it would not be a parabola, it would just be a different slope. Actually I got . . . the same slope, but it would go through—I don't know—it would go at a higher intercept, *y*-intercept.

He slipped at first, picking slope rather than intercept as the changed feature, but ended up correctly applying his knowledge of linear functions to this case which appears, for reasons he has not discovered, to be a line. He then graphed the new function (Figure 9-2) and was quite satisfied that his analysis was correct. Can he derive a formula from the graph? Yes, he has that knowledge as well. He saw the crossing at -1 and knew from the formula on the screen that the *y*-intercept is 6. Working entirely in his

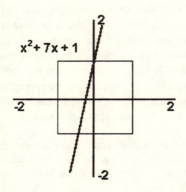

Figure 9-1

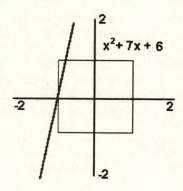

Figure 9-2

head, he almost instantly derived an equation and wrote down $y = 6x + 6$, a perfectly plausible formula for the graph he saw.

But this behavior is full of paradoxes. So I pressed him further, asking him explicitly "Does that mean these two functions (the $y = x^2 + 7x + 6$ that the computer claims it graphed and the $y = 6x + 6$ that he derived from that graph) are the same?"

> 101 S Mathematically, I would think they would be, because they have the same graphs. See what, what you're doing up here is the $x^2 + 7x$, would equal the $6x$ in the area that we're talking about . . . .

Again, his statement raises some questions. From further questioning it became clear that he saw the constant 6 in both functions $6x + 6$ and $x^2 + 7x + 6$, and reasoned that "$x^2 + 7x$ would equal the $6x$" by subtracting the constant. He could, one presumes, have just as easily gone further to conclude that $x^2 + x = 0$, but he did not. But what did he mean by qualifying his answer with the word "mathematically" and by saying "in the area that we're talking about"? Was he trying to state (correctly!) that these functions are *numerically* close in the *neighborhood* in which we are viewing them? Apparently not, because when he later attempts (line 105) to demonstrate the equality of the two, he is apparently indifferent to the neighborhood, choosing $x = 1$ where the functions have quite different values rather than $x = -1$ where they intersect.

> 105 S So because the y-intercept doesn't change between those two, that means the x^2 and the $7x$ has to in some way equal the $6x$. So when you're using, when you're using 1 for x, that'd be 1 (*quadratic term*) plus 7 (*linear term*) plus 6 (*constant*), 13, 14—14, so y equals—and then— (*mumbles*)

If the question had been presented only in symbols, this student would certainly have asserted with complete confidence that $6x + 6$ and $x^2 + 7x + 6$ are not the same function. He would have appeared the good student that he is, but we would have learned little else about his thinking. Faced with a strangely scaled graph of the quadratic, however, this student did not treat the graph as *additional* information, but saw it as *conflicting* information. In his attempts to resolve the conflict he chose to abandon certain ideas while using others: He gave up on his expectations about the graph of a function containing an x^2 term, but derived (even using information from the quadratic form) the linear expression $6x + 6$ for the graph of $x^2 + 7x + 6$ and then went through elaborate effort to defend the equality of these two functions.

The presence of a second representation simultaneously brought out more genuine mathematical power in this student than we might otherwise have seen, and also exposed an absolutely unexpected fragility in some of his ideas.

How Does Computer-Based Multiple-Linked Representation Help?

Fostering and Exposing Dialogue with Oneself: The Computer's Contribution

Even without multiple representation, the interactive nature of the computer can contribute measurably to the researcher's information about students' thinking.

When students perform mathematical tasks mentally or on paper, they often—wittingly or unwittingly—conceal parts of their thinking even when they intend to explicate their ideas and methods. Their own internal dialogue may not be fully conscious, they may "assume" that the researcher sees the steps they take (as may the researcher), and they may combine many steps or assumptions into a single act.

On the other hand, when students ask a computer to perform whatever manipulations are needed to solve a problem, they must express each required step explicitly, making visible certain operations that might otherwise be performed mentally. Software can be designed to highlight whatever level of detail is of interest—high-level operations like "solve this equation," intermediate-level operations like "factor this expression," low-level steps that detail each element of a calculation. In any of these cases, the researcher becomes a witness to the student-computer communication and is thereby afforded a more direct window on the student's strategies.

The interactive nature of the computer allows students to become engaged in dialogue with themselves. They perform a manipulation, get a response, and react to that response. If they are truly exploring, we get to observe how they build their strategies, how they design their experiment, how they react (including expressions of surprise or puzzlement) to the outcomes of their experiments, and how they classify and explain these outcomes and organize them into patterns.

Multiple-Linked Representations

There are four intertwined ways in which multiple-linked representations help: enriching dialogue with self, raising conflict and surprise, affirming (if not paralleling) students' own internal multiple representations, and helping us distinguish between students' expressed models and the ones they act on.

The dialogues that students engage in with themselves can be vastly enriched when they translate across representations. The increased variety of representations through which students can express themselves, as well as students' preferences for one representation over another can be a wealth of information to the researcher.

Problems in which only a single representation is used draw less broadly from the students' store of internal representations, giving (1) a narrower view of the students' model in the first place, and (2) less opportunity for the students' multiple models to come into conflict with one another. Such conflict gives us rich information about the students' strategies for resolving the internally generated conflict.

Further, when students need to manipulate one representation in order to achieve some goal expressed in another, the act they choose gives evidence about their theory about how the two representations are linked—a theory that the students may not be able to articulate, and may not even recognize. The students' education comes principally from the feedback they get, but the researcher's education begins right as the students choose their very first act—and students' expressions, remarks, and gestures as they receive their feedback are additional sources of information to the researcher.

Actually, it is not merely the multiplicity of representations, but their dynamic linking—the immediacy and accuracy with which the computer ties two or more representations together—that affords the full benefit to the researcher. Working in an algebra world that dynamically links graphical and symbolic representations, our students often express surprise when some manipulation does not produce the effect they had expected. Surprise is a flag marking a spot that we, as researchers, should endeavor to understand. Moreover, it is a pointer to something that students might never think is worth expressing. Without the surprise of contradiction, students have little reason to suspect that there is anything remarkable in their thinking.

We have not so often seen surprise among students performing similar manipulations without the aid of a computer. This may be partly because, in a paper-and-pencil translation among representations, so many mechanical steps intervene between expectation and outcome that the two are not so readily compared—no conflict may be noticed. Furthermore, so many mental or paper-and-pencil transactions may take place between a critical thought-step and its expression as an observable result that even when conflict is noticed, neither student nor researcher can identify which step was the original source of that conflict.

Perhaps the most important reason for using multiple representation as a vehicle for understanding Understanding is that it is quite apparent that students themselves multiply represent their concepts. A family of graphs that differ only in their vertical displacement may be described as differing in their *y*-intercept, their "height," their constant term, and in various other ways, each representing with greatest fidelity some feature of the family at the expense of others. Which feature the student selects as salient in a particular problem, or what problem characteristics help to call the different representations into play is information the student may not otherwise supply.[3] Students may *know*, for example, that points have location only and no size, and therefore may respond correctly to any probe that questioned this knowledge explicitly. At the same time, if the problem is not posed explicitly, students may *act* under the perceptual influence of representational systems that "show" points as visible blobs. In effect, these students are storing both the official line and their own home-grown theories. If we test only in the official modality, we may hear only half the story.

Understanding *uses* multiple representation, and so to understand Understanding, we must tap that use.

An Example

The wealth of information available when students solve problems in a multiple linked representation environment on the computer is perhaps best illustrated by example. The following is a sequence of excerpts from an interview with the same bright, successful high-school senior whose work was illustrated previously. Headings for each section highlight particular features of the interview—for example, the student's affect, gestures, and focus of attention—that served as information to the researcher. Even in these excerpts which were selected to present the interview features as distinctly as possible, you will see how intertwined the communicative elements really are.

It is important to keep in mind that this chapter presents less than 10% of a single 40-minute interview with this student. Even with such a brief example—roughly four minutes' worth of data—we are pointed to some very deep issues about the student's understanding, and we can illustrate how we use the interview to raise conjectures about that understanding. Confirmation or rejection of our conjectures, of course, require supporting data. Remarkably, the remaining 36 minutes provide most of that support.

Student Selection of Salient Features as Information

Having shown the student how to enter a function on the computer, the interviewer (I) asked the student to enter some function he was reasonably familiar with. The student entered $f(x) = x + 2$, and watched the graph appear on the screen. (See Figure 9-3.)

I confirmed that this matched the student's expectations, and then asked the student to change the function in some way. S changed the constant from $+2$ to -2 (see Figure 9-4) and, in response to a query from the interviewer, described the change as follows.

> 16   S   Well, basically the y-intercept is, I mean, when you plug in 0 to the x——when you do $f(x) - 2 =$, uh, $x - 2$ the y-intercept ends up being -2, and when you have $f(x) = x + 2$, the y-intercept would be 2. So what you're ultimately doing is just changing the y-intercept.

The student's choice of features to describe is information. The student might, for example, have described the change as a change in the constant term, or under influence of the graphs, a change from fourth quadrant to second quadrant, or an addition of 4 to the previous function. But he chose to mention the y-intercept. How shall we interpret this? It seems likely that for the two functions he has defined—$f_1(x) = x + 2$ and $f_2(x) = x - 2$—he knows that $f_2 = f_1 - 4$ for all values of x, but his answer—"What you're ultimately doing is just changing the y-intercept"—could be interpreted as if he meant that only the y-intercept were affected. If that is what he meant, why might he have slipped in this way? And if that is *not* what he meant, what are some reasonable alternatives.

Possible explanation 1: A high level of abstraction and an analysis of the function

We might explain his language by assuming that "just changing the y-inter-cept" means "not changing other essential features of the function, such as

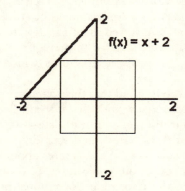

Figure 9-3

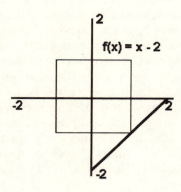

Figure 9-4

slope, degree, and so on." At this level of abstraction, he might fully recognize the function as a mapping for *all* values of x and does not mean that the only value that changes is the value at $x = 0$. Rather, he ignores changes at values of x other than 0 (or, perhaps, is not talking about *values* at all because he is operating *above* that level of detail). The only *feature* that changes (in some set of critical features he has in mind) is the y-intercept.

Possible explanation 2: A reliance on definition or perceptual features

A similar, but slightly different way of explaining his language is that "y-intercept" is his coding of the role played by the constant term in a linear function. The difference between this explanation and the first is that this one doesn't require that the student have a clearly articulated set of distinctive features of *functions*, but merely that he has learned the usual things about translation of functions and recalls what he was taught about the linear form: $y = mx + b$. If this is the correct explanation of his language, he is essentially stating a definition—"the change between $x + 2$ and $x - 2$ is a change in b, so by definition it is a change in y-intercept"—rather than using some understanding of the critical features of a function. Alternatively, he may be basing his response on a visual rote, invoking selected (taught) features of the geometric shape in the graph (in this linear example, slope and vertical distance from the origin). In either case, he may not be thinking about changes in a *mapping* from x to $f(x)$ at all, even *at* 0.

Possible explanation 3: Weak concept of mapping defined on a set

Despite what is likely to be his *ability* to affirm the translation for all values of x, it may be that he does not *spontaneously* think of functions as such a mapping. Many students respond in ways that hint that even though they might, under proper questioning, recognize that functions express a relation between two *sets*, a domain and a range, their *notion* of function is dependent on *particular* values rather than this general relation. They may see the particular values by "plugging in points" or by reading values off of graphs, or they may see geometric gestalts, but they do not really have an image for any mapping from one infinite set to another. Here S explains what I refer to as "the change between those two graphs" by referring to what happens when you plug in a single, *and special*, value. It may not be obvious to S—that is, it may not be S's image, even if it is, at some level, something he could claim to know and perhaps even work out—that $g(q) - f(q) = 4$ for some arbitrary and "unfriendly" value of q (such as π).

We will try to learn how much of each of these three explanations contributes to this student's reasoning as the interview continues.

Gesture, Surprise, Temporal Order in Selecting Features

Responding to the interviewer's probing for more explanation, the student describes his two lines as "like the same slope but just being translated." The interviewer then asks if the student can make a line with a different slope.

20   S   OK. (*Types f(x) = 2x and sees graph shown in Figure 9-5.*)

21   I   OK. And, what would happen if you made that, say $2x + 1$?

22   S   Then you would be (*gesturing along the x = 1 column*) up 2 because of the, of the dilation of the x and then you translate over the 1, over 1 more in the x direction (*points to the right!*).

This is most remarkable. What is he really saying here?

His words *up* and *over* suggest images of coordinate plotting, in particular through a rise-and-run maneuver. Is his immediate gesture to $x = 1$ further evidence of that strategy, or is he drawn to the 1 because it is the new feature in the symbolic expression he is interpreting?

One interpretation: He may be saying that the way to graph $2x$ is to go

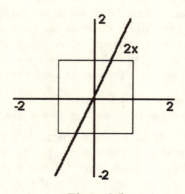

Figure 9-5

"up 2" in the $x = 1$ column "because of the dilation of the x." Then, to get $2x + 1$, "you translate [some unspecified set of points] over the 1, over 1 more in the x direction." If this *is* his intent, there are two puzzles. First, although $2x + 1$ and $2(x + 1/2)$ are algebraically equivalent functions, each notation suggests a particular mapping from $2x$. The notation $2x + 1$ describes vertical displacement, but the student speaks of a horizontal translation. Moreover, in pointing to the right, he translates in the wrong direction regardless of his image of the mapping, perhaps influenced by the (positive) sign of the change.

A second interpretation: Because, as he has told me, his most recent math classes have focused on "translations and dilations," he is, at the moment, more used to thinking about forms like $m(x - r)$ than about polynomial form. If the function had actually been $2(x + 1)$ instead of $2x + 1$, his wording "up 2 because of the dilation of the x" would have been particularly appropriate and entirely accurate. Unfortunately, if this is the slip he has made, it still leaves a puzzle: though the slip itself may "just" be a case of mind-set over reading matter, it cannot explain why, after giving a correct description of the incorrect reading, he goes on to talk about "and then you translate . . . over 1 more."

In both cases, his gesture to the right is puzzling. That gesture appears to describe still a third function $2(x - 1)$. A possible reconciliation of this conflict (supported by evidence elsewhere in the interview) suggests a third interpretation: His mind-set has, indeed, led him to see an $m(x - r)$ form, and he is secondarily confusing the sign inside the parentheses. The fact that he calls attention to the dilation—"up 2 because of the dilation of the x"—suggests that he is explaining something that he treats as non-obvious. If so, he is not reiterating the up-2-over-1 as an explanation of the $2x$ slope itself—that would be too obvious—but is, instead, explaining that the addition of 1—the horizontal displacement of 1—has the effect of displacing the graph vertically not 1, but 2 "because of the dilation"—a newer idea to him and therefore less obvious and more in need of the additional clarifying words.

We will need to look further for a possible solution to the puzzles.

I asked him to graph the function so that we could see it. He typed $f(x) = 2x + 1$, but as the graph appeared (see Figure 9-6), he said with obvious surprise:

24   S   Hold it!
25   I   Um, you look surprised. Tell me what happened . . . Where was the last line (the $2x$)?
  26   S   The last one was over here.

He held the edge of his hand roughly along where the $2x$ line had been, but so imprecisely that I had to crane way over to see. I asked him to hold a pencil along the indicated line. This additional use of gesture would clarify both the line and what aspects of the line he attended to most.

The student immediately and correctly set his pencil through the origin

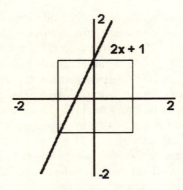

Figure 9-6

but seemed very hesitant about slope. He adjusted the slope of the pencil several times, sometimes passing it through the corners of the oblong graphing window, sometimes running parallel with the current graph. It took many spontaneous changes before he settled on a slope that roughly matched that of the line on the screen. His strategy for setting the pencil's position clearly did not lead him to preserve the current graph's slope and change its intercept. Rather, his gesture and expression showed that he was trying to recall the slope of the previous graph, as if that feature might not have been preserved under the transformation $2x \rightarrow 2x + 1$. It is as if he was certain about what a change in the constant term does do, but uncertain that it never does anything else. (In line 69 of the interview, quoted earlier, we see a similar kind of uncertainty: The quadratic term determines that the graph is a parabola, but perhaps, at least in some circumstances, some combination of linear and constant terms can "change the whole equation.") This is a particularly clear example of how gesture is information. His correct answer by itself would not have led us to question the solidity of his thinking.

28   S   —Something like that.

29   I   Something like that?—So you're keeping, from my angle, keeping the same slope, and where are you putting it through?

30   S   Over at negative ¹/₂.

His answer is a surprising slip. Even though he has been asked about the placement of his pencil, which unambiguously passes through the origin, he becomes distracted by the graph on the screen and describes its x-intercept. In response to a query from the interviewer, he readily confirms that he meant to say 0, but why did he get distracted at all? We may speculate that this student maintains a fragile concept of function, that any one function is represented as a bundle of not too tightly related features, and that the resulting forest of details makes it relatively easy to lose track of one or another from time to time. It is also interesting to note his reference to the x displacement rather than the y. This is not an error, for the line $2x$ may be translated in many ways to coincide with the line $2x + 1$, but it is not the explanation we might have expected. Does this further support the view that his most recent mathematics classes on horizontal translation are dominating his thinking? Or is he again, as in line 69, being captured by the powerful perceptual phenomenon (see, e.g., Goldenberg, 1988) that the line has moved to the left?

Access to Multiple Internal Models as Information

35 I   OK. OK. But why were you surprised? Isn't that what you had explained?

36 S   Yeah, but I was just thinking that, uh,——(*gesture of embarrassment*)——I just didn't move it over in terms of——. 'Cause it's affecting the y, ultimately the $+1$ and, you know, the x stays the same. (*waves error away*). Getting out of math class last block. (*chuckles*).

This response makes it clear that he *has* both ways of thinking available to him. What influences his choice? In this case, it appears that he is heavily influenced by his most recent math class, and is not operating from a stable internal image of the mapping.

The slip seems almost inconsequential but is, in ways, a central matter. At one level, algebra is all about tautologies: the various forms $y = mx + b$, $y = m(x - r)$, and $(y - y_1)/(x - x_1) = (y_2 - y_1)/(x_2 - x_1)$, for example, can all express the same functional relation between x and y. Algebra classes teach students how forms like these can be derived from one another. But to appreciate the *purpose* of an algebraic transformation—the content behind the syntax, so to speak—a student must understand *both* the equivalence of the different forms *and* the special information that each one conveys. If the student does not understand that it is possible to derive information from an identity, many algebraic manipulations become hollow exercises. Faced with a specific form, this bright student fails to find its peculiar information because his current lessons are about something else. This is yet another sense in which multiple representations—in this case, various representations of the same functional relationship—are at the heart of algebra. We cannot understand a student's understanding of algebra if we examine only one representation at a time.

Line 36 raises a new question. What does "the x stays the same" mean to this student? Does he mean that in this type of translation we are not talking about any movement in the x direction? Or is he thinking (much more subtly) about the "immovability" of the domain of the function—that is, that the notion of "$\forall x$" cannot change, since all values of x are already included. Or is he thinking of the (related) independence of x?

Although there is no direct evidence, there is a lot of explanatory power in theorizing that notions of "$\forall x$" are difficult for this student, although he may appreciate something like that idea in a piecewise fashion, that is, as "for *this x* and for *that x* and, as we seem to be seeing as we try more cases, for all the other *particular x*'s we can think of."

There is no way to know for certain from this interview, but this student's tendency to ground his analyses on "plugging in points" suggests a concrete version of the independence-of-*x* explanation. Thus, he is saying that "if you plug the same value for *x* into two functions, the difference between the functions is just 'affecting the *y* . . . and . . . the *x* stays the same.'"

> 39   I   OK. What would happen if you change that to $2x + 2$?
>
> 40   S   Then it, it would go, translate more, more to the left. (*shows with hand*).

Even though this student explains in line 36 that "it's affecting the *y*" and recognizes that his mind-set from "math class last block" may be getting in the way, he still does not abandon his focus on horizontal instead of vertical movements. He clearly knows better, but does not act on that knowledge. The interviewer tries to find out why.

> 41   I   OK. More to the left. I'm not sure that I understand that, because I thought you were talking about *up* movements with that, with that 2.
>
> 42   S   Well in terms of——when you're talking from the origin, you know, the line, the point that would be at the origin is moving over.

Two things of note. He qualifies his explanation with the words "when you're talking from the origin." He also begins to explain about "the line" but shifts to explaining about "the point." Both, but especially the latter, may be the result of what seems to be a common student discomfort with the notion of function as mapping from one entire set (the "''∀x") to another. The initial qualification and his repetition of that qualification in "the point that would be at the origin" seem to continue hinting that not all points are created equal—that certain points are more important or more graspable than others. (See line 16.)

The interviewer repeats the question about the confusion between left and up.

> 50   I   Why did you refer to this as the line moving over rather than up?
> 51   S   It's, well the fact that lines are ultimately infinite. The actual movement would be the *y*-intercept moves up. But if you're looking at an infinite line . . . The *y*-intercept actually moves up, it also moves the lines comparatively, and if you're looking straight at the origin you move it over. You know, it looks like it's going left even though it's just a raising of the——

The student has invoked ideas about geometry, infinity, and perception and has used these to explain an observation about algebra. This rich use of related knowledge is common when the problem situation clearly permits multiple representations. It stands in sharp contrast to the "move-it-over-here-and-change-the-sign" explanations that often accompany purely symbolic manipulations.

Afterword

In the introduction, I said that I would restrict my examples to one domain for ease of exposition. Perhaps I should add that this restriction allowed me to speak of the domain I know best and the only one I have researched firsthand. Keeping that limited perspective in mind, I will take a moment to explore my claim that the arguments for computer-based multiple representation as a valuable tool for research on understanding were transportable to other domains. Of course, to transport the arguments one must be able to transport the phenomenon: the selected domain must be multiply representable in some suitable ways.

The writing tool I am using right now allows me to view my composition either as full text or in various levels of outline form. Like most text editors, it also allows me to manipulate variously sized linguistic structures as I edit: letters, whole words, sentences, paragraphs, arbitrary blocks of text, and units defined by the outline. This is not the richest of imaginable alternatives for representing the ideas I wish to set down in writing, but already it recalls some of the points made earlier in this chapter. My alterations at various levels of detail—from outline to draft and back to outline—do expose aspects of the dialogue that I am having with myself about what I am trying to communicate. They also foster that dialogue by making it easy for me to move fluently among various levels of abstraction as I write. Although I am not exploring in quite the same sense as the mathematics students I described earlier, I am playing with the structure and wording of my ideas both to clarify them to myself and to present them in as unambiguous a way to you. Without an outline feature, I would still be able to perform these edits—and an observer could still watch me perform them—but without that more abstract representation of my text it would be less clear to the observer (and perhaps even to me) when my moves treat the text as amorphous blocks of prose and when they identify structural elements of my argument or the plot of my story. In a similar way, when I change a name of a character in the paragraph I am editing, an observer has no immediate way of knowing whether I am correcting a local slip that I made or responding locally to a much more radical change I have planned—a global change of that character's name. The observer can identify the level at which I am dealing when I use a search-and-change-all-instances feature.

The parallels are not perfect—possibly because the nature of multiple representation in the writing example is not as rich and well linked as in the mathematics example—but they are suggestive. The existence of more than one way of looking at the task helps to enrich the writer's internal dialogue, and conforms with what (I am already disposed to believe) is the

$$\mathcal{T}ruth = \lim_{\text{experience} \to \infty} \mathcal{B}elief$$

Figure 9-7

writers' own internal multiple representation of the chapter. To act on the text, the writer engages in a dialogue with the machine, rendering observable much of the thinking that might otherwise have been obscured as a single global act of rewriting. At the most fundamental level, the observer is availed more observable behavior. And, as in the mathematics example, a variety of ways in which the text is represented may help observers to distinguish between the writer's expressed goals in an edit and the goals that the writer acts on, by aiding in identifing what features the writer chose as salient.

Of course, inferring the nature of understanding remains a tricky business. Even when there is more than one representation to observe, the particular choices of representations made available by a particular tool will encourage certain behaviors, inhibit others, and thus skew the picture we get of the student's internal representations of the understandings we hope to study. A friend enamored of mathematical notation once characterized Truth as shown in Figure 9-7.

That itself may not be Truth, but the truth in it reminds us that the richer and more varied our experiences of students' understandings, the more we may trust our inferences about them.[4]

Notes

1. Most of these interviews were conducted either by me or by Marlene Kliman, but corroborative interviews and observations were made by a number of other colleagues, especially Phil Lewis.

2. All the interview data given in this chapter were drawn from a single 40-minute interview with one articulate pre-calculus student. Lines in the protocol were numbered sequentially. These numbers are retained in the excerpts here to give some sense of where in the dialogue the statements occurred. The current illustration is drawn from the middle of the interview. Excerpts from earlier segments of the interview are included later in this chapter.

3. An example of the effect of switching from the use of the "*y*-intercept" to height as a mental representation of this feature can be found in Goldenberg, 1988.

4. The preparation of this chapter and the generation of some of the ideas behind it were supported in part by the National Science Foundation, grant number MDR-8954647. The views represented here are not necessarily shared by the NSF. Special thanks to Judah Schwartz and Cynthia Carter for helping me think through the issues discussed here.

References

Goldenberg, E. P. 1988. Mathematics, metaphors, and human factors: Mathematical, technical, and pedagogical challenges in the graphical representation of functions. *Journal of Mathematical Behavior* 7(2):135–74.

Schwartz, J. L., M. Yerushalmy, and W. Harvey. 1988. *The Function Analyzer*. Pleasantville, NY: Sunburst Communications.

10

The Right Size Byte: Reflections of an Educational Software Designer

JUDAH L. SCHWARTZ

In this chapter, I set down some ideas I have developed over the last decade about the problems of designing educational software. These ideas have evolved out of my own experience designing educational software in a variety of subject areas and for a range of audiences. I make no claim here that these views offer deep truths about educational software design, and the reader should be aware that they do not represent the thoughts of the majority of educational software designers.

Choosing a Topic

The first issue an educational software designer must address is the choice of content for the software that he or she is about to design. This choice will often, although not always, imply a relatively specific audience. For example, a piece of software on special relativity is likely to be used in a high school or college physics class but not in elementary school. A piece of software on color names may be appropriate for kindergarten and early elementary grades but not for the later years of high school.

Whoever the audience, we can think about choosing content in the following way.

Old content using old approaches
New content using old approaches
Old content using new approaches
New content using new approaches

For the most part, traditional Computer-Assisted Instruction (CAI) uses old approaches to old content. By and large, the instructional content of the majority of CAI materials is already part of traditional curricula. The pedagogical technique employed in most CAI materials has an authority, in this instance, the computer, posing a question to the student, waiting for an answer, assessing the quality of the answer, and choosing the next pedagogical interaction.

Some educators at another extreme, bedazzled by the apparent potential of the microcomputer to affect education, have raised a clarion cry for new curricular content using new approaches. No longer will it be necessary for youngsters to learn to spell; there will be spelling checkers. No longer will it be necessary for youngsters to learn to divide; there will be calculators. These enthusiasts similarly anticipate that the presence of memory resident thesauruses, atlases, and dictionaries all hiding just behind the next *hyper-something-or-other* will make room for totally new content in the curriculum. The claim is made that these tools will make it possible for children and teachers to bypass the "curriculum of the culture" and to generate for themselves whole new subject areas to replace those traditionally taught and learned.

Without commenting on the intellectual depth and solidity of these claims (and the examples offered in support of the claims, which are for the most part very uneven), the sparkle and shine of new content does little to hide the quite traditional pedagogy that many of the "new content" people use. They tend to confuse the use of new media with new pedagogical approaches. Thus many, like the CAI traditionalists, use the computer to ask questions and assess answers. Others who are equally enthusiastic about the promise of the new technology, but seemingly unwilling to put forward concrete examples of their visions, abdicate responsibility and abandon students to find their own ways in the electronic intellectual treasury they now have access to.

In and of itself, there is clearly nothing either wrong or silly about the call for new content. Much of what we teach is indeed outdated or foolish. Moreover, it is important to rethink continually the content of what we teach and to revise that content to reflect the realities of the world around us. There is, however, a pragmatic difficulty. New content, in any medium, is frightening to many school boards and to some teachers. The problem is more severe in the case of new content and a new medium, in this instance the computer.

Does this mean that the promise of the microcomputer will not be realized in education until we overcome the intellectual inertia of those who want to keep teaching forever what they were taught as children? I suggest that judiciously chosen traditional content, implemented in thoughtful and engaging new ways that both promote and scaffold new learning and teaching approaches, is the key to bringing the new technology, and in the end new content as well, into the lives of our students and teachers in a serious way. In this chapter, I will discuss the design of software that takes this approach.

Choosing this approach has the virtue of making change more acceptable and more workable in schools. It also has a longer term and potentially far more important entailment: dealing with old material in new ways will press teachers to rethink and reformulate their own understanding of what they are teaching. Ultimately, I believe they will be led to introduce new topics and materials with enthusiasm and freshness. The value to students, and to society as a whole, of teachers modeling this behavior should not be underestimated.

What Responsibility Should the Software Have?

Having chosen a subject for the software, the designer must next consider the question of how much instructional responsibility the software should have. The extreme stances on this question are:

1. The software runs the conversation with the user, making inferences where necessary about the intentions of the user.
2. The software simply responds to the user, displaying the consequences of the user's actions.

My own position on this question is unequivocally on the side of the second option. I take this position for several reasons. First, I think understanding a user's response well enough to make inferences about his or her intentions is the central problem of artificial intelligence research. In general, this is a very difficult problem that has never been satisfactorily solved. Each of the partial solutions that do exist represents an enormous investment of human and financial resource, is pedagogically flawed, and requires hardware environments that are not likely to be affordable by schools for some time.

Even if these difficulties did not exist, I would still be uncomfortable with the first option. Normally in human discourse, when A asks B a question, B presumes that A cares about the answer. No student is ever going to believe that the computer that poses a question cares about his or her answer. We have more than sufficient evidence of the alienation of our youngsters from school settings in which they are asked questions with known answers or asked to do tasks that have no "clients" for their products.

There is one circumstance under which I am willing to take a different position on this question. When and if a student gives "informed consent," I am willing to use a piece of software that runs the conversation. Here is an instance drawn from my own experience. I do not know how to touch-type, and I feel no compulsion to learn. But if I did, I would be more than happy to use a normative, didactic, conversation-running piece of software to learn how to touch-type. I would not, under those circumstances, resent in the least the fact that the software was telling me what to do, how often, and when.

How to Think About the Intellectual Scope of a Program

Just as it is possible to prepare written materials that address a specific topic, and thus can be "used up" in the sense that students master the content and are ready to move on, it is also possible for sharply targeted software to be "used up." It is not a criticism of a piece of software to say that it addresses a narrow range of curricular concerns.

It is also possible to write software that has very wide, domain-independent utility. Perhaps the extreme case of software of this type is the programming language. A programming language is a tool for making tools. There is no reasonable way it can be "used up" in the sense previously mentioned. Obviously, it is not a criticism of software to say that it is a tool-making tool.

Though I believe both extremes of software types are useful and desirable, I think there is reason to consider where on this spectrum of specificity to generality lies the possibility of making the greatest educational impact. Practical problems of classroom and computer lab management accompany a heavy reliance on software that can be "used up." There is a continuing need to find the right piece of software for students to be using at any given moment as well as the logistical task of keeping track of many disks and manuals.

The pragmatic difficulties that attend the use of the open-ended end of the spectrum of software type are different in kind but no less difficult to resolve. Open-ended programming languages are marvelous tools in the hands of teachers who have both mastered the language and know how to use it interestingly and imaginatively to challenge students to do projects in subject areas that schools will recognize as legitimate. Unfortunately, such people are rare.

I believe the greatest potential educational impact of microcomputer software lies neither in narrowly targeted software that can be "used up" nor in general purpose tools. I believe that the promise of educational software and the most exciting creative challenges lie in the design and programming of a kind of object intermediate to these two. In the kind of software environment I have in mind, the intellectual domain is bounded by the functions the software puts at the user's disposal, but within that domain users are unconstrained in what they may do. Software environments of this type do have a subject matter. They are not general purpose tools. They are certainly not tool-making tools. On the other hand, like tools, they do not question, judge, or assess their users' intentions. They simply display the consequences of users' actions and allow them to raise their own questions and assess their own actions.

Guided Inquiry—An Appropriate Pedagogy

I have explored the characterization of software along two dimensions. On the first dimension, that of constraint to open-endedness, I have given my reasons for preferring the open-ended end of the spectrum. On the specific to general dimension, I have tried to argue the importance of an intermediate position between narrowly targeted software on the one hand and programming languages on the other.

Having thus located myself in a kind of instructional space, I turn to the question of what kind of pedagogical style is most appropriate to the stance I have adopted.

I believe that the kind of microcomputer use I favor dictates a sharing of learning and teaching roles among teachers, fellow students, and the individual student. The computer, like the encyclopedia, the atlas, the dictionary, and the thesaurus, can serve them all, either collectively or individually, when needed.

The teacher's responsibility is to challenge, to lead, and, above all, to *educe*, to draw out of students their understandings and misunderstandings, their insights and their inventions. Our rhetoric about teaching, for the most part, honors this role. It gives substantially less prominence, however, to the teacher's role as continuing learner of the subject that he or she teaches. For a teacher to be a continuing learner of the subject, he or she must be a careful listener to the words of students. Students often have fresh and interesting ways of both understanding and misunderstanding a subject. Close attention to what students say can help teachers continue to broaden their own grasp of the subject and the ways students come to learn it.

Listening to students carefully, while necessary, is not sufficient. Teachers must actively seek to extend their own knowledge and understanding of their subject. Often they do this in professional groups and in courses. I believe that software of the type I have been discussing offers yet another avenue for the professional intellectual growth of teachers. It is a particularly desirable avenue of growth because, in contrast to coursework and professional associations, it involves the very same medium their students use. The opportunity for students to see their own teachers acquiring and making new knowledge is certain to make a both a lasting and desirable impact on them.

Students also have roles and responsibilities. They must learn the "curriculum of the culture" in some depth. By this I mean both their own culture as well as enough of others' cultures so that they come to respect and cherish the diversities of both groups and individuals. They must also learn that what there is to learn is not static, but rather is a live and growing body of knowledge to which they can, and indeed are obliged to, contribute. Traditional school practices do not make the learning of this latter lesson easy. Such learning cannot happen without teachers who encourage and challenge. Given teachers who do so, I believe it is easier when students have access to curricular environments in which they can explore their nascent inventions and hone them to the point where they are willing to share them with others. These inventions will sometimes extend the previously known. At other times they will challenge previously held beliefs.

In summary, teachers must guide, but they must also inquire. Groups of students must inquire and help to guide one another. Clearly, for this to happen, teachers and students must come to formulate their roles and responsibilities in these ways. They will need curricular environments that permit these activities to happen easily and well.

Before closing this section, I want to add a comment about motivation. I believe it is important for the software designer to design software in such a way as to make the intellectual content of the software appealing and engaging. If it is necessary to have a "cover story" that drives users through the software by a series of external motivating "gimmicks," then, in my view, the design is not yet as good as it can be.

The Problem of Simplicity and Complexity

Having selected a topic, a position on the constraint-open-endedness dimension, a position on the specific-general dimension, and a pedagogic style, I now turn to the problem of designing a piece of software. One way to formulate this problem is to ask the following two questions.

1. What actions do you want users be able to carry out in this software environment?
2. What elementary tools do you wish to put at the disposal of the users to make it possible to carry out these actions?

The first question is really about the operations of greatest complexity that the designer is willing to allow the user to be able to carry out in the software environment. The second question deals with the other end of the problem, that is, how simple should the simplest possible operations in the environment be? Perhaps the best way for me to answer these questions is to draw on the example of *The Geometric superSupposer*, a software environment designed by Michal Yerushalmy and me.

This is not the place to describe this software environment in detail. For our present purposes, it is sufficient to say that the *superSupposer* allows the user to make a series of geometric constructions on a shape such as a triangle, rhombus, a set of intersecting circles, and so on. The software tracks the user's construction as well as any measurements that are made and records them. The construction and measurements can then be repeated effortlessly as many times as desired on new shapes of the same sort. The pedagogic position of the *superSupposer* is consistent with the stance I outlined earlier. I believe that, in the long run, we must help our youngsters learn to pose, as well as solve, problems. In my view the best way to do this is to allow them to practice posing problems in an environment in which it is inviting to do so, and, having done so, to explore potential solutions. Thus, the *superSupposer* does not pose problems for the user.

Let us turn now to a more detailed look at some of the design issues the *superSupposer* raised for Michal and me. Two facilities characterize the *superSupposer*. The first of these is a construction facility, and the second is one to operate on and manage the constructions one has made.

The construction facility of the *superSupposer* contains such primitive operations as the ability to draw angle bisectors, perpendicular and parallel lines and circles that circumscribe and inscribe triangles, as well as the ability to label intersections, subdivide segments into N equal length segments, reflect both points and lines in lines, and place random points inside, outside, or on geometric shapes.

The facility to operate on and manage constructions includes the ability to measure angles, lengths, distances, and areas, as well as the ability to rescale the construction, to clear the construction, and most important of all, to repeat the construction on a new primitive shape, that is, a new triangle, quadrilateral, and so on.

The design of the construction facility was not intuitively obvious to us. Indeed, it took a fair amount of time for us to understand two important issues about it. These were the problem of making the primitive operations of the software environment too simple and the problem of making them too complex. In addition we had to come to realize that we were building a pedagogical tool for learning, teaching and making plane geometry, not a Computer-Aided Design (CAD) system.

Let me expand on these problems a bit. The mathematically trained person is likely to fall prey to a temptation to conceive of the primitive construction operations of a computer environment in geometry as the ability to make straight lines and arcs of circles. After all, is it not possible to derive all of Euclidean geometry from these simple and elegant beginnings? It is, of course, but at a price. The price is the tediousness of the task. If a user of the software must make an elaborate series of straight line and circular arc constructions in order to draw a median or an angle bisector, that user is unlikely to explore playfully the properties of geometric constructions that are rife with medians and angle bisectors.

The reader will no doubt object to this point, arguing that in a computer environment it should be possible to capture a series of commands and define them as a "macro," that is, to create and name a composite command that consists of the sequence of commands that have been captured. In fact, is this not what the *superSupposer* itself does? If it were possible to construct "macros," then the user would not have to undergo a painful repetition of intermediate constructions to arrive at a perpendicular bisector or a median.

This point is logically correct, but pedagogically somewhat less compelling. Building and naming a procedure as a way of extending a language is a subtle and delicate idea. Although it is a very important idea and one that is certainly worth learning, it seems not to be an easy idea for many people to grasp. One need only look at the many widely used spreadsheet and word processing programs in which powerful macro facilities are present and unused. We felt that it would be unwise to confound the problem of learning geometry with another set of important ideas about formulating and naming procedures. To be sure, the *superSupposer* contains the ability to name and store procedures. But the primitive objects in the *superSupposer* are not straight lines and arcs of circles. Instead, the *superSupposer* contains as primitive objects a rich collection of geometrically interesting structures such as orthogonal circles, obtuse isosceles triangles, quadrilaterals inscribable in circles, regular hexagons, and so on.

Having argued against making the primitive operations of the software environment too simple, let me now discuss the problem of making them too complex. It seems to me there are several good reasons to avoid too great a degree of complexity in the primitive operations available to the user in a software environment. The first of these reasons is that complexity of primitive operations conflicts directly with ease of use. The more "bells and whistles" that are present in a piece of software, the less obvious its operation is to the naive user and the longer it takes to learn to use the program to accomplish useful work. It is a source of some pride to Michal and me that the *superSupposer* seems to require no computer background or experience of the user. It does, of course, require some geometrical knowledge, but that, we believe, is as it should be.

A second reason for not making the primitive operations of the environment too complex is pedagogical: The software should provide an environment in which the user can formulate an extended line of argument. If the primitive operations provided the user by the software allow for complex ideas to be instantiated instantly with no hint of their internal structure and composition, it is likely that intellectual opportunities will be lost.

Yet another reason for not making the primitive operations of a software environment too complex is to avoid a trap that Michal and I fell into early on. We managed to extricate ourselves from the trap before we were embarrassed into doing so by a community of users, but there is little guarantee that the software designer will always be so fortunate. In an early version of one of the *Geometric Supposers,* the predecessor environments to the *Geometric superSupposer,* we included a primitive that allowed the user to subdivide an angle into N angles of equal measure. The subdivision of an angle into an arbitrary number of equal angles is not a construction that can be made using the primitive Euclidean construction tools, that is, straightedge and compass. We had lost sight of the primacy of the Euclidean geometry and were seduced by the capabilities of the software environment. If we had left such a primitive in place, we would have crippled the ability of the software to serve as an environment for the making and exploring of conjectures about Euclidean geometry.

Before leaving this discussion of the merits and demerits of simplicity and complexity, it is worth adding a comment about the distinction between tools for doing things and tools for learning how to do things. It is not difficult, for example, to imagine a Computer-Aided Design (CAD) system that would incorporate the features of the *Geometric superSupposer* among many other capabilities. Would such a system be a more appropriate tool for the geometry classroom? I believe not. CAD systems, no matter how elegant, enable users to manipulate spatial constructs in order to design specific objects. They address fundamentally synthetic ends. The implicit agenda of CAD systems is to provide a tool to do things with, and they are not fashioned with an eye for inducing users to reflect on their actions. The implicit agenda of the *superSupposer* and one that it seems to address well is to help users to learn *how* to do things. It tries to seduce users into addressing analytic and reflective ends: wondering, conjecturing, and finally proving things about the general categories to which the spatial objects manipulated in the program belong.

Jumping into an Interesting Middle

Our attempt to avoid the overly simple as well as the overly complex is an illustration of a broad pedagogic approach that I think of as "jumping into an interesting middle." What I mean by this is finding a way to engage learners by letting them interact with and manipulate aspects of a subject that are complex enough to be interesting and simultaneously simple enough to be understood. Thus, in the case of the *Geometric superSupposer* environment for Euclidean plane geometry, we chose, for example, to make the median of a triangle a primitive tool for the user. The median of a triangle is a moderately complex object in its own right. In terms of the logical development of the subject of plane geometry, it needs to be constructed from straight lines and arcs of circles, the constructions that form the logical foundation of the subject. If however, students using the software were obliged to construct each median they were interested in using in a painstaking fashion from arcs and straight lines, it is highly unlikely that they would have arrived at the rich collection of geometric theorems, both already known and totally new, that they have.

The pedagogic point here is larger than the geometric context from which it emerges. It seems to me that in order to engage a student in a subject, one must show the student quite early on something of the true nature of the subject and why it is that human beings are willing to expend effort in it. If one is introduced to a subject at a level of complexity that allows real problems to be wrestled with, then the point of studying the subject is clear. Furthermore, if it becomes clear to the student why the subject is worth studying, then it is likely that the student will be willing to expend the effort to understand its intellectual foundations. The level of complexity must be such that students can work their way back to the foundations without too much difficulty.

Satisfying the constraint of simultaneously not being too simple and not being too complex is a central challenge in the design of all curricular materials. The need to do this in the design of educational software should not come as a surprise.

Conclusions

Other much more detailed design questions are also worth discussing, but I have limited myself in this chapter to those that directly engage pedagogical questions. In so doing I have tried to focus on the problem of selecting a subject matter topic, recognizing one's pedagogic ideology, implementing it in the software medium, and finally steering a course between the problems that inhere in both simplicity and complexity of design.

It is likely that others who design educational software will take issue with the views expressed here. I can think of little else as salutary for our emerging field as for them to express their views publicly so the debate among us can proceed in a way that benefits from the views of students and teachers.

III

Connecting Educational Research
and Practice

Computers in the schools may be an idea whose time has come. But it is not the first time around for the notion that technological means might powerfully serve pedagogical ends. There was, for example, the audio-visual revolution—slides, filmstrips, and movies remaking the educational enterprise through the language of imagery. Then there was the television revolution, with its agenda of video bringing to learners the best of information in accessible visual form duplicated on a wide scale for the collective classroom of a nation.

But the question might well be, "What revolutions were those again?" Because these transformations in education somehow never made it much past the talking stage. To be sure, schools are widely equipped with projectors and VCRs. But, by and large, classroom business proceeds as usual, with only occasional recourse to the technological fairy godmothers that were to have waved their magic wands over the curriculum.

It is not hard, of course, to point up trenchant advantages of the new information-processing technologies in comparison with slide projectors and VCRs—perhaps most notably, the prospect of interactive learning systems that respond sensitively to the learners' actions and that give learners the freedom to explore conjectures and construct conceptions of complex subject-matter topics, as discussed in Part II.

Nonetheless, to ignore the lessons of the past is surely risky. After all, if in some respects the latest wave of technology is different, it shares features with past waves that may be crucial—costliness, unfamiliarity, a general scarcity of high-quality materials to use *with* the hardware, and so on.

183

Moreover, innovation in education, technologically based or not, has generally come hard. One of the recurrent reasons appears to be that innovators have persistently ignored the climate and culture of the classroom and the educational institution, the need of teachers to feel empowered and not beleaguered by innovations, the demands of the community for educational objectives and means that they can understand and subscribe to, and related factors.

Accordingly, Part III of this book turns to the challenges of converting pedagogical theory and technological potential into robust practice that recognizes and deals with the problems and potentials of the educational setting. Chapter 11, "A Cultural Perspective on School-University Collaboration," opens Part III. In this chapter Martha Stone Wiske examines the implications of the constructivist learning theory for the process of collaborative educational research. She defines the knowledge construction paradigm as one in which the context is collaborative; the responsibility for teaching and learning is shared among members of an intellectual community. This contrasts with the traditional "transmission" culture that treats knowledge as a fixed commodity to be passed along in a unidirectional way in a hierarchical setting.

Wiske presents the work of the Educational Technology Center as one model of a collaborative process that combines educational research, curriculum development, and support for the process of change in classroom practice. In discussing the work of the Center, Wiske also examines certain tensions that predominate in school/university collaborations and suggests ways of dealing with them.

The next three chapters analyze specific approaches to integrating new technologies into teaching for understanding in the classroom. In Chapter 12, "Managing the Tensions in Connecting Students' Inquiry with Learning Mathematics in School," Magdalene Lampert explores the problems that arise in teaching practice when student inquiry and authentic academic understanding are introduced into the typical school classroom. Lampert addresses the practical dilemmas in conducting inquiry in schools and suggests practices that support inquiry teaching. Focusing on research with a set of mathematical software called *The Geometric Supposers*, the author concentrates her discussion on three teaching tasks: (1) guiding social interaction in a class discussion, (2) interpreting learners' language and connecting it with the conventions of the discipline, and (3) navigating the subject-matter terrain in response to student inquiry.

In Chapter 13, Joseph Snir and Carol Smith shift the focus from mathematics to science and offer another perspective on the challenges of using new technologies to help students build conceptual bridges. In "Constructing Understanding in the Science Classroom: Integrating Laboratory Experiments, Student and Computer Models, and Class Discussion in Learning Scientific Concepts," Snir and Smith describe successful strategies for teaching with computer models like those discussed in Chapter 7.

Their methods serve to build bridges between student conceptions and computer models while helping students develop an understanding of the role of model building in science. They conclude that such teaching strategies can not only foster student understanding, but also inform observant curriculum developers and teachers about students' thinking.

In Chapter 14 Steven Schwartz and David Perkins address the problem of achieving widespread educational change, beyond the classrooms of pioneer teachers. In "Teaching the Metacurriculum," the authors propose an approach to deepening subject-matter learning in ways consonant with classroom realities—the "metacourse." In the conception of Schwartz and Perkins, a metacourse is a set of supplementary ideas and activities that augments the regular curriculum, providing metacognitive and metaconceptual support to students new to a particular subject matter. Not a separate course, but rather supplementary lessons and activities, a metacourse works with conventional content to add an emphasis on mental models, thinking strategies, and metacognitive reflection.

The authors describe their empirical work in developing and testing a metacourse for beginning students of BASIC, and in developing a similar course for algebra. The positive findings suggest that, for any subject matter, it is worth considering an appropriate "metacurriculum" of mental models, problem-solving strategies, and related matters, to augment the usual instruction.

Part III concludes with Chapter 15, "Integrating Computers into Classroom Teaching: Cross-National Perspectives," by Margaret Vickers and Jane Smalley. The authors review some of the difficulties many countries have faced, and the successes some have achieved, as they attempt to assist teachers in learning to use computers as a tool integrated with other educational practices across the curriculum. Their article outlines broad patterns of classroom computer use in Europe, the United States, and Australia. More detailed case studies of four countries' policies provide alternative models of integrating new technologies into schools. The authors analyze aspects of technology integration, such as the relationship between software development and the development of related course materials, the potential impact of technology-enhanced practices on classroom and school dynamics, and the stages and forms of support that teachers need as they encounter the changes in curriculum content and educational methods that new technologies may provoke. The authors argue that teachers must be included in making decisions about all these aspects of educational technology in order to promote effective use of computers in schools.

Altogether, the five chapters of Part III address a range of curricular areas and encompass the scope of educational technology innovation from research, to development, to change in classrooms, schools, and national school systems. The clear message emerging from these accounts is that new technologies call for complementary curriculum materials, extended

11

A Cultural Perspective on School-University Collaboration

MARTHA STONE WISKE

> The university stands—or should stand—behind enquiry in school
> as the curator of that uncertainty without which the transmission of
> knowledge becomes a virtuoso performance in gentling the masses.
> We do not live up to our principles, of course, but it is of the first
> importance that we do not rest from trying to do so, routinely
> from day to day. Whenever we assert and bully with our authority
> instead of reasoning on an equal base with those we teach and
> helping them to liberate themselves from our authority as the
> source of truth, we invite them to faith rather than knowledge.
>
> Lawrence Stenhouse, as quoted by Rudduck and Hopkins (1985).

The conviction that knowledge is constructed, not given, carries implications for the social context of education. If knowledge is viewed as fixed and objective, then teaching can be seen as a process of transmission, of telling truths. But if one believes that understanding requires the learner actively to make sense, then teaching must be a process of construction, of building with, not merely of instruction. The context for constructing knowledge is a collaborative, not autocratic, setting where responsibility for teaching and learning is shared among members of an intellectual community.

The notion that learning involves collaborative inquiry has implications for the social organization of every educational setting, including classrooms, schools, and universities, and of every educational process, including research, curriculum development, and efforts to support change in educational practice. In each case the knowledge construction paradigm implies that responsibility for teaching and learning is shared, that everybody contributes and nobody dictates.

This paper examines the implications of the knowledge construction paradigm for the process of collaborative educational research. The Educational Technology Center's efforts to involve school and university people in collaborative working groups provide cases in point. They offer one model of a collaborative process that combines educational research, curriculum development, and support for the process of change in classroom practice. They also reveal certain tensions endemic to school/university collaboration of this sort and suggest ways of dealing with these tensions.

Background

The Educational Technology Center's Mission and Approach

The Educational Technology Center was established by the U.S. Department of Education as one of its national research centers in the fall of 1983. Its mission was to "find ways of using computer and other information technologies to teach science, mathematics, and computing more effectively" (Educational Technology Center, 1984). In short, its aim was to conduct research to improve practice.

This goal must be distinguished from related endeavors such as curriculum development, teacher education, and client-centered school development. ETC's work ultimately included activities that might be recognized under these other rubrics, but they were undertaken in the service of the Center's research agenda. Some observers, frequently members of ETC's collaborating school districts, wished the Center provided such services directly to schools. Their preferences, combined perhaps with hopes raised by ETC's efforts to bend its research toward practical ends, sometimes led them to lose sight of the Center's prime objective and responsibility. Clarification and reiteration of ETC's research goals became an important component of the collaborative process.

The Center's architects realized that its mission required the combined expertise of a range of participants: subject matter specialists, cognitive psychologists, experienced teachers and curriculum developers, technology experts, and supporters of school-university collaboration. Accordingly, they formed ETC as a consortium, based at Harvard University's Graduate School of Education, including Children's Television Workshop, the Education Collaborative for Greater Boston (a school service agency supported by member school districts), Education Development Center (a nonprofit research research and development organization), Educational Testing Service, Interactive Training Systems, WGBH Educational Foundation (affiliated with the local public television station), and the public school systems of four Massachusetts communities: Cambridge, Newton, Ware, and Watertown.

Members from these various institutions were brought together at two levels. At an executive level, a key administrator from each consortium organization joined ETC's administrators to form an Agenda Group, whose purpose was to define, refine, and monitor the Center's overall research agenda. The Agenda Group included the superintendent of each participating school system and the director of the relevant unit within each of the other consortium organizations. This executive level structure provided a mechanism for relating ETC's agenda to the long-range interests of the member organizations and helped sustain their institutional commitment to the collaboration. A second level of connection involved representatives from the member institutions who took on responsibility for ETC's day-to-day work. This working level included teachers, university researchers, currriculum developers, and technology designers who defined and conducted ETC's research. Other school/university collaborative endeavors have found that such two-tiered structures of affiliation help to sustain both institutional commitment and ·close communication among those who do the daily work of collaboration (Gomez et al., 1990; Greenberg, 1991).

The working level of collaborators was initially organized as three large committees—one each in science, mathematics, and computing—to specify research projects in each domain. A fourth committee was charged to define research on the educational potential of emerging technologies, without such clear constraints on subject matter. Recognizing that ETC's agenda could not address all of the K-12 curriculum in these three areas, the Center's directors asked each committee to identify a limited number of "targets of difficulty." These were to be particular topics that met several criteria:

- They were widely recognized by teachers as perennially difficult topics to teach and to learn.
- They involved central concepts in the discipline that students must understand in order to lay a firm foundation for further study of the subject.
- They played a central part in the school curriculum.
- They appeared likely to be made easier with new technologies.
- At least some university people and some school people on the committee were interested in participating in research on the topic.

The Science, Mathematics, and Computing committees met in the fall of 1983, each including several university-based and school-based members, as well as people assigned to facilitate the collaborative process. The facilitators included two staff members from the Education Collaborative for Greater Boston (EdCo), a nonprofit school service agency serving some 20-member school systems in the area, and the author, who was then the ETC Assistant Director and its school liaison. The first task of these committees was to nominate targets of difficulty. Over a series of meetings, members debated candidate topics in relation to the criteria previously listed. In the science group, for example, after several lively meetings, the group decided to vote on their set of candidate targets of difficulty. Next to each topic a university person's vote was registered as O and a school person's vote as X. At the end of the process the three topics that had attracted a combination of Xs and Os were selected as the ones to study. The science committee decided to focus on heat and temperature, weight and density, and understanding science as a process.

Simultaneously, the other two committees identifed their targets. The mathematics group selected fractions and word problems as their topics. The computing committee decided to focus one group on programming and a second on the educational applications of general software tools such as word processors, electronic spreadsheets, and data base managers. Once the targets of difficulty were defined, the committees subdivided into collaborative research groups, each focused on a particular target. Each Working Group, as they were called, included from 1 to 4 teachers, one or more university-based researchers, and sometimes software or curriculum developers.

Working Groups were asked to develop a detailed research agenda. The actual writing of this document was undertaken by an academic member of each Group, who subsequently became known as the Project Leader. By the spring of 1984, once these research agendas were reviewed by the Agenda Group and approved by the Center directors, most Project Leaders hired research assistants to help carry out their Group's research. In most cases the research assistants were graduate students from Harvard or the home university of the Project Leader.

Usually Project Leaders devoted 15 to 25% of their time to the project, research assistants worked from 25 to 100% time, and teachers were expected to devote approximately 1½ days per month or 5 to 10% time to the project. [All participants were paid for their ETC work.] Teachers were encouraged to devote more time to the project if they wished, but few were able to do so. Given full-time jobs at school, along with other professional and personal obligations, few teachers could commit more than a few days per month to ETC work during the school year. The author attended most Working Group meetings, as did a staff member from EdCo, in order to promote effective communication between school-based and university-based members.

Methods

Much of the information and insight reported here was gathered through participating in and observing the collaborative research process at ETC over five years. The author attended most Working Group meetings especially during the first year, as well as many other formal and informal meetings devoted to overall management of ETC. Minutes of these meetings, prepared and circulated at the time, served as one source of information for this chapter. At intervals throughout the project meetings, interviews, and less formal conversations were conducted with participants in ETC collaborative research groups to discuss their experiences with this process. Some of these investigations were reported earlier by McDonald (1986).

Near the end of ETC's five-year contract with the U.S. Department of Education a series of meetings was convened with groups representing the range of participants in ETC Working Groups, to review their experience with collaborative research. Three meetings were led by an EdCo staff person whose leadership skills and neutral organizational affiliation enabled her to stimulate an honest and open sharing of sometimes painful views. One meeting included school people who represented different school systems, had participated in the entire range of Working Groups, and had joined ETC at various times during its four-and-a-half year history. The second group included research assistants whose tenure and participation in Working Groups were similarly varied. The third included Project Leaders. The agenda at each of these meetings was similar. People were asked to look back on their experiences, clarifying their initial expectations about the roles that participants would play in the collaborative research process, the ways in which collaboration was accomplished, and the conflicts that emerged. They were asked what insights they had developed about the ingredients of effective collaboration and the recommendations they would make for structuring future collaborative research projects. Several people with particular responsibility for facilitating collaboration at ETC attended all three meetings and met afterwards to review themes that emerged.

This chapter draws heavily on these discussions and is structured accordingly. The phases of work undertaken by ETC Working Groups are described and illustrated with vignettes that focus on episodes where conflicts arose. These tensions are analyzed as reflections of cultural differences between schools and universities. Finally, in light of this analysis and building on the recommendations made by ETC participants, suggestions are offered of ways to structure effective collaborative research.

Initials are used throughout to refer to individual people. This format is intended to provide some measure of anonymity and to downplay the importance of particular people. While individual characters may strongly shape collaborative ventures, this chapter's aim is to examine the influence of organizational cultures and structures on collaborative research efforts.

Process of Collaborative Research—A Chronicle

All ETC Working Groups faced basically the same assignment—identify a "target of difficulty" and then study ways of using new technologies to improve teaching and learning of this particular topic. Looking across their life histories, one discerns that they all undertook a roughly similar strategy. First they defined the target of difficulty and clarified its position within the structure of related subject matter—what one ETC researcher called "getting the intellectual story straight." Then they diagnosed its root causes (i.e., the reasons it is hard to teach and to learn), reviewed existing teaching strategies and materials, designed and developed interventions to improve the teaching and learning of the topic, tried these out in clinical research settings, and then proceeded to revise them for whole-class teaching experiments. At intervals along the way they analyzed the results of their work and published reports. Individual projects varied significantly in the depth of attention they paid to each step and in the pace of their progress through this sequence of activities. This progression is typical enough, however, to structure examination of the collaborative research process.

Define Targets of Difficulty

The first step was to define a target of difficulty that met the rather stringent and complex criteria mentioned earlier. In some Working Groups, the school people and the academics seemed rather easily to circumscribe a topic they all agreed was worth addressing. In others, this stage was more complicated.

The Heat and Temperature Group, for instance, settled promptly into agreement that students confuse these two concepts. The two ideas must be distinguished if students are to proceed to understand energy transfer. The university professor on the group invited a colleague whose research focused on the history of scientific thinking about this topic and the applicability of this history to understanding the development of students' thinking. The group was also joined by a developer who had designed Microcomputer Based Laboratory equipment. This technology helps students deliver calibrated "dollops" of heat to a substance, accurately measure the resultant changes in temperature, and display temperature graphically as a function of time. The early stages of defining and diagnosing a target of difficulty and develping a technology-enhanced teaching intervention proceeded fairly speedily in this group.

Other subjects did not gel so readily. For example, one of the topics identified by the mathematics committee was "Word Problems." The teachers on the committee, when asked about topics that were perennially difficult to teach and to learn, noted that word problems are notoriously challenging. Such problems describe a situation in verbal form and ask students to solve some mathematical problem presented by the situation. They typically appear at the end of a chapter or unit on particular mathematical operations and require students to use the concepts and algorithms presented on the preceding pages. Teachers reported that students often had no idea what operation to use in solving word problems. They tended to rely on ritualistic ploys rather than examining the structure of the quantitative relationships presented in the problem.

The university professor in this group perceived students' difficulties with word problems as a symptom of a more fundamental lack of understanding about the mathematics of particular kinds of quantities. Specifically, he identified intensive quantities as the bulls-eye in this target of difficulty. These quantities, sometimes called "per quantities," include ratios, rates, and proportions. Their central feature is that they specify the relationship between two numbers. The academic pointed out that intensive quantities are conceptually difficult, in part because their arithmetic is counterintuitive. Suppose you have two piles of coffee beans—one that weighs 2 pounds and costs $10 dollars, and a second that weighs 3 pounds and costs $12 dollars. If you combine the piles, you add the weights and the costs of the separate piles but you can't just add their costs PER pound.

The teachers defined the word problem problem in terms of the types of problems, taken from their texts, tests, and workbooks, that students frequently failed. The professor, called S, defined the problem in terms of an underlying mathematical concept, described with language that was unfamiliar to most of the teachers. Through his lens, S could see the problem in relation to his overall map of mathematics, recognizing this fundamental topic as part of a set of neighboring mathematical ideas.

S recalls the early conversations with teachers about the heart of the word problem problem as full of conflict. He and the teachers became "polarized" over the way they defined the important questions worth investigating. "I remember a range of emotions in myself that went all the way from rage to anger. . . . I thought I was respecting what teachers brought to the table, and I thought what I brought to the table was going to be respected. What I brought to the table was analysis going back on the order of ten years as to the guts of the problem, building widely on what others had done." Instead, he recalls that his analysis of intensive quantities "was largely construed as abstruse and theoretical and without purpose." Remarks made by at least one of the teachers made him "feel that this formulation was too remote from the concerns and questions of the teachers, and that despite my ideological commitment to collaborative work, I damn well better find somebody else to do this because I was not temperamentally suited."

A second professor, who later became the leader of this project, experienced a similar incongruence between the conceptual framework he used to define this target of difficulty and the one teachers seemed to use. He responded by proposing that the group read and critique some papers that had shaped his views. He suggested that members of the group take turns leading discussion of the readings during part of their regular meetings. He recalled that teachers "read the stuff and began to make sense of what I was pushing, which was to get at the . . . cognitive foundations of what appeared to be behavioral syndromes that the teachers had a tendency to want to attack directly." He felt the group functioned for a while like a graduate seminar where participants developed a shared vocabulary and conceptual framework that enabled them to converse meaningfully as they continued their collaborative research.

Diagnose the Roots of the Target of Difficulty

Having defined a topic on which to focus, the Working Groups proceeded to clarify the reasons behind its difficulty. This might include reviews of related literature, further analysis of the subject matter to get the intellectual story line straight, review of common curricular materials to learn how the topic was typically presented in schools, and diagnosis of the ways students tended to understand and think about the topic. Researchers associated with ETC tended to believe that learning of hard concepts requires students not simply to take in new information, but to construct a new understanding by actively changing their minds. From this perspective, knowing what students already have in mind is a necessary step in designing materials and activities to help them challenge and change their ideas.

Conflicts around the merits, methods, and appropriate duration of this diagnosis of student thinking arose in several groups, but were particularly apparent in a project aptly titled Complex Systems. This group had formed at the request of one science teacher who feared that the "target of difficulty" strategy was too conservative. He wished ETC would include at least one topic thought to be too challenging for school children, which might now be made accessible by new technologies. He nominated the analysis of multivariate systems as a candidate topic. Although none of the academics originally involved in the ETC Science Committee was inclined to lead a research group on this topic, a developmental psychologist deeply devoted to the "constructivist" theory of learning was persuaded to become the group's leader.

Like Word Problems, Complex Systems constituted a large ill-defined set of difficult ideas. Clarifying the root of the problem was a complex undertaking in itself. In keeping with her research interests and accustomed methodology, the university professor, called D, proposed to conduct clinical interviews with some students to clarify their ways of thinking about systems. She wanted to engage students in active exploration of an interesting system, simple enough to be analyzable yet complex enough to puzzle children. She and her research assistant devised a system of helium balloons trailing strings long enough to cause the balloons to hover in mid-air neither rising nor falling. They proposed to use this system to clarify how students think about dynamic equilibrium, a key concept in many complex systems and an important idea in science. Tension mounted in the group as teachers who were used to knowing and telling answers confronted a researcher whose life work had been to resist this urge, in order to reveal the confusions underlying apparent knowledge and to support people's capacity to develop ideas.

D's research assistant C recalled that the conflict between teachers and researchers came to a head as she and one of the teachers on the group jointly conducted a series of clinical interviews with students from this teacher's school. According to C, the teacher, J, "didn't agree with our premise—she didn't like kids not to know the answer. She didn't want them to feel frustrated." The first time the teacher raised this concern, C dismissed it because she thought the teacher simply did not understand or value this kind of research. The second time, C realized that the teacher was "saying something about the credibility of this research for practitioners. Teachers would ignore the results of this research because it was conducted under circumstances very far from their current practice." As they argued between interviews during lunch one day, C felt each finally managed to express her views in terms the other could understand. "That was real collaboration. We each had to butt our heads."

As a result of this exchange, C reconsidered her response to a situation that came up in the afternoon's clinical interview. A student who was frustrated by her own confusion about the balloons blurted out in exasperation, "What is the answer? Would you *please* just tell me?" Sensitized by J's remarks at lunch, C responded, "I need to understand your question. Then maybe I could use my words to explain to you how *I* understand the answer. OR then we could work together until you figure out how *you* understand the answer. Which would you rather do?" The student thought a moment and then said, while J continued to watch, "I want to understand the answer." C reported that J later told her she was amazed by the student's response and wondered how C had backed her into answering in this way. C regarded this incident as a seminal collaborative experience where she finally understood how J viewed her responsibility and together they found a way of proceeding that was ethically and educationally acceptable to them both.

Despite this happy story, both this Group and others dealt with struggles between researchers eager to understand how children's minds work and teachers who felt pressed to educate those minds.

Design Interventions and Pilot Test Them Clinically

Based on their analysis of the subject matter, the existing curriculum, and students' thinking, the groups designed experimental lessons, involving computers as well as more traditional technologies. Basic differences in priorities and assumptions were revealed when either researchers or teachers designed lessons without regularly consulting the other group. An example from the Scientific Theory and Methods Project (STAMP) illustrates this common problem.

STAMP focused on teaching students about the process of conducting scientific inquiry. Two teachers in the group had a running argument with the Project Leader about the feasibility of teaching middle school students simultaneously about particular content and the process of reasoning scientifically. The teachers claimed that most students this age were not cognitively capable of attending to both matters at once. They cited Piaget's research in arguing that the students were not yet developmentally at the formal reasoning stage. Meanwhile, the Project Leader M claimed that students could understand the purpose and process of scientific reasoning *only* within the context of experimenting and revising their theories about some specific phenomenon. She argued that even young children build theories and, as they gather more information, they refine their concepts and revise their theories. Challenging common interpretations of Piaget's work, she believed children's development over time is more a reflection of their increased knowledge than of some fundamental shifts in the kind of reasoning they are capable of conducting.

This continuing disagreement resurfaced as the group began to design experimental lessons. The teachers offered to prepare some lessons, building on the ones used in their school system to teach about scientific methods. They knew these lessons held students' attention, and believed they served to help students understand the structure and steps of a scientific experiment. Each of the several lessons they prepared dealt with a different phenomenon: for example, rates of absorption by paper towels of water containing different concentrations of soap, heights of different balls when bounced, and factors affecting pendulum swings.

When the Project Leader M reviewed the lessons, she found they violated her basic principle, to wit, students cannot truly appreciate the process of scientific reasoning unless they see its value in helping them develop and revise a theory about *something*. She firmly believed that the lessons must deal at length with one phenomenon, rather than deal more superficially with several different subjects. She therefore decided not to use the lessons developed by the teachers, but to insist that the group develop a series of lessons around a particular topic.

One of these teachers recalled this episode with distress. "We spent several summer evenings writing up these lessons, trying to use the same terminology of 'hypothesis' and all [that the other experimental units employed], and then it was never tried out. We just were not heard."

M's memories also conjure up frustration. "I came close to exploding when people would lecture me about what Piaget had shown that seventh graders can and cannot do." Reflecting on the group's history, she perceived that the group had unclear goals from the outset, leaving room for different members to hold conflicting expectations.

> If we had been totally clear about what we wanted to start with, we might have been able to engage in a more collaborative way from the beginning. But as it became clear what our [the university-based researchers'] goals were, it was hard to communicate with them [the school teachers]. In the end, the way we communicated with them was to develop our own materials. When we developed our own materials, their reaction was 'that's not possible, that won't work, that's too ambitious, you can't do two things at once.'

Another ETC researcher saw the conflict in this group as a reflection of the different nature and quality of the kinds of knowledge brought by different participants to the collaborative research endeavor. "The character of knowledge that the successful practitioner-collaborator brings is empirical knowledge and the character of knowledge that the successful academic collaborator brings is analytic knowledge. In the case of [the teachers who denounced M's approach], [their] empirical knowledge was not empirical, and [their] analytic knowledge was faulty," he declared.

Design and Conduct Teaching Experiments in Classrooms

This conflict in the STAMP group eventually eased as the group proceeded to try out their teaching unit with students. Some teachers in the group agreed to pilot test the materials developed by the researchers. After one cycle of pilot testing, the materials were revised and then taught by a teacher W who had not been part of the original Working Group. Without the legacy of conflict, and perhaps because she was introduced to the ideas when they were already instantiated in a classroom-ready approach, W found the underlying conceptual framework acceptable.

M and other university-based members of the group found actually trying out theoretically grounded lessons was a very valuable stage of collaborative research. They discovered that W was extremely knowledgeable and helpful in revising and extending the experimental lessons to make them more feasible for classroom use.

W said she also found this work satisfying, though not free of conflict. She participated in pilot testing some lessons with small groups of students after school and recommended several significant alterations to make the lessons more practical with whole classes of seventh graders. Her recommendations were based on two concerns. First, the "flow of ideas" was not sufficiently clear and, second, the lessons involved too much telling by the teacher.

> It was the mind-set of telling students what to do, rather than trying to take what the students come up with and working from there. You have to be open to take all kinds of ideas, and yet bring it together, and lead them where you want them to be. . . . You don't just tell the student to do this . . . you have a dicussion so that they understand what they're doing.

When she was asked a few months later to teach the revised experimental unit to her class, she found that "some of the things we had said absolutely would not work had been put back into the lessons." W felt the researchers ignored what she said until the research assistant co-taught these lessons with her. The research assistants agreed that co-teaching with the teacher, trading the roles of teacher and observer, helped them hear the teacher's voice in a new way. One research assistant said:

Teaching the unit myself put me in a whole different position to criticize the unit. . . . You find yourself thinking, of course this can be done. When the teachers say it's not possible you think, well, they just don't understand. . . . But the fact is you don't know until you do it . . . with the first five minutes getting the kids to sit down and the last five getting them settled before the bell rang. It was an incredibly great experience. . . . Having to think what you want to do and do it at the same time is not easy.

As another research assistant put it,

I learned a lot about how to actually implement a technique we were discussing. We often planned too much for too little time, or it's something you could do once, but you couldn't do it five times in a day. . . . It's a whole elaborate procedure, trying to make connections in kids' heads. You have an idea on paper, but when you try to chunk it up into classes, the connections get lost. . . . Watching one kid [in a clinical study], you forget how much of the problem comes from the constant distractions in a class.

Another research assistant was thoughtful about the reasons that teachers and researchers have difficulty taking each other's wisdom into account.

I think there were times when senior researchers forgot what had been learned about some lesson. They forgot that teachers had tried out something . . . not everything got written up from the pilot work. Teachers were extremely offended and rightly so. They thought, "I did that a year ago and now you're going to do it again. You try it and it doesn't work. I told you that a year ago." In part it's that different people are involved and may not always have heard things. It's very hard to hear things that you don't agree with.

Analyze Research Results

Some university-based participants described tensions that arose when teachers who participated in teaching experiments collaborated in interpreting the results. Research assistants noted that teachers had valuable insights to share about their students' responses in the clinical studies, based on intimate knowledge of what a student had been previously taught and how the student typically approached such tasks. "But the trade-off was that during the discussion of the student, the teacher sometimes gave the impression that she felt she was being evaluated. . . . One example doesn't discourage a confident, veteran teacher, but you don't want want to see a lot of these things creep into the discussion. It was sometimes awkward, but it was a trade-off because if you work with other teachers' students you lose [their insight]."

The mirror image problem arose when researchers *did* think that the teacher was part of the problem. One research assistant recalled working with someone whom she thought was an excellent teacher, but "She had low expectations for her students and thought half of them shouldn't be in this class. That's something we might have wanted to discuss [in analyzing the results of the teaching experiment], but we wouldn't do that with her."

Teachers who participated in analysis of results sometimes questioned researchers' methods, especially regarding the validity of clinical studies. Teachers were often amazed that researchers were prepared to draw conclusions about students in general based on observations of only a few students or classes. One project began by closely observing a few students work on problems in order to understand how they reasoned. A teacher in this group said, "I didn't think that was a sufficient sample . . . I would want to chose a group of kids with a lot of differences among them in their learning styles, with different learning abilities and backgrounds in mathematics."

She also thought the clinical methodology was vulnerable to bias. In reviewing the protocol of a clinical interview conducted by one of the researchers in her group, she noted that the student had offered several responses to a question. She thought researchers had interpreted the student's response as indicating more understanding than she herself believed the student actually demonstrated.

> I know kids who know how to read your face, and when they say something, and they see a twitch, they'll change their answer. They know how to read every line on a teacher's face. I think that if you're not a teacher of kids, or if you're not aware of that, and you want to [hear] something [in the kid's answer], then you can.

The most effective way of coping with these uncomfortable differences in the interpretations of research results appeared to be the open discussions made possible by the kind of trading roles described earlier. As one research assistant put it:

> You can say that we're evaluating the curriculum, not the teacher, but one thing that really helps make that point is when you have a research assistant teaching for the teacher to observe. The teacher gets a really good view of what's happening in her class from a different perspective and she can offer a lot of insights that the regular observer couldn't because they don't know the kids. Also, when you have a teacher and an RA teaching the same curriculum, they can exchange information and learn from each other how to teach it. Then the teacher is not alone in receiving criticism. And then it becomes a communal effort in how are we going to make this curriculum work.

Endorsing this approach, another research assistant said, "When you teach and then the teacher teaches . . . you are *equal* sharers. Each of us was open, we traded ideas, then the teacher was able to step back and think about the theory." Tensions were more likely to remain undiscussed and unresolved if participants had not made this kind of effort to view the work from the others' point of view.

Report Research Results

Further differences in perspectives of teachers and university people were apparent in their reactions to reports of research results. For a variety of reasons, including the much greater time commitment of university-based participants, academics rather than teachers wrote most research reports. To respect the collaborative spirit of the work, Project Leaders were urged to circulate drafts of reports among members of their group and take their comments into account in preparing final drafts.

Project Leaders reported that they rarely received any feedback from teachers in return for the significant nuisance of distributing copies of the draft report as submission deadlines loomed. Teachers noted that they had several reactions when faced with these technical reports. First, they were often written in obscure jargon that was sometimes as difficult to interpret as a foreign language. One consequence was that teachers required hours to wade through the reports. By the time they were able to devote this much time to the endeavor, the submission deadline had often passed. Second, the reports often treated topics at length that had little meaning for teachers, while ignoring the teachers' experience and the implications of the reseach for teacher's work. One teacher was particularly disappointed to read pages of "verbiage" which in his view simply attempted to explain away the fact that the experiment had failed. As a teacher, he knew when a lesson did not work, and regularly had to revise and try again. His perception was that researchers are not willing simply to admit failure and move along.

Another source of tension around research reports concerned the different purposes that people expected a document to serve. One clear example emerged from the work of the ETC Laboratory Sites Project. This project was initiated in the fourth year of the Center's life to study how ETC-developed innovations might be carried out in a range of regular school classrooms. Teachers from five different secondary schools were recruited, trained, supported, and studied to learn about the processes and requirements of incorporating these innovations into regular classroom practice.

An illuminating conflict arose around teachers' reactions to an interim report on the process of teaching the unit developed by ETC's Heat and Temperature group. This research group's lessons involved fairly complicated apparatus including computers with peripheral devices, as well as more traditional "wet lab" equipment such as beakers, graduated cylinders, hot plates, water, and ice. Lab site teachers working with this innovation found they must design additional lessons to weave the experimental unit into their regular courses. These teachers also provided vivid, detailed accounts of the many kinds of prerequisite skill and knowledge that students needed to benefit from the research group's lessons. Students had to be able to keep track of materials and ideas from one class to the next during the unit; they had to be able to set up and operate complex fragile apparatus and know how to cope when it broke as it often did; they had to be able to divide up tasks among the members of the small groups who worked together at each lab station; they had to understand the overall structure of the experiment well enough to know when and how to make and record critical observations. These significant requirements had not been revealed during the previous field tests, involving only a few students or handpicked, carefully supported classroom settings.

The problem arose in reporting on these valuable insights. After reading the draft report, science teachers in the laboratory sites were quick to acknowledge the accuracy of the classroom picture: equipment malfunctioning, students not realizing when to watch the computer monitor for critical real-time data, one student in a trio missing half the experiment by going to the bathroom while his partners continued. But some did not want these images included in the case study. "I'd hate for my superintendent to read this," said one teacher. "I'm sure he'd blame us teachers for not having better control of the class." What the Project Leader regarded as a powerful revelation of the gaps between clinical research and classroom life, the teacher regarded as an indictment of her colleagues' professional competence.

Themes and Cultural Differences

Several themes emerge from this set of vignettes about collaborative research that reveal differences in the culture of schools and universities. Other researchers have noted differences in school and university cultures that may foil their attempts to collaborate. Greenberg (1991) notes that differences in funding and resources, in student bodies, in teachers and teaching conditions, in faculty roles in decision-making, and in the institutional methods of valuing performance constitute a cultural discontinuity between schools and universities. Collaborative research of the sort conducted by ETC makes certain aspects of this cultural discontinuity especially salient.

Map of the Subject-Matter Domain

Academics tend to focus on key concepts in a discipline. They chart them as part of a web of related ideas forming the conceptual foundation for theory building within a domain. They perceive multiple ways of approaching such concepts from various related ideas that form part of the theoretical web.

Teachers' views of the subject matter—especially when they think about teaching it to students—tend to be informed primarily by the structure of their textbooks, workbooks, curriculum guides, and standardized tests. One feature of textbooks is that they typically focus on a much smaller grain size of information than the "big ideas" in terms of which academics map the intellectual terrain. Intensive quantity, for example, is nowhere mentioned in the typical mathematics textbook, although the concept appears in multiple guises under the headings of multiplication, division, rates, proportions, ratios. These topics in the textbook are further subdivided into short and long division, multiplying with single digits versus two or three digits, and so on. As these topics appear in quite different places in the text, and across different grade levels, their common underlying conceptual basis that the university-based academic perceives may not be at all apparent to the teacher.

A similar sort of distinction about the grain size of ideas became clear as teachers and researchers discussed the process of mathematical or scientific reasoning. Teachers, often influenced by the types of questions found on standardized tests, were accustomed to teaching students definitions of terms like dependent variable, independent variable, hypothesis, and conclusion as distinct elements in a generic process of scienctific reasoning. The researcher worried that learning the separate elements in this way amounted to a meaningless ritual unless their relationships and value became apparent in developing, testing, and revising a theory about some particular phenomenon.

Besides chunking knowledge into smaller and more discrete bits than university-based scholars often prefer, textbooks also present subject matter as a linear sequence of topics. Teachers often teach topics in the same order as they appear in their textbooks, and may believe that this order reflects the best sequence for building students' understanding. If they commonly map the subject in this linear way, they may not recognize the multiple relationships that connect ideas in the academic's web and the multiple paths that can be used to relate students' notions to the teachers' curricular agenda (Lampert, 1988).

When academics and teachers can describe their maps to each other and explain how they use them to guide their work, as the Word Problems Group ultimately did, they are less likely to misunderstand and devalue the other's framework. Discordant maps and vocabulary, leading people to use the same word to mean different things, may undermine the apparent consensus researchers and teachers achieve in defining a research focus causing it to deteriorate as they proceed to work through the project (Wagner, 1986). In order to conduct collaborative research that makes sense in both worlds, school and university people must define a shared vocabulary and recognize some correspondence between elements and relationships of their different maps of the subject matter. This process of negotiating a shared language and gaining fluency in using it to discuss educational practice can require a great deal of time and trust among collaborators.

Nature of Research

The Educational Technology Center's mission, to conduct research on ways of improving education, encompassed a range of goals spanning the middle of a continuum. At one end of this continuum lies basic research, whose purpose is the production of knowledge without concern for its practical application. At the other end lies educational practice not based on any explicit theoretical foundation. In between lie a range of other activities. These might include research into children's cognitive development as a foundation for designing an educational intervention or theory-based design and experimental use of lessons in regular school classes. Understandably, ETC researchers and teachers tended to have different priorities. Lawrence Stenhouse helps clarify their priorities by distinguishing between "research acts" undertaken to "find something out" and "substantive acts" which are "justified by some change in the world" (Rudduck and Hopkins, pp. 56–57). Some ETC researchers were content to build cognitive theories without pressing on to develop educational interventions. Some teachers became impatient with years of preparatory research that produced neither materials nor strategies that could be used in normal classrooms.

Features of the research/practice tension, the "paradigmatic pinch" that McDonald (1986) and others (Barzun and Graff, 1977; Eisner, 1985a; Popkewitz, 1980; Sirotnik, 1988) interpret as reflecting different underlying epistemologies, can be discerned in the story about the helium balloons. The choice of helium balloons, selected by the researchers because they were engaging and illustrated dynamic equilibrium, was denounced by some teachers because the balloons would be so impractical in the classroom. The teacher regarded the clinical interview as an educational experience for the student. She wanted the child to be treated as the teacher would have treated her in class, not allowed to feel stupid or discouraged by a prolonged period of ignorance unlike anything the teacher would willingly sustain in class. While the researcher studied how students learn, the teacher was worried about how teachers teach. Some teachers recognized that research activities might not lead directly to classroom-ready approaches, but most were reluctant to postpone asking, "How will this work in a school classroom?"

Disparate assumptions about the purpose of research help explain the science teacher's discomfort with the case study revealing classroom implementation difficulties. She interpreted the case primarily in personal terms of its effect on her colleagues within her particular school setting. Eisner (1985b) notes that practitioner accounts tend to treat "individual agency" as a central ingredient, a tendency that tugs against the "impersonal" conventions of researchers reaching for generalizable findings. To the extent that the teacher considered the report's more general implications, she assessed its probable effects on people working in schools. The researcher interpreted the same case primarily in terms of its capacity to illuminate important features of classroom life for researchers. Each had a different audience in mind, and their assumptions about the value of research reflected their expectations about how those audiences would interpret and act on the research results (Erickson, 1986).

Teachers' focus on local interpretation and practical application in schools helps explain, too, some of their discomfort with clinical research results. Their responsibility is to educate groups of 20 to 30 students usually in the context of 45-minute periods packed tightly into a 6 to 8 hour teaching day. Living in this environment, they are rightly wary of findings derived from closely watching one or a few students in quiet little corners away from the many distractions of classroom life. Teachers are challenged to respond to many different kinds of students with a range of intellectual styles, levels of knowledge, and ways of relating socially and emotionally. Teaching a few students under ideal circumstances does not necessarily reveal anything that will work with most students in classroom situations. Competency indicated by a posttest at the end of a teaching experiment or even a month or two later does not necessarily constitute mastery of the sort a teacher seeks. The proof of the research pudding for teachers is quite remote from the results that many researchers find sufficiently satisfying.

Nature of Knowledge, Teaching, and Learning

Most academics, especially those based in major research universities, conceive of knowledge less as a product than as a process of ongoing study and communication. Most see themselves as knowledge makers who continue their own study and stay abreast of developments in their field. Their responsibility to their students includes an obligation to help their students learn how to be knowledge makers, cultivating in them the taste and capacity to invent, critique, and synthesize powerful ideas. Ultimately, the distinction between teachers and learners blurs in higher education. At least most academics espouse these views, even if their classroom lectures do not appear to enact them.

Many school teachers share these ideas about knowledge to some extent, but most work in settings that emphasize teachers' obligations to transmit knowledge to their students rather than to construct and critique knowledge with their students (Cohen, 1988; Cohen, Mclaughlin, and Talbert, 1993). School teachers feel obligated to "cover curriculum requirements." They are responsible to students for preparing them for the standardized tests they must take before they can pass on to the next grade. This requirement is especially potent in secondary school where the tests can open or block entry into college. Principals, department chairpeople, and parents may pressure teachers to assign materials from particular texts and exercise books to establish the legitimacy of what is to be taught (Powell et al., 1985). Under these circumstances, knowledge takes on a more determined, fixed, and sacred character. Gaps widen between those who make knowledge, those who transmit knowledge, and those who absorb knowledge. University scholars may belong to the first group, school teachers to the second, and school students to the third.

Interestingly, school teachers—so often portrayed by researchers as locked into a "transmission" rather than a "constructivist" pedagogy—

may be more alert to the dangers of teacher talk than academics. More than one teacher involved in ETC research projects complained that the lessons prepared by academics called for teachers to present too much information didactically.

So long as different assumptions about the nature of knowledge, of teaching, and of learning remain tacit, researchers and school teachers can easily misunderstand each other. They may assume a shared perspective, each using the same words to mean different things, and becoming increasingly annoyed as they talk past each other. Without clarifying their assumptions about educational agendas and pedagogical philosophies, the stage is set for confusion and frustration. Without understanding the structures and incentives of schools and universities, neither group is likely to understand or value the others' frame of mind.

Time

Differences in perceptions of time in schools versus universities appeared throughout this project. Scheduling meetings of the collaborative groups created tensions. University people scheduled the first meetings during the school day, knowing that ETC had promised to provide substitute teacher coverage and thinking teachers would dislike after-school meetings. But teachers objected, saying that preparing for and cleaning up after an ineffectual substitute meant a one-day meeting took three days of their time. They preferred to meet after school.

Teachers noted that researchers had much more time available to invest in the project. First, researchers were paid to devote 15 to 25% of a full-time equivalent to the project while teachers were expected to fit 1 to 2 days of time per month around their full-time commitments at school. Second, teachers perceived that reseachers had much more control over their time at the university than teachers whose entire school day was tightly packed into a completely structured time grid. Teachers rarely have time to get a drink of water during the school day, let alone time to read or think.

The month-to-month calendars for schools and universities are also mismatched enough to create significant inconvenience in planning joint activities. The beginning and ending of terms, vacations, and examination periods make for incongruence in convenient times for teaching experiments.

Finally, researchers had a different perspective on the pace at which a project was expected to proceed. As Barzun and Graff (1977, p. 5) note, "School people are very firmly rooted in the present. Their focus is, of necessity, on currently available answers to immediate problems." Teachers connect with their students for usually no more than one year. If they do not succeed in educating the student during that time period, their opportunity is lost. While professors may face a similar constraint in their classes, they normally expect their research to require a period of years to bear fruit. Thus "projects which appear to be proceeding in a timely fashion for one group may well be experienced by the other as entirely out of synchronization and consequently counter-productive" (Gifford & Gabelko, 1987, p. 383).

Ownership and Responsibility

Like the research assistants quoted earlier, teachers who participated in ETC research projects found the work most satisfying when researchers became part of their world at school. "I found that [the work] became much more interesting when we could focus on some concrete experiences and discuss our perceptions of them rather than just talk about theoretical stuff." Teachers thought that researchers would understand better what teachers were saying at meetings if the researchers had spent time in the classroom. "I think a day in the classroom would do it," suggested one teacher. "They're so much smarter in their field, and we're so much smarter in our field. We know kids and we know classrooms and we know a lot of the reality they don't know. They know theory that I could live twice and not understand. Somewhere along the way we have to bring that out and respect each other for the strengths that we both bring."

In response to this suggestion, another teacher replied, "I don't perceive it as one group being smarter than the other—I think it's who's controlling the game, who is going to have the last say, and who is going to be listened to. You know that if [school people] were running this game, the reports would have looked different, the meetings would have looked different, the activities and time lines would have looked different. The people who have charge of the money hold the cards that dictate the game."

In the collaborative research project examined here, the prime contractor was indeed the university, the various projects were led by university scholars, and the project sponsor expected the resulting work to meet the standards set by university-based researchers. Under these circumstances, the university-based participants were "more equal" than the school-based members. While most ETC participants recognized that the academics made a good faith effort to collaborate, school people found that the university people's world view tended to predominate in the design, conduct, and interpretation of the research. McDonald (1986, p. 131) pointed out that because ETC's work was very much the work of the university—knowledge expansion—it included "the inevitable tension involved in maintaining a full partnership on one partner's terms."

In essence, teachers wanted assurance that even if researchers did not espouse all the same goals as teachers, at least they would hear teachers' voices and respect their concerns. If the teachers were to help researchers address their agendas, they wanted to know that the researchers would reciprocate by sustaining their connection with the project until it produced results that address the teachers' agenda.

Researchers voiced parallel concerns. They explained that the teachers on their group sometimes acted like a Board of Directors, with the power to veto any ideas but no responsibility for moving the work along. Many researchers came to value the contributions that teachers could make, but resented objections unaccompanied by constructive assistance.

Recommendations

Sustained Commitment

On reflection, nearly all participants in ETC research realized that teachers' contributions were often severely limited by the small amount of time they were able to devote to the work. If teachers are to be full partners in collaborative research projects, they must be involved for as much time as other actors. This might involve an ongoing arrangement of 25% or more time, accomplished by buying a secondary school teacher out of one or more courses. The structure of elementary schools makes this arrangement difficult. Alternatively, a leave of absence and summer work might be arranged to free a teacher full-time during a critical period of the research. A less intense involvement could sustain commitment between these periods of full-time engagement.

Continuous involvement of both school-based and university-based participants throughout the various phases of this kind of research is another boon to effective collaboration. Over time members can define a shared vocabularly, clarify disagreements, trade favors, learn to fight productively, and develop loyalty to their shared work. All these steps are necessary for members to learn how to make their expertise useful to an endeavor that only partially coincides with their individually held goals.

Reciprocal Exchanges

ETC's experience confirms other reports (Blumenfeld et al., 1994; Clark, 1988; Gifford and Gabelko, 1987; Gomez et al., 1990; Greenberg, 1991) of successful collaboration that emphasize the importance of engaging participants in mutually beneficial exchanges. People are both altruistic and selfish. Their commitment to a relationship grows if they both contribute and receive something of value in the course of their participation. The focus must be on useful activities and products, not the machinery of collaboration (Maeroff, 1983).

Mutual respect and understanding grew among members of ETC Working Groups as all participants contributed to getting the work done. Once the work of ETC projects progressed to the point of developing materials and strategies for classroom use, the teachers' knowledge and expertise became especially obvious and valuable. At that point the researchers clearly gained from a relationship that some of them might have previously regarded as more trouble than it was worth to their personal agendas.

Collaborative research could be structured to ensure reciprocal exchanges throughout the process. For instance, teachers' expertise could be tapped from the beginning stages of defining targets of difficulty and diagnosing their roots. Teachers are in a good position to map the ways schools normally teach about the selected "target of difficulty" by analyzing commonly used textbooks, local and state curriculum requirements, and standardized tests. Teachers might also review alternative instructional approaches by examining the guidelines issued by professional organizations and collecting materials from other research and development efforts that had enjoyed widespread use in schools.

As the comments of several ETC research assistants make clear, teachers can also play a valuable part in conducting research with students. Here, their familiarity with the way students respond in school settings as well as the knowledge they may have of particular subjects' characteristics can make teachers valuable partners in interpreting findings.

The teachers' assistance in designing experimental lessons and research materials was frequently the most apparent and valuable contribution to many researchers. Yet the anecdotes from ETC's experience indicate that university-based researchers may actively discount or passively ignore the teacher's voice unless they are primed to hear it.

Mutual Education

Satisfactory reciprocal exchange clearly requires that each party develop an appreciation of the other's contribution. Reporting on their own experience with collaborative research, Gifford and Gabelko (1987, p. 382) attest to the primary "power of overcoming the we/they thinking that usually separates university researchers and school-site practitioners" based on "trust built evenly over time . . . that has to lap over into implementation of findings." In relationships between university researchers and school teachers, a history of mutual disrespect must be overcome. This process entails explicit education by both university and school people regarding their own cultures, to wit, the values, assumptions, and structures of their organization settings that constrain and reward their activities. Wagner (1988) calls this process "interpretive consultation" through which university researchers teach school practitioners about research findings while the latter teach researchers about the nature and problems of practice. He believes that links between research and practice can be substantially improved through such discourse, especially when it is augmented by teacher-to-teacher exchanges.

The merits of explicit education of this sort were indicated by several examples from ETC Working Groups. When the Project Leader of the Word Problems group shared readings that informed his conceptual framework, other members of the group were able to join him in further refining and applying this framework to their shared work. When a researcher and teacher sat together long enough to explain to each other their expectations about an appropriate way to conduct a clinical interview, they were able to invent a way of proceeding that made sense to both of them. When researchers traded roles of teacher and observer with collaborating teachers, their eyes were opened to insights previously invisible to them.

Several features of most school-university collaborations make this mutual education endeavor rather lop-sided. First, there is a basic status differential between faculty members from prestigious universities and teachers from school systems that gives preferential weight to the former's views (Gross, 1988; Trubowitz, 1984). Second, university professors are rewarded in their own institution for articulating their views orally and in writing. In contrast, school teachers are rewarded for teaching students, not for learning to articulate their wisdom either orally or in print. Consequently academics are more likely to be personally skillful at arguing their position, and they are much more likely than teachers to find support for their views in the literature. Finally, the structure of many research efforts places the work more nearly in the university camp than the school's. ETC's mission, financial structure, and physical location made this true. Under such circumstances, the university-based members of the collaborative project must make themselves particularly receptive to being educated.

Learning to hear the teacher's voice is a crucial aspect of the researcher's responsibility in collaborative research. Teachers and those research assistants who ventured into the classroom world believed that a good way to cultivate this receptivity was for researchers to spend some time in the school world. In this way, teachers and researchers blended the roles of "participant observer" and "observant participant" (Florio and Walsh, 1978). As Wagner (1988) points out, firsthand experience in the classroom sensitizes the academic to features of this setting that are difficult to grasp from secondhand accounts. McDonald (1986) emphasizes the paradigmatic obstacles impeding researchers' efforts to hear teachers' voices; "that is certain habits of thinking, believing, and working can handicap the effort to attend" (p. 46). He recommends that school-university collaborative projects make use of interpreters specifically assigned to tune into the teacher's voice as "message rather than noise" (p. 32). These interpreters must be sensitive to both teachers' and researchers' views and skilled at helping them make sense of each others' ideas.

Reward Collaboration

The recommendations so far have addressed the conditions that might promote effective communication between school-based and university-based participants in collaborative educational research. Yet individual actors cannot be expected to sustain such demanding efforts unless their home institutions reward them. Most teachers and professors work under circumstances that discourage them from collaborating. Teachers are rewarded for teaching their students the required curriculum and participating in extracurricular activities required by their district. Few are rewarded for taking time to reflect, experiment, and inquire. Professors are rewarded for conducting research and presenting results for their own professional group, which does not usually include school people. In most university settings applied research, teacher education, and work in schools are not so highly regarded as scholarly work unfettered by such practical concerns. Until the demands of collaborative research are understood and the products are valued in both settings, teachers and researchers willing to undertake this important work will be rare.

Building support for collaborative research requires commitment from administrative leaders, attention to evaluation and reward systems, and backing from funding agencies. Academics who extend their research beyond the ivory tower must be appreciated by their administrators, supported by funding agencies, and endorsed by professional colleagues. Teachers who strive to develop and carry out instructional innovations must be rewarded, not constrained by testing practices geared solely to the traditional curriculum. They must be given time and recognition for devoting themselves to professional renewal. Changing organizational values and structures to reward collaborative research is a gradual process, as is all education, but it is necessary to link schools and universities in their joint effort to sustain the culture of inquiry.

References

Anderson, B. L., and P. L. Cox. 1987. *Configuring the education system for a shared future: Collaborative vision, action, reflection.* Unpublished draft.

Barzun, J., and H. Graff. 1977. *The modern researcher.* 3rd ed. New York: Harcourt Brace Jovanovich.

Blumenfeld, P., Krajcik, J., Marx, R. W., and Soloway, E. 1994. Lessons learned. A collaborative model for helping teachers learn project-based instruction. *Elementary School Journal* 94(5): 539–51.

Clark, R. N. 1988. School-university relationships: An interpretive review. In *school-university partnerships in action: Concepts, cases, and concerns* edited by K. A. Sirotnik and J. I. Goodlad, pp. 32–65. New York: Teachers College Press.

Cleveland, H. 1985. *The knowledge executive: Leadership in an information society.* New York: E. P. Dutton.

Cohen, D. K. 1988. Teaching practice, plus que ca change. . . . In *Contributing to educational change: Perspectives on research and practice,* edited by P. W. Jackson, pp. 27–84. Berkeley, CA: McCutchan Publishing Co.

———, M. W. McLaughlin, and J. E. Talbert. 1993. *Teaching for understanding: Challenges for policy.* San Francisco: Jossey-Bass.

Educational Technology Center. March, 1984. *The use of information technologies for education in science, mathematics, and computers: An agenda for research.* Tech. Report TR84–1. Cambridge, MA: Harvard Graduate School of Education, Educational Technology Center.

Eisner, E., ed. 1985a. *Learning and teaching the ways of knowing: Eighty-fourth yearbook of the national society for the study of education.* Pt. 2. Chicago, IL: University of Chicago Press.

————. 1985b. *The art of educational evaluation*. Philadelphia: The Falmer Press.

Erickson, F. 1986. Qualitative methods in research on teaching. In *Handbook of research on teaching, third edition: A project of the American Educational Research Association*, edited by M. Wittrock, pp. 119–61. New York: Macmillan.

Florio, S., and M. Walsh. 1978 . *The teacher as colleague in classroom research*. Occasional paper no. 4 (February). East Lansing: Michigan State University, College of Education, Institute for Research on Teaching.

Gifford, B. R., and N. H. Gabelko. 1987. Linking practice-sensitive researchers to research-sensitive practitioners. *Education and Urban Society* 19(4): 368–88.

Gomez, M. N., J. Bissel, L. Danziger, and R. Casselman. 1990. *To advance learning: A handbook on developing K-12 postsecondary partnerships*. Lanham, MD: University Press of America.

Goodlad, J. I, ed. 1987. *The ecology of school renewal: Eighty-sixth yearbook of the National Society for the Study of Education*. Chicago: The University of Chicago Press.

————. 1988. School-university partnerships for educational renewal: Rationale and concepts. In *School-university partnerships in action: Concepts, cases, and concerns* , edited by K. A. Sirotnik and J. I. Goodlad, pp. 3–31. New York: Teachers College Press.

Greenberg, A. R. 1991. *High school-college partnerships: Conceptual models, programs and issues*. ASHE-ERIC Higher Education Report No. 5. Washington, DC: The George Washington University School of Education and Human Development.

Gross, T. L. 1988. *Partners in education: How colleges can work with schools to improve teaching and learning*. San Francisco: Jossey-Bass.

Haberman, M. 1971. Twenty-three reasons why universities can't educate teachers. *Journal of Teacher Education* 22: 133–40.

Lampert, M. 1988. *Teachers' thinking about students' thinking about geometry: The effects of new teaching tools*. Tech. Report TR88-1. Cambridge, MA: Harvard Graduate School of Education, Educational Technology Center.

Lieberman, A. 1986. Collaborative research: Working with, not working on. *Educational Leadership* 43: 28–32.

Maeroff, G. I. 1983. *School and college: Partnerships in education*. Princeton, NJ: The Carnegie Foundation for the Advancement of Teaching.

McDonald, J. P. 1986. *The teacher's voice in collaborative school improvement projects*. Thesis, Harvard University. Cambridge, MA: Harvard University.

Popkewitz, T. S. 1980. Paradigms in educational science: Different meanings and purpose to theory. *Boston University Journal of Education* 160: 28–46.

Powell, A. G., E. Farrar, and D. K. Cohen. 1985. *The shopping mall high school: Winners and losers in the educational marketplace*. Boston: Houghton Mifflin.

Rudduck, J., and D. Hopkins, eds. 1985. *Research as a basis for teaching: Readings from the work of Lawrence Stenhouse*. Portsmouth, NH: Heinemann Educational Books.

Sirotnik, K. A. 1988. The meaning and conduct of inquiry in school-university partnerships. In *School-university partnerships in action: Concepts, cases, and concerns*, edited by K. A. Sirotnik and J. I. Goodlad, pp 169–90. New York: Teachers College Press.

————, and J. I. Goodlad, eds. 1988. *School-university partnerships in action: Concepts, cases, and concerns* . New York: Teachers College Press.

Trubowitz, S. 1984. *When a college works with a public school: A case study of school-college collaboration*. Boston: Institute for Responsive Education.

12

Managing the Tensions in Connecting Students' Inquiry with Learning Mathematics in School

MAGDALENE LAMPERT

What is entailed in engaging students in authentic academic inquiry in school mathematics? Is it possible? Does student inquiry actually result in their learning what they need to know? Does it result in mathematical understanding? If so, why does it not happen more regularly?

The psychological relationship between inquiry and understanding has been taken up in an earlier section of this volume. In this chapter, the question to be examined is what happens when teachers try to engage students in inquiry in school. It is not assumed that inquiry by itself will produce understanding; instead inquiry is taken to be a component of the sorts of activities that might lead to a deeper knowledge of mathematics than is now being produced by more conventional approaches to curriculum and instruction. In addition to the perspectives provided by cognitive science on the relationship between inquiry and learning, this chapter also considers inquiry as an authentic *mathematical* activity in which students might engage for the purpose of learning about what is entailed in *doing mathematics*.

Researchers and reformers stress the idea that the learning environment should be structured so that students can pursue questions of interest or concern to them, bringing their intuitive knowledge and reasoning skills to bear and using them to extend their understanding into new domains (Brown, Collins, and Duquid, 1989; Greeno, 1990; National Council of Teachers of Mathematics, 1989; National Research Council, 1989; Pea, 1987). The literature on how students think about mathematics is rich with examples of invented solutions to relatively complex problems in which learners seem genuinely interested, suggesting that the teacher's job should be a relatively simple matter of refining and connecting informal understanding with what we want students to learn in school (Behr and Hiebert, 1988; Carpenter, Fennema, and Peterson, 1988; Resnick, 1988; Romberg & Carpenter, 1986). But little attention has been given to the problems of teaching practice that must be addressed if student inquiry and authentic academic understanding are to be related in ordinary school classrooms (Cohen, 1988; Cuban, 1984; Desforges and Cockburn, 1987).

Practical Dilemmas in Conducting Inquiry in School

When school teachers try to engage students as active inquirers and at the same time attend to their responsibility for teaching a subject coherently and equitably to all students, they are faced with a series of practical dilemmas (Berlak and Berlak, 1981; Jackson, 1968; Lampert, 1984, 1985). Individual students are interested in different questions, but the teacher must teach the class as a whole. Students' inquiry may propel them deeply into one topic, but the teacher is responsible for their acquaintance with a broad set of topics. Students' conjectures propel them in different directions through the subject matter, but the teacher is responsible for keeping track of who knows what and what they still need to learn. Students may learn a great deal from making a hypothesis and then mustering the evidence to show that it was wrong, but school knowledge is measured in terms of students' capacity to produce correct answers. Students may develop idiosyncratic systems for structuring their understanding, but they are also supposed to learn to communicate with a wider community of scholars who use agreed on structural conventions. And so on. These are all problems of practice for the teacher who embraces the belief that students' inquiry will produce valuable knowledge. They stem from conflicts that are inherent in the very idea of universal public education (Bidwell, 1965; Cohen, 1988; Waller, 1932). It is unlikely that they will go away, even if institutional structures are modified, as long as we continue to care about equity and efficiency. Teachers who want to teach in other than conventional ways need to find strategies for managing these dilemmas if their practice is to succeed.

How do teachers organize and teach lessons so that learners can and will explore a topic from the perspective of their own understanding, and teachers can and will take account of that understanding in what and how they teach? How can intellectual and social coherence and equitable education be maintained in classrooms where teachers do let students' ways of thinking about mathematics become a substantial part of the agenda of mathematics lessons? How can a different social organization be created in the classroom, so that the teacher retains social and intellectual authority, but also takes seriously the need for students to search out and verify knowledge for themselves in order to learn what is being taught? How can teachers attend to the idiosyncratic ways of understanding a mathematical idea that students will bring to a topic, and also conduct lessons that are orderly and predictable enough to fit the school's institutional structure? How can students' inquiry be plausibly linked with the content goals that are assigned to schools?

At least since Socrates, we have been caught in the irony of setting things up so that learners will have the experience of "discovering" exactly what teachers want them to know (Cobb, 1988; Petrie, 1981). This irony is not lost on students who are invited by teachers, in courses they are required to take, in schools they are required to attend, to "inquire" into a subject and "discover" its truths. The invitation seems duplicitous, even when it is genuinely extended, and it is even more complicated by the fact that students often feel that unnecessary work is being asked of them. Teachers wouldn't be teachers if, students say to themselves, "they did not know what I need to know, so why am I being put through the difficult task of finding things out for myself?" Yet if students are to learn what it means to do mathematics, to invent and justify assertions in the mathematical domain, they must do more than learn about the record of mathematical knowledge that others have produced. Within mathematics, and within mathematics education, the dilemmas that arise from bringing both inventions and conventions into the learning environment are a matter of long-standing argument (Steiner, 1988; Tymoczko, 1985).

Teaching Practices That Support Inquiry in School

Managing the tension between students' inquiry and schools' agendas is not only a problem of how to teach subject matter in a way that takes account of what students bring. It is also a problem of building a culture of understanding that legitimates students' active involvement in creating their own knowledge (Cazden, 1988; Bereiter and Scardamalia, 1983; Lampert, 1989). In addition to whatever conceptions of mathematics students carry to learning the subject, they also carry assumptions about what they are supposed to do and what teachers are supposed to do to cause their learning to happen (Ball, 1988; Cooney, 1987). To be able to guide students' inquiry toward the learning of the mathematical content in the syllabus, teachers must first convince students that inquiry is a legitimate, safe, and productive way to learn in school.

Once students are willing to engage in inquiry and the classroom is set up to support their engagement, the teacher faces other problems. Communicating with students about their understandings and guiding them toward the central ideas of the discipline means that the teacher must be adaptive and able to use conventional knowledge in flexible ways. The language (and other representations of ideas) that are used by students who have not yet been initiated to disciplinary conventions needs to be interpreted by the teacher and refined through conversation among the class members and the teacher (Lampert, 1989; Resnick, 1988; Vergnaud,

1988). This conversation cannot be dominated by disciplinary formalisms if it is to include the authentic expression of students' understanding. At the same time, class discussions must also serve to make students familiar with the terms of discourse that are commonly used in mathematics. Traditionally, these terms are communicated through the curriculum. But following a syllabus or a textbook from one important topic to another is not a useful organizational tool once a teacher acknowledges that students are making their own constructions of relationships among mathematical concepts (Lampert, 1989, 1993). Since discourse is constructed in response to student activity in inquiry-oriented classrooms, the teacher takes on a much greater responsibility for representing the discipline to students.

To better understand the sort of teaching practice that is indicated by these conditions, I would like to examine three teaching tasks more deeply: guiding social interaction in a class discussion of students' ideas, interpreting learners' language and connecting it with the conventions of the discipline, and navigating around in the subject-matter terrain in response to student inquiry. Each of these tasks can be seen as a strategic response by teachers to the essential tensions that arise from attempting to engage students in academic inquiry in school. These three tasks are interrelated in the actual activity of teaching, and they are by no means a complete list of what teachers need to do to support inquiry or mathematical understanding in school.

My analysis of mathematics teaching in terms of these three aspects of pedagogical practice will be based on research in teaching geometry that has been conducted during the first five years of operations at the Educational Technology Center at Harvard University in five "Lab Sites" where secondary school teachers have been experimenting with new tools designed to support a pedagogy of guided inquiry (Wiske, 1988).

High School Geometry: A Case of Trying to Teach Mathematics Through Inquiry

The *Geometric Supposer* is a set of computer software designed to enable teachers and students to examine patterns in geometrical relationships by quickly constructing and measuring figures in the plane, namely triangles, quadrilaterals, and circles (Yerushalmy and Houde, 1986; Schwartz, Yerushalmy, and Gordon, 1985). Because it can produce, measure, and compare figures quickly and accurately, the *Supposer* software supports the process of making conjectures about spatial relationships based on induction as a prior step toward establishing the generality of the relationships with a deductive proof. An understanding of the process of creating mathematics is thus enabled by giving students and teachers a tool they can use in the service of producing data to support mathematical conjectures (Schwartz, 1993).

Guided inquiry is an approach to curriculum and instruction that gives the teacher the responsibility for introducing content in a way that is illuminated and modified in response to students' questions and ways of thinking about that content. The teacher defines the focus of inquiry by posing problems for the class while students take an active part in acquiring knowledge by generating not only answers, but formulations of problems, definitions of the terms of discourse, and analyses of alternative solutions. Students collect data and analyze it, making conjectures about mathematical relationships that they observe in the course of their work. What the teacher aims to teach is supplemented and complemented by the discussion of student findings. Conjecturing is the currency of mathematical discourse (Lakatos, 1976; Polya, 1954). It is also thought to be an important activity for students who are learning mathematics (NCTM, 1989; Romberg, 1983). In mathematics, inquiry begins with assertions that are generated intuitively or inductively, and formal knowledge is established by examining the extent of the domain to which an assertion might apply. This sort of disciplinary inquiry is what the *Supposer* materials were designed to support.

The *Supposer* is used in many secondary school classrooms across the country, and ETC has been working closely with teachers in some of those classrooms to better understand the work that is entailed in developing inquiry oriented lessons around the activity of students' conjecturing about geometrical relationships (Wiske et al., 1988; Wiske and Houde, 1993). In this chapter, I will draw on particular aspects of the *Supposer* experience to illustrate the tensions in teaching mathematics using guided inquiry in school, but these tensions extend into many classrooms across the entire spectrum of mathematics instruction (Cobb, 1988; Cooney, 1987; Desforges and Cockburn, 1987; Lampert, 1985; Rubin, Roseberry, and Bruce, 1988; Stephens, 1982).

Managing the Tension: Risking Conjectures Versus Learning from an Established Authority

One of the teachers who had been using the *Supposer* in her geometry classes for a few months surveyed her students to find out what they thought about using the computer software to produce and collect data from which they could make conjectures about geometrical relationships. The students had been spending one or two days a week in the school's computer lab, exploring definitions and problems with the constructions they produced on the computer screen. When they were back in class, on the other days, the teacher attempted to integrate the findings of their explorations with discussions, lectures, and homework assignments that were organized according to a standard textbook. For some of the students, this integration was experienced in the way it was intended, as an attempt to engage them in actively constructing their own knowledge. One young woman from the class wrote:

> Instead of just feeding us the information and expecting us to understand
> it instantly, [working with the *Supposer*] makes us draw our own figures in

our own ways and makes us figure out the questions by ourselves. It makes us use our brains a little more; for example, to draw a figure, we must use some property of it which we then learn much better, since we must use it for our construction. As we are doing our own little things in creative ways it is forcing us to discover new geometry facts and conjectures. We are, in a way, with the teacher's guidance, teaching ourselves. . . . It is also sort of rewarding when you've discovered something and you, for a short fleeting moment, feel like a genius.

This student was not only acquiring geometrical information; she was acquiring the conviction that what she was learning is true by verifying it for herself, and she was sorting out important information from the superficial characteristics of figures. She was, with the teacher's guidance, "teaching herself" geometry, and learning that mathematical knowledge is knowledge that can be discovered inductively.

But this student's sense of how one learns mathematics is unusual, both in classes using the *Supposer,* and in mathematics classes more generally (Ball, 1988; Stodolsky, 1988). More typical is the student who wrote:

I feel that the *Supposer* could be of help if it was used in conjunction with a teacher who also retaught the material, making sure everyone knew exactly what was going on. What would be good would be to have the teacher teach the material, then have students see it for themselves on the computer. But if the teacher teaches the material, then why bother with the *Supposer?* . . . A good teacher emphasizes important facts; minor things that you would spend four or five periods on in the computer room can be emphasized in one class, and move on to more important information. I feel that time spent in the computer room has been pretty much a waste.

This student believed it was the teacher's job to figure out what he needed to know, and that he would learn most efficiently if the teacher told him what was important to know. He did not want to "waste time" exploring problems to figure out for himself what facts were important. He saw geometry as a subject that could be transmitted from teacher to student in a direct form, rather than one in which the important facts are determined inductively and deductively by the learner, working on the sorts of problems the subject was invented to solve. This student did not consider it efficient to follow his own lines of inquiry as a route to learning what he thought he needed to know about geometry in the school setting. He did not think it was safe to rely on his own reasoning powers to figure out what was relevant or important about geometrical relationships in the process of solving problems.

This is the "problem space" in which teachers who want to enact a pedagogy of guided inquiry do their work. The second student's perspective on how knowledge is acquired fits very well with the way schools are generally organized, and he would probably be a very successful student in a traditional setting. If their students are going to learn what they need to know through engaging in guided inquiry, teachers must challenge such traditional assumptions about how knowledge is acquired. And they must do this, even as the norms of the situation in which they teach work against students taking their own thinking seriously as a route to being successful (Powell, Farrar, and Cohen, 1985). Engaging students in inquiry is something that teachers must work at. It does not simply come as a by-product of changing the curriculum or adding new tools to the learning environment. The broader culture in which schools operate does not value such intellectual activity, and teachers must counter that culture in order to engage students in classroom inquiry (Cohen, 1988; Hilton, 1988).

To counteract students' tendency toward more familiar ways of learning and knowing, the *Supposer* teachers invented various strategies, in the form of alternative social arrangements for instruction, that would encourage students to believe that it would not only be safe to share their ideas with one another and with the teacher, but that this sharing would also lead to their acquiring the knowledge of geometry that they needed. They tried in a variety of ways to make connections between students' conjecturing and the more formal aspects of learning the discipline of geometry. Making the connection remained difficult, perhaps because the teachers themselves were not fully convinced that students' inquiry was an appropriate route to their learning what they needed to know.

Letting anyone know what one is thinking before one has a sense of whether that thinking is correct is risky business, especially in the social environment of the classroom where the student's sense of self-worth is tied up with the ability to produce right answers in recitations and on paper. Creating a classroom culture in which students are willing to expose their ideas for experimentation and revision—even if it is done in private conversation with the teacher—requires a radical change from the way students and teachers typically think about the relationship between what one knows and who one is (Barnes, 1976). Asserting and examining mathematical conjectures can just as easily lead to dead ends as to important theorems. Scholars in the disciplines have rituals (such as blind peer review of publications and sharing new ideas with a trusted group of insiders before going public with them) that protect them somewhat from the risks of conjecturing (Davis and Hersh, 1981; Gleick, 1987) but these rituals do not automatically "trickle down" to patterns of interaction in schools. For teachers to carry on instruction that is aimed toward making connections with learners' inquiry, they need deliberately to initiate similar rituals in the classroom.

The easiest place for *Supposer* teachers and students to experiment with the social arrangements that affect how activities and learning are related was in the computer lab. In the lab classes, students usually worked two to a terminal, and they were expected to produce one report of the data they were collecting and the conjectures derived from them. In the pairs, one student would make an assertion about a pattern in the data, and the other would challenge the assertion as they decided what to put down on paper.

They refined their thinking in this back-and-forth manner, until they could agree on assertions that seemed both plausible and worth noting. The first step from individual thinking to public mathematical inquiry was taken when the pairs of students talked with one another about what they thought might be patterns in the measurements they had taken. As they worked together on deciding "what to put down" on paper while pointing to figures on the screen, they negotiated with one another about what might be worth saying about the figures, developing their own idiosyncratic language for communicating about geometric properties and figures. This negotiation was relatively private, out of hearing of the teacher for the most part, and often conducted with a chosen and trusted peer.

In the lab, teachers walked around and observed the work that pairs of students were doing at the computers, and they attempted to respond to the geometrical issues that were raised by the particular data that each pair of students was collecting. Although this strategy was exhausting and time consuming, it made it possible for the teachers to time instructional interventions differently for different students and to legitimate private idiosyncratic exploration as a way of learning mathematics in school. As one teacher commented:

> In the large group you have your agenda, but you may overlook the individual student's agenda. So it's hard to be sure that each student has contributed or that each student's questions have been answered. . . . Facilitating a discussion is not something I am good at, and I don't think most math teachers are.
>
> In the lab, they have their agendas, and I am literally running around like a maniac. . . . But it is intellectually exciting to see some of the things the kids were coming up with. Things I didn't predict.

Some of the *Supposer* teachers tried to import the activity of conjecturing from the lab into classroom discussions by building regular whole-group lessons around the software used on a large monitor. This attempt to bring conjecturing into the public forum of classroom discussion and connect it with the content of the syllabus represents a progression from the relatively safe and private inquiry-driven discourse that occurred between pairs of students in the computer lab to the public and standardized knowledge exchanges represented by teachers, textbooks, and syllabi. But it is still one step short of the most impersonal and perhaps most threatening forum in which students are required to expose what they think to teachers: the graded assignment. Here "right answers" earn you an evaluation that places you in a hierarchy of knowledge in relation to other members of the class. The *Supposer* teachers recognized that they could not evaluate conjectures generated from a lab activity on the same sort of "correct versus incorrect" standard that they had been using for traditional homework and tests. Not having enough evidence does not make a conjecture "wrong" in the same way that not having appropriate reasons makes a proof "wrong." The differences between a more and a less insightful conjecture are subtle;

even those teachers who had some sense of the difference had a hard time communicating their standards to students. Indeed, the issue of how to judge the quality of an as yet unproven conjecture is one that is continually debated within mathematics itself (Davis and Hersh, 1981; Tymoczko, 1985). Throughout the two years that the *Supposer* experiment occurred in these classrooms, teachers and students struggled with how to evaluate students' conjectures (cf. Wiske and Houde, 1993). One teacher remarked:

> I feel very nervous about grading. Very nervous. In terms of quizzing and testing, I am very nervous, because you want kids to think it is a serious experience and a learning experience, and then you go, "How in the world do I get everything together in a test from the book and the *Supposer*?" I am nervous, but I am willing to wait and see what happens.

Another teacher commented:

> Homework is hard, too. When they're in the lab, there is sometimes no homework I can give because they are still in the process of discovery. But to some extent, you want to be able to say, after they have had two or three labs, "You've got to have it finished." And so you have to evaluate the written work.

Although these comments are focused on the problem of grading, they express the more general tensions that the teachers were feeling as they tried to redefine authentic academic achievement in terms of inquiry and communicate their expectations to their students.

Managing the Tension: Eliciting Students' Constructions of Mathematical Ideas Versus Initiating Them to the Conventions of the Discipline

Once it is made legitimate within the classroom culture, students' inquiry into geometry must be connected with the important ideas in mathematics in such a way as to assure that all students have the possibility of acquiring disciplinary knowledge. In classroom lessons, teachers needed to find ways to connect students' intuitions with the content of the syllabus, which is primarily devoted to the idea that geometry is a set of deductively related abstractions. To do this, they had to create the visual, verbal, and social means with which to engage students in mathematical discourse about important geometrical relationships and guide that discourse into a kind of mathematical thinking that was not familiar to students. They had to build forms of communication that would accommodate *both* inquiry that was meaningful from the perspective of students who did not know formal geometry and the expression of the central ideas of the subject matter.

Neither students and teachers, nor mathematicians, can authentically argue about their assertions unless they agree on a set of rules that will determine the level at which the discourse will be conducted and common definitions for the terms they are using. How you decide whether a conjecture is true and what constitutes evidence are questions that have both personal and disciplinary significance. If students and teachers talk about subject matter using language and symbols that are connected to students' thinking, both in their content and in the level of their abstraction, there is a greater possibility for both students and teachers to be able to make authentic assertions about the structure of the domain, prove them, and refute the ones that are untrue (Lampert, 1993). But if students are also supposed to learn things that will connect them with mathematical discourse that occurs outside their classroom, they must also be taught the formalities of the discipline.

Issues of connection and communication were addressed in *Supposer* classrooms on two fronts: making definitions and proving assertions. In the case of making definitions, many teachers began work on the *Supposer* by having students first explore the regularities and distinctions among the different figures that the software menus would produce, and then they invited students to make definitions that fit their observations. In one class, this resulted in a debate about whether different sorts of triangles should be defined in terms of the characteristics of their *sides* or the characteristics of their *angles*. Students replayed familiar disciplinary considerations as they tried to resolve their disagreements, and they confronted the tensions between "what makes the most sense to me" and the formal definitions they found in their textbook. The teacher was challenged to portray the role that inventing definitions plays in mathematics, a lesson that required some sophisticated appreciation of the rules of discourse in the discipline as well as an understanding of the sort of understanding students were expressing with their invented definitions. In another class, a teacher regularly tried to use the *Supposer* at a large monitor in front of her whole class to elicit students' conjectures about mathematical relationships before they read about them in the textbook. She was often put in the position of reformulating students' observations in terms of *general* relationships among parts of figures rather than those that are *particular* to an actual figure, teaching them about the ambiguous position that the drawn figure has in deductive geometric proofs. Her students often made conjectures that she knew were true, but which they were unable to prove because they had not established the prior necessary arguments. Although she attempted on several occasions to readjust the agenda to mediate between conjectures that arose from induction and those that students could prove deductively as a class, she was frustrated by this situation.

This teacher was confronting one of the deepest issues in mathematical epistemology, and teaching with the *Supposer* required her to manage it "on line" while at the same time being responsible for her students acquiring the knowledge that would serve them in future mathematics courses. She had initiated a classroom discourse that had students "conjecturing all over the place" and that excited her, but at the same time she said she felt personally threatened by her perceptions of what she saw students doing with the *Supposer*. She reported that one of the reasons she liked teaching was her appreciation of the "beautiful logical development of the whole corpus of Euclidean geometry." She wanted her students to like geometry for its "self-contained completeness." But her goal was at risk as she watched her students conjecture about what might be true of the shapes they had generated on the *Supposer*. She was both excited and worried about the fact that her students were

> making generalizations all over the place that they did not have the background to prove. . . . We did some of these projects [in the *Supposer* materials], just to get a sense of the *Supposer* and collecting data. We made conjectures and then just threw them in there [without proving them] to explore what similarity was. . . . They've got a lot of neat conjectures, and they can't do anything with them because they don't have the theory yet; that is, they can't do anything in the sense of proof.
>
> This bothers me because one of the things that is neat about geometry for me is that you can really do a deductive process with it. My teaching the deductive process has gone out the window. . . . It's like I'm in a totally new ball game and I don't know what the rules are.

To this teacher, "not having the theory yet" means that students do not have a corpus of already proven theorems that they can use to go on to prove the conjectures that result from their observations of the measurements produced by the *Supposer*. This contradicts what it has meant to her to "do geometry," because the ideas that students are encountering are not coming in logical deductive order. In her view, doing geometry means

> You have to be clear about what you know is true at the start and where you want to end up; you have to have that set out in your mind and you have to have available some place up here [in your head] what relationships exist that you know about and then be able to put them in the right places to apply them to this situation. And that comes from where you are in the course of the year. You can begin with something as simple as proving triangles congruent and wind up with proofs about the internal and external triangles on a circle. The progression is really remarkable.

What is at stake here is finding some means by which the students can legitimately make discoveries, and the teacher can communicate what connection these discoveries have to the formal, generally stated theorems and proofs that are in the textbook.

In order to communicate in the classroom in a way that would accommodate both students' intuitions and deductive mathematical "truths," the teachers spoke of "conjectures" in a way that blurred the distinction between students' discoveries and the theorems in the textbook. They tried to structure the lab activities so that they would be perceived as a route to students' acquiring what they called "ownership" of the ideas that they wanted them to learn. But building a system of communication that connected students' inquiry with the contents of the syllabus that they wanted students to master continued to create practical dilemmas in their practice.

Managing the Tension: Navigating Along Different Paths Through the Mathematical Terrain Versus Covering the Standard Curriculum

Since school teaching occurs in real time, one problem that teachers have to solve is what to do first, then next, and next, and next. At the very least, teachers need some way to keep track of who knows what already and what they still need to learn. This task is more difficult for teachers who take mathematical understanding as their instructional goal than for those who see their job as training students to use computational skills or remember mathematical facts. Teachers with these more conventional goals can rely on the textbook or syllabus to guide and pace their instruction (Leinhardt, Putnam, and Hattrup, 1992; Putnam, 1987). But to teach for mathematical understanding is to see mathematics as something other than discrete bits of knowledge that can be acquired one after another in a sequence determined independently from the learner (Zarrinia, Lamon, and Romberg, 1987). In the current thinking of educational psychologists, knowledge about mathematics is conceived as an intricate web of relationships, and understanding it means being able to move around in that web in a way that is appropriate to the problem being considered (Hiebert & Behr, 1988). It is assumed that students must create their own conceptual webs or "maps" of the terrain if they are to understand the subject. In Dewey's (1902/1964) terms, the map provided by the curriculum, even though it may be a logical representation of the subject, cannot substitute for the psychological map that students construct as they participate in active inquiry; teaching must be about "transforming logically organized subject matter into psychologically meaningful experience for students" (Stanic and Kilpatrick, 1989, p. 19).

If teachers take seriously the idea that instruction should be related to what students already know and the idea that their knowledge is structured in an idiosyncratic web of relationships, then they cannot simply "keep track" of where learners and teacher have been together by following the textbook chapter by chapter, assuming that the way it connects one mathematical idea to another is the way that those ideas will be connected in students' thinking. But they must still keep track, for the sake of producing coherent lessons as well as for the purposes of reporting to others on students' progress. If classroom activity is organized by teachers to engage students in working with problems for which solution strategies need to be invented, the mathematical knowledge that will go into those inventions will be extremely varied from person to person. At the same time that teachers are observing and appreciating the knowledge that students bring to the solution of problems, they also have in mind some collection of knowledge that students should acquire. The elements of that collection need to be available in a way that makes them usable in the act of teaching in response to what students bring.

We might think of the pedagogical work involved in this task to be figuring out where each student in a class *is,* identifying where he or she *should be going,* and then providing some sort of guidance for *how to get there.* By analogy with learning about an unfamiliar place by visiting different locations in that place, we might consider two alternative sorts of guidance that could be provided: step-by-step directions on how to get from one important landmark to another, and a map of the place to be explored and understood. The textbook is like step-by-step directions for how to get from one place to another, in which the importance of the locations to be visited is determined by some external authority, who also decides the order in which these places will be visited. It does not give any information that would enable either teacher or student to construct alternative routes around the territory, nor does it tell you what to do if you get lost. A map, on the other hand, would leave the construction of a route and the choice of destinations up to the travelers. It would allow for digression without getting lost. And it would enable different travelers to take different routes and visit different locations, thereby building unique understandings of the place. Either a map or a textbook can serve as the navigational tool that a teacher would use to guide the interaction between students and subject matter, but a map of the intellectual domain seems more usable if one is aiming to teach mathematics for understanding. In the main, the *Supposer* teachers did not have such maps, or, if they did, they were unable to use them regularly. But they recognized the need for some way of thinking about the content they were responsible for teaching that would enable them to be more flexible in guiding students' inquiry.

High school geometry offers a special opportunity to explore this issue because it is the most self-contained piece of the K-12 mathematics curriculum; its territory is thus somewhat more constrained than, say, sixth-grade mathematics. It has traditionally been taught as the quintessential example of formal mathematical reasoning, beginning (in Chapter one) with Euclid's axioms, and building the whole corpus of plane geometry from there by orderly deductive steps. This progression follows the form of the record that Euclid put down, showing how what was known about shapes and their relationships could be logically established. What this record does *not* express, however, is how these relationships came to be discovered or understood (Romberg, 1983; Steiner, 1988). Acquiring mathematical knowledge involves intuition and induction, and moving back and forth among examples and general assertions about logical relationships (Davis and Hersh, 1981; Hadamard, 1945; Kitcher, 1984; Lakatos, 1976).

In attempting to establish the reasons why their conjectures might be true for some general class of figures, students "range all over" the territory of plane geometry, as they assert conjectures about angles, or parallel lines, or similar triangles. This way of doing mathematics is in stark—and to the experienced teacher, confusing—contrast to the corpus of geometry as it was formally recorded by Euclid, starting with a very small number of assumptions from which could be generated a large body of seductively provable theorems. One of the teachers observed:

> The textbook is a logical progression, it absolutely is. As a matter of fact, the nature of geometry is sequential; that's how Euclid did it. You accept some statements as true because they make logical sense and then you deduce things from them. That's how geometry progresses.

Another teacher commented that the textbook was laid out so that students would prove theorems that they could then use as "reasons" in the proof of theorems in the next chapter. At the end of each chapter was a set of problems making use of the theorems proven in that chapter. The problems that were designed to be used with the *Supposer* did not follow this organization, and were intended to generate thinking about relationships between classes of figures rather than as an application of discrete bits of knowledge. But they caused a sequencing problem because they made it hard for the teachers to keep track of where they and their students had been and to plan where to go next. As one teacher commented:

> In terms of specifics, I'm very confused, because it's so nitty gritty in the book, and then when you go to use the *Geometric Supposer,* its kind of "Well, they'll get that idea when they do problem #18, so do I really even have to discuss it?," I mean in terms of the postulates you need for doing that proof or whatever.

This teacher was trying to use both the *Supposer* problems. which were designed to have students connect geometric knowledge in ways that would serve to invent solutions, and a conventional textbook in which geometric knowledge was lined up as a progression of axioms, definitions, theorems, postulates, and more theorems. She struggled to build an instructional agenda that would mediate between the two very different epistemologies underlying the *Supposer* problems and the textbook.

When they were interviewed near the end of the school year, the *Supposer* teachers all expressed concern about what they had accomplished, often in terms of worries about their divergence from the familiar sequence. They talked at length about the difficulties they were having trying to *both* give time for exploration *and* complete the syllabus. One teacher said she thought others had done better at integrating the two, but she was still going back and forth in a "linear" way. Although she wanted to integrate, she thought it would be "much more of an effort for me to think that through." She hoped to do a better job on that the following year. Then she spoke about her "sabotage" of the deductive process she enjoys so much: "I've sabotaged it all, I give the kids all kinds of axioms, but—it's because I so value the problem-solving experience." By "giving kids axioms" this teacher feels she has been disloyal to the Euclidean ideal. But without those axioms, her lessons could not "proceed," and she would have to find another way to conduct students' inquiry with formal geometry.

Another teacher also talked about how much she valued the "problem-solving experience" that the students had when they were working with the *Supposer,* but she, too, said it made her concerned about what she needed to do to make conjecturing a worthwhile classroom activity.

> My mind is so straight and all I see is what I know and my mind doesn't
> go off on all the tangents like the kids do. . . . You've got to take the time
> to study a lot and you have to think a lot before you give the projects out,
> and that's what I have to do more of. . . . I never realized the kids would
> come up with so many more ideas, or so many different things than what
> I thought of.

As the teachers saw what their students could come up with while looking for patterns in geometric data, they felt that the job of teaching became more difficult rather than easier, even though it seemed as if the students already knew many of the things they felt they needed to teach in the past. When they taught in conventional ways, there was little opportunity to seriously consider what students might bring to the occasion of learning geometry. Recognizing what students bring means they may have less to teach, but a more difficult job to do: "I see that they know an amazing amount. Not only do they know stuff I haven't taught them, but they know stuff it never would have occurred to me to teach them, and they know it in their gut."

As the work of these teachers changed from information transfer to guided inquiry, it made the task of keeping track of what students know more difficult, and it meant that the teacher had to do the work of connecting students' informal knowledge with the formalities of the discipline—not only so that they could perform successfully in school, but so that they would learn something about the nature of the relationship between induction and deduction in mathematical discourse.

What Is Entailed in Teaching
Mathematics for Understanding?

As students were taught to collect data about geometrical relationships, look for patterns, and make conjectures about what sorts of relationships might be "always true" of figures in a certain class, they became engaged in working on problems that were posed neither by teacher nor textbook. They could construct their own intellectual roadmaps through geometry as they asserted geometrical relationships and tested their reasonability. As they proceeded to make and test conjectures, they were able to take off in many different directions through the subject matter. *Supposer*-related conjectures—in contrast to theorems in the textbook chosen by the teacher for the teaching of proof—could be experienced by students as geometric relationships that needed to be proven before they could be accepted as true. Thus, the work of proof could be "owned" by students in a way that it had not been in the traditional curriculum.

When it occurred, this student "ownership" of the agenda represented a radical contrast to what had occurred in these classrooms before the *Supposer* became a tool for teaching and learning, when the roadmap that defined the content of the geometry course and the journey a class was going to take through it was determined by how the teachers decided to proceed through the textbook. If one sees guided inquiry as the ideal sort of pedagogy for promoting mathematical understanding, then student ownership of the agenda should be considered as an admirable accomplishment. Making conjectures and arguing with their peers about the conjectures' plausibility engaged these students in authentic mathematical activity. But from the perspective of the teachers who experimented with the *Supposer,* it did not always seem that they were doing what they were supposed to be doing as teachers of school mathematics. They felt a serious conflict between encouraging student thinking and getting through the syllabus that students would be tested on at the end of the year. Their worries about this conflict were exacerbated by students' complaints that they might not be learning what they needed to learn, a concern that was often expressed, particularly in the higher tracks of the courses in each of the schools. The culture of the schools in which they were working had not prepared either the teachers or their students to feel secure that, if students followed their own intellectual roadmaps, they would learn what they were supposed to know. Yet the new technology was seductive—to both students and teachers—and drew them along mathematically interesting paths that did not coincide with the routes through the subject defined by the textbook. Students went off on mathematically productive tangents that no one was able to keep track of. As they made conjectures that they wanted to prove, teachers were barraged with questions. Even teachers went off on tangents as the *Supposer* captured them in some interesting mathematical puzzle. This was both exhilarating and frustrating; the participants enjoyed what was happening, but they were not sure what connection it might have with what they had come to know as learning high school geometry. They were faced, at a very practical level, with figuring out how to "guide" the inquiry process once students were engaged in it.

The situation the *Supposer* teachers experienced was something like that of a tour operator whose bus (the textbook) has been replaced with a collection of glitzy motor scooters (computers booted with the *Supposer*) in the middle of the Place de la Concorde with roads leading out in all directions to the attractions of Paris (geometry). Many of the tourists (students) could see places they wanted to explore, but did not know how to get to them. Others did not even know where to go or how to begin to make choices. Everyone was complaining because their expectations for the tour were not being met, while at the same time they were anxious to jump on a scooter and take off down the road toward some interesting looking destination. To make matters worse, the cameras (tests), that were to serve to record where everyone had been, were left on the bus.

As they worked at creating a social environment in which students felt that it was safe and productive to express their ideas about geometrical relationships and tried to organize communication in the classroom so that connections could be made between students' thinking and the mathematical ideas that teachers wanted them to learn, the *Supposer* teachers— and the researchers who shared their struggles—learned firsthand what would be required to run school classrooms in a way that supports students' inquiry. We need to know more about what the maps they developed to accomplish this might look like, and how they are used in planning and in spontaneous reactions to what teachers hear when they listen to students express their thinking about a mathematical topic. Learning about their maps might help us think about how to better prepare teachers, in both subject matter and pedagogy, so that they have the intellectual resources to do this kind of work. We also need to know more about what sorts of communication strategies are effective in developing a language and social organization for classroom discourse that is both expressive of students' ideas and genuinely mathematical. And we need to know how teachers construct assignments that encourage conjecturing and mathematical argument rather than the memorization of "proofs." Learning about these pedagogical strategies may help as we think about how to restructure teaching to secure a relationship between inquiry and school learning.

References

Ball, D. 1988. *Knowledge & reasoning in mathematical pedagogy: Examining what prospective teachers bring to teacher education.* Unpublished doctoral dissertation, Michigan State University.

Barnes, D. 1976. *From communication to curriculum.* Harmondsworth: Penguin Education.

Bereiter, C., and M. Scardamalia. 1983. *The psychology of written composition.* Hillsdale, NJ: Erlbaum.

Berlak, A., and H. Berlak. 1981. *Dilemmas of schooling: Teaching and social change.* New York: Methuen.

Bidwell, C. 1965. The school as a formal organization. In *Handbook of organizations,* edited by J. G. March. Chicago: Rand McNally.

Brown, J. S., A. Collins and P. Duquid. 1989. Situated cognition and the culture of learning. *Educational Researcher* 18(1): 32–42.

Cazden, C. 1988. *Classroom discourse: The language of teaching and learning.* Portsmouth, NH: Heinemann Educational Books.

Cobb, P. 1988. *Multiple perspectives.* Paper presented at the American Educational Research Association, New Orleans.

Cohen, D. K. 1988. *Teaching practice: Plus ca change . . .* (issue paper 88–3), East Lansing MI: National Center for Research on Teacher Education.

Cooney, T. 1987. *The issue of reform: What have we learned from yesteryear?* Paper presented at the Mathematical Science Education Board & Center for Academic Interinstitutional Program Conference, UCLA.

Cuban, L. 1984. Policy and research dilemmas in the teaching of reasoning: Unplanned designs. *Review of Educational Research* 54(4): 655–81.

Davis, P. J., and R. Hersh. 1981. *The mathematical experience.* Boston: Birkhauser.

Desforges, C., and A. Cockburn. 1987. *Understanding the mathematics teacher: A study of practice in first schools.* New York: Falmer Press.

Dewey, J. 1902/1964. *The child and the curriculum.* Chicago: University of Chicago Press.

Gleick, J. 1987. Chaos: *Making a new science.* New York: Viking.

Greeno, J. G. 1990. *Number sense as situated knowledge in a conceptual domain.* (Report No. IRL90–0014). Palo Alto, CA: Institute for Research on Learning.

Hadamard, J. 1945. *An essay on the psychology of invention in the mathematical field.* Princeton, NJ: Princeton University Press.

Hiebert, J., and M. Behr. 1988. *Number concepts and operations in the middle grades.* Hillsdale, NJ: Erlbaum. Reston, VA: National Council of Teachers of Mathematics.

Hilton, D. 1988. *Contemporary science and natural explanation: commonsense conceptions of causality.* Brighton: Harvester.

Jackson, P. W. 1968. *Life in classrooms.* New York: Holt, Rinehart and Winston.

Kitcher, P. 1984. *The nature of mathematical knowledge.* New York: Oxford University Press.

Lakatos, I. 1976. *Proofs and refutations: The logic of mathematical discovery.* Cambridge: Cambridge University Press.

Lampert, M. 1984. Teaching about thinking and thinking about teaching. *Journal of curriculum studies* 16(1): 1–18.

———. 1985. How do teachers manage to teach? *Harvard Educational Review* 55(2): 178–94.

———. 1989. Choosing and using mathematical tools in classroom discourse. *Advances in research on teaching.* Vol. 1. Greenwich, CT: JAI Press.

———. 1993. Teacher's thinking about students' thinking about geometry: The effects of new teaching tools. In *The Geometric Supposer: What is it a case of?*, edited by J.L. Schwartz, M. Yerushalmy, and B. Wilson. Hillsdale, NJ: Erlbaum.

Leinhardt, G., R. Putnam, and R. Hattrup. 1992. *Analysis of arithmetic for mathematics teaching.* Hillsdale, NJ: Erlbaum.

National Council of Teachers of Mathematics. 1989. *Curriculum and evaluation standards for school mathematics.* Reston, VA: National Council of Teachers of Mathematics.

National Research Council. 1989. *Everybody counts: A report to the nation on the future of mathematics education.* Washington, DC: National Academy Press.

Pea, R. D. 1987. Cognitive technologies for mathematics education. In *Cognitive science and mathematics education*, edited by A. H. Schoenfeld. Hillsdale, NJ: Erlbaum.

Petrie, H. G. 1981. *The dilemma of enquiry and learning.* Chicago: University of Chicago Press.

Polya, G. 1954. *Induction and analogy of mathematics.* Princeton, NJ: Princeton University Press.

Powell, A., E. Farrar and D. K. Cohen. 1985. *The shopping mall high school: Winners and losers in the educational market place*. Boston: Houghton Mifflin.

Putnam, R. T. 1987. Structuring and adjusting content for students: A study of live & simulated tutoring of addition. *American Educational Research Journal* 24(1): 13–48.

Resnick, L. B. 1988. Treating mathematics as an ill-structured discipline. In *The teaching and assessing of mathematical problem solving*, edited by R. I. Charles and E. A. Silver. Hillsdale, NJ/Reston, VA: Erlbaum/National Council of Teachers of Mathematics.

Romberg, T. 1983. A common curriculum of mathematics. In *Individual differences and the common curriculum. Eighty-second yearbook of the National Society for the Study of Education, Part 1*, edited by G.D. Fenstermacher and J.I. Goodlad. Chicago: University of Chicago Press.

Romberg, T. 1986. Research on teaching and learning mathematics: Two disciplines of scientific inquiry. In *Handbook of research on teaching*, edited by M. C. Wittrock. New York: Macmillan.

Rubin, A., A. S. Roseberry, and B. Bruce. 1988. *ELASTIC and reasoning under uncertainty*. (Report Mp/6851) BBN Laboratories.

Schwartz, J. L., M. Yerushalmy and M. Gordon. 1985. *The Geometric Supposer:Triangles* and *The Geometric Supposer: Quadrilaterals*. Pleasantville, NY Sunburst Communications.

Schwartz, J. L. 1993. A personal view of the supposer: Reflections on particularities and generalities in education reform. In *The Geometric Supposer: What is it a case of?*, edited by J. L. Schwartz, M. Yerushalmy, and B. Wilson. Hillsdale, NJ: Erlbaum.

Stanic, G.M.A., and J. Kilpatrick. 1989. Mathematics curriculum reform in the United States: A historical perspective. In *International journal of education research*, edited by H. J. Walberg, et al. New York: Pergamon Press.

Steiner, H. G. 1988. Two kinds of 'elements' and the dialectic between synthetic-deductive and analytic-genetic approaches in mathematics. *For the learning of mathematics* 8(3): 7–15.

Stephens. 1982. *Mathematical knowledge and school work: A case study of the teaching of developing mathematical processes*. Madison: Wisconsin Center for Educational Research.

Stodolsky, S. 1988. *The subject matters: Classroom activity in math and social studies*. Chicago: University of Chicago Press.

Tymoczko, T. 1985. *New directions in the philosophy of mathematics*. Boston: Birkhauser.

Vergnaud, G. 1988. Multiplicative structures. In *Number concepts and operations in the middle grades*, edited by J. Heibert and M. Behr. Hillsdale, NJ/Reston, VA: Erlbaum/National Council of Teachers of Mathematics.

Waller, W. 1932. *The sociology of teaching*. New York: Wiley.

Wiske, M. S., D. Niguidula, and J. Shepard. 1988. *Collaborative research goes to school: Guided inquiry with computers in classrooms*. Technical report 88–3. Cambridge, MA: Harvard Graduate School of Education, Educational Technology Center.

Wiske, M. S., and R. Houde. 1993. From recitation to construction: Teachers change with new technologies. In *The Geometric Supposer: What is it a case of?*, edited by J. L. Schwartz, M. Yerushalmy, and B. Wilson. Hillsdale, NJ: Erlbaum.

Yerushalmy, M., and R. Houde. 1986. *The Geometric Supposer:* Promoting thinking & learning. *Mathematics Teacher* 79(6): 418–22.

Zarrinia, E. A., S. J. Lamon, and T. A. Romberg. 1987. *Epistemic teaching of social mathematics*. Program report 87–3. School Mathematics Monitoring Center, University of Wisconsin School of Education.

13

Constructing Understanding in the Science Classroom: Integrating Laboratory Experiments, Student and Computer Models, and Class Discussion in Learning Scientific Concepts

JOSEPH SNIR and CAROL SMITH

Science education involves introducing students to new ideas and theories that scientists have developed to understand and explain the observed phenomena of nature. There is now considerable evidence that students have great difficulty in understanding and internalizing these concepts and theories, in part because they come to science class with ideas that are often incommensurable with the ideas of scientists. Such cases arise, for example, when the student's conceptual framework includes undifferentiated concepts that are incoherent from the point of view of the scientist's theory (e.g., weight/density as described in Smith, Carey, and Wiser, 1985; dead/inanimate in Carey, 1985; heat/temperature in Wiser and Carey, 1983; force/energy/pressure/momentum in Viennot, 1979). As Strike and Posner (1985) have cogently argued, for conceptual change to occur students must not only become aware of and dissatisfied with their old conceptions, they must also find the new conceptions of scientists to be intelligible, plausible, and fruitful. Hence in cases where students begin with undifferentiated concepts, science educators must help students to represent and understand the ideas of scientists as part of the process of bridging between students' and scientists' conceptions.

One promising technique for making the scientist's ideas intelligible to students involves finding student concepts that have a similar structure to concepts in the desired theory and using these points as anchoring or bridging analogies to the desired conception (Brown and Clement, 1987). In cases where students do not have direct access to relevant analogies from their everyday experience, one can extend this approach by creating conceptual models and simulations implemented on a computer. A conceptual model gives students a way of visually representing abstract concepts that are themselves not "seeable" by exploiting more intuitive, immediately apprehensible visual analogs. Students then can use the visual analogs to provide guidance in how their concepts need to be restructured. Such computer-based conceptual models and simulations have been developed and successfully used by a variety of researchers in teaching students about difficult subjects such as the distinction between weight and density (Smith, Snir, and Grosslight, 1992), heat and temperature (Wiser and Kipman, 1988; Wiser, Grosslight, and Unger, 1989), and the nature of momentum as a vector quantity (White and Horwitz, 1987, 1988).

When using computer models in a science curriculum, however, one needs to consider how to bridge between student conceptions and predesigned computer models, and how to use the computer models in ways that genuinely support and respect a constructive approach to both learning and science. In this chapter, we present and analyze a teaching unit we designed that used conceptual models to help sixth- and seventh-grade students differentiate weight and density. In this unit students had the opportunity to express their own ideas about natural phenomena and the concepts by which those phenomena are explained. Students were involved in a cycle of activities that included structured laboratory experiments, data collection and organization, model building on paper, manipulation of predesigned conceptually enhanced computer simulations, and class discussion about the process of modeling. We present our views on how this cycle of activities helped students construct and internalize the scientific ideas and how we believe such a cycle of activities may be applied in teaching other concepts to promote a deeper understanding of both the concepts themselves and the process of model construction in science.

Our chapter is organized into four main parts. The first part identifies the three levels of understanding a natural phenomenon that should be addressed in school science. We thus define both the goals we would like to achieve in science education in general and in this teaching unit in particular.

In the second part we describe the flow of activities and student ideas throughout the teaching unit. These are based on a detailed research study that followed the implementation of the unit (Smith, Snir, and Grosslight, 1992).

In the third part we analyze the components of the teaching unit, discuss how they were sequenced to foster student understanding, and suggest implications for designing other science lessons. We especially emphasize the importance of creating, using, and discussing models to help students reflect on their own concepts, construct and internalize scientific concepts, and develop an understanding of the nature of model building itself.

The paper concludes with a reflection on how we as curriculum designers learned from students through the implementation of the unit and how this kind of teaching can inform teachers about students' thinking.

Learning Goals: Three Levels of Understanding in Science

As we have argued in more detail elsewhere (see Chapter 7, this volume), we believe science education should address three types of learning goals and deepen students' understanding of natural phenomena on three different levels. First, students need to learn some basic facts about natural phenomena and form some simple generalizations based on these facts (e.g., "wooden objects float on water," or "metal objects expand when heated"). We call this a "concrete" or "object" level because it is based on a direct observation of everyday objects.

However, science involves much more than amassing facts. It is concerned with developing explanations of those facts in terms of some core principles, laws, and hypothesized causal mechanisms. Thus, students need to learn the current scientific theories by which the facts observed at the first level can be conceptualized and explained. One of the difficulties in learning about these theories is that they make use of webs of concepts defined in relation to each other that cannot be simply or directly observed. Further, students often bring their own quite different concepts and theories to science class that they use to explain the basic facts they have observed. For example, the concept of density is useful in explaining why some objects float and others sink in certain liquids. However, one cannot directly "see" the densities of objects or liquids. Rather, density is a characteristic property of a material that is inferred by observing that objects made of a given material have a constant mass-to-volume ratio under standard conditions of temperature and pressure. We call this a "theoretical" or "conceptual" level because it is concerned with relations among a set of theoretical (conceptual) entities rather than relations among the objects themselves.

On the third level, students need to learn about the purposes and methods of science itself. For example, scientists develop models and theories to help them understand natural phenomena. Thus, students must become aware of the choices scientists face when constructing models and theories and some of the principles they use in deciding what is a good model or theory. We call this third level a "metatheoretical" or "metaconceptual" level because it involves reflection about the epistemological basis of the conceptual level, for example, how scientists use concepts and observations to construct knowledge.

We argue that properly designed and integrated teaching units can be used to help students make changes at all three levels. To explain more fully how such teaching units are designed, we start by describing the sequence of lessons and student progress in the unit we created.

The Teaching Unit

Our teaching unit had two main parts. The first part centered on the phenomenon of flotation, the second on the phenomenon of thermal expansion. These phenomena were carefully selected to motivate the development of an understanding of the concept of density, which is central to understanding both phenomena. Recent research has indicated that most sixth- and seventh-grade students do not have distinct concepts of weight and density, but unite components from both concepts in one undifferentiated weight-density concept (Smith et al, 1985). The core of students' notion of weight is felt weight, a property of some but not all physical objects. Further, students' notion of weight is inherently a comparative one, and, in making judgments of weight, they always make comparisons with an implicit (and somewhat variable) standard. When they say an object is heavy, they may mean it is heavy for them, heavy for objects of its type, or heavy for its size. Thus, they unite the components "heavy," "heavy for me," and "heavy for size" in one undifferentiated weight/density concept. In this particular unit, no attempt was made to teach students the distinction between weight and mass. Hence density was simply defined as "weight per unit volume" rather than "mass per unit volume."

A complete description of the lessons and worksheets is given elsewhere (Grosslight, S. Smith, Unger, Snir, and C. Smith, 1988). In this section we describe the main flow of activities and their internal structure. An analysis of the unit, highlighting the importance of different teaching elements, is given in the next section.

Part 1: Thinking About Sinking

The first part of the unit consisted of ten lessons in which students investigated the phenomenon of flotation and the concept of density of materials.

Exploring students' intuitive ideas about flotation and density:
Laboratory experiments and structured worksheets

Students started by making and testing predictions about whether different sized objects (made of different materials) would sink or float in water. This first class helped us identify the intuitive ideas students had about flotation. At this point, students used several different ideas in their predictions: the kind of material the object was made of, the weight or the size of the object, whether they imagined the object was hollow, solid, or had holes, whether the material had air in it or could absorb water, and how much water there was in the container.

Over a two-day period, we worked with students in articulating some of their hypotheses and testing them with various objects. We tried to get them to come up with a consistent rule, one that could be applied to all objects. After two days of experimentation, the majority of students had come to believe that the kind of material an object was made of was particularly relevant, although they were not very clear about which feature of materials was important.

Students were reminded how some people thought that the weight of the object and the weight of the material was important for predicting whether the object would sink or float. To make it clearer to students that they were using two different senses of heavy when talking about "heavy objects" versus "heavy materials," the teacher next asked them to order a set of objects by their weight and by "the heaviness of kind of material" the objects were made from. Students found it relatively straightforward to order the objects by weight (using balance scales as well as feeling). However, students found it much more confusing to order objects by the density or heaviness of the kind of material because they unknowingly moved back and forth between two senses of weight. On the one hand students thought a large piece of wood was denser than a small copper penny because it was so much heavier. On the other hand, they thought the copper penny was heavier than the large wood because copper is "heavier" than wood (in the sense of "heavier for size"). With help and discussion, most students reached agreement that the small copper object in their kit was made of a heavier kind of material than the big absolutely heavier piece of wood. After the ordering, the objects were placed in the water. Students saw that the heaviness of material and not absolute weight of the object is the better predictor of sinking or floating behavior.

Introducing the scientific concept of density and the idea of a model:
Student model building and class discussion

At this point, we formally introduced the word density and reviewed a procedure for telling whether one object was made of a denser material than another by comparing the weights of equal amounts of each material. Then we introduced the idea that models could be used to help clarify our ideas. We challenged students to try to invent a model that would show the density of different materials. Students began with a set of three equal-size cylinders of different materials (wood, hard black rubber, and copper) and then were given two additional objects (a very large heavy piece of wood and a small penny) that they were to portray in modeled form.

One of the common ways students portrayed density differences was by using shading of varying intensity. A few students represented density by how "filled up" the object was; a couple of students represented density by the crowdedness of dots. More than half the students were able to

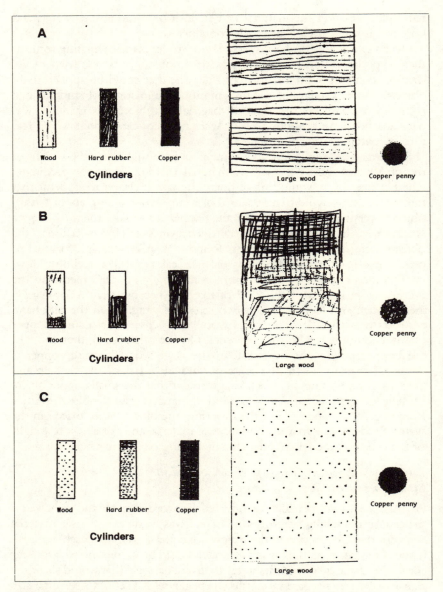

Figure 13-1 Three examples of student models portraying the density differences of wood, hard rubber, and copper using either (A) an intensity shading model, (B) a "how filled up model," or (C) a dot crowdedness model. The five objects portrayed were three same-size cylinders of wood, hard black rubber, and copper; a large block of wood; and small copper penny.

follow through on their ideas and show that the large heavy wood was made of a light material (the same shading intensity as the wooden cylinder in their model) and the small light penny was made of a heavy material (the same shading intensity as the copper cylinder in their model). (See Figure 13-1 for examples of consistent student models). The others were less consistent in their use of codes, or omitted a representation of density for the penny and wood block.

In discussing the merits of their various models, we stressed the importance of creating consistent codes (codes that could be used the same way for all objects) and codes that clearly represented the relevant dimension. We also noted that intensity shading and dot crowdedness were two good ways to represent density. Students were then asked if they could tell anything about the absolute weights of objects using their modeling codes. From this discussion, one limitation of the intensity-shading model emerged: It does not provide an explicit representation of the total weight of objects. We then introduced our own grid-and-dots model (which students later saw on the computer screen) and discussed the way it provided a representation of size, weight, and density. We told students we had designed some computer programs that used our models, and we hoped the computer models would help them keep track of the differences between weight and density. In this model a box stands for a unit of volume, a dot stands for a unit of weight and the number of dots per box stands for the density of the material (see Figure 13-2 for an example of the grid-and-dots model used in the flotation programs).

Searching for the flotation rule: Manipulation of conceptually enhanced computer simulations

In the next class, students used the computers for the first time to help them explore sinking and floating. In the program, students could choose materials for the objects and liquid and then perform a simulated experiment to see what happened. There were five materials ranging in density from 1 dot/box to 5 dots/box. Students were encouraged to start with the first kind of material for the liquid, to systematically try objects made of the five different materials, and then to move on to the next liquid. At the conclusion of their exploration, they were asked to formulate a general rule.

Students liked this program very much, and now the majority of students focused on the density of materials as the variable relevant to sinking and floating. Further, half the students formulated an explicit rule that talked about the relation between the density of the objects and liquid (i.e., an object will float if it is less dense than the liquid it is in; it will sink if it is more dense than the liquid it is in). The rest who talked about density simply said, for example, "Dense things sink, less dense things float." No student when dealing with real-world materials alone had formulated the rule in a fashion that explicitly compared the density of the object to the density of the liquid. Thus, working and experimenting with

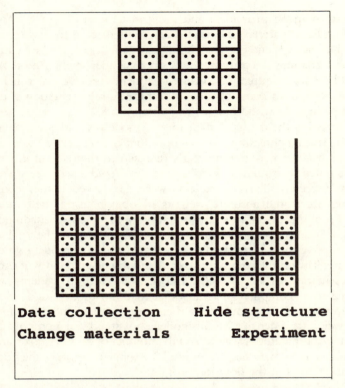

Figure 13-2 Screen from the sink and float program showing the object and liquid represented, using our grid-and-dots model.

the objects in modeled form not only helped students focus on the density of the material as the relevant variable but it also made salient that it was important to consider a relation between two densities. Significantly, only two students formulated a rule simply in terms of the model (dots or dots per box) rather than in terms of underlying physical magnitudes such as weight and density. This is a sign that most students were genuinely interpreting the model as a representation of physical objects, not viewing it as an unconnected microworld.

In a subsequent class, students were able to use the computer microworld to explore whether the absolute size (or weight) of an object was useful in predicting sinking and floating above and beyond knowledge of the object's density. Most were able to understand that the three variables were distinct and concluded that the variable of relevance to sinking and floating was still relative density. However, it was our impression that at this point most students were actually seeing the three quantities as entirely independent of each other rather than as mutually interdefined.

Making links between the computer model and real objects: Computers used in the laboratory setting

We then returned to the topic of modeling real objects and materials using the grid-and-dots models. Students were given pieces of aluminum and steel, both the same size and asked if they thought one of them was denser than the other and, if so, how they could represent it. At first students approached the problem qualitatively: they represented steel with more dots per box than aluminum. They were not asking themselves the question of how much denser steel is than aluminum. We then gave them further information (3 cm³ of aluminum balanced with 1 cm³ of steel) that allowed them to think more quantitatively about the problem. Now, with help, students were able to see that the steel was three times denser than the aluminum and to capture that in their models. They also could make some predictions about how many pieces of aluminum would be needed to balance 2 cm³ of steel and so on.

As homework, students were given three more problems to work on alone. In two problems, students were shown a quantity of one material that balanced with a different quantity of another, and they were asked to infer which material was denser and to draw a grid-and-dots model of the objects. Almost all students performed perfectly on these problems, correctly inferring the ratio of the two densities (in one case 2:1, in the other 5:1).

Finally, we asked students if they could generate a rule that would allow them to determine the density of an object if only the weight and the size of the object were known. More than two-thirds of the students were able to formulate a rule in terms of division, although they were not clear that it was the weight that was to be divided by the size. One group thought the larger number should be divided by the smaller number, because it was impossible to divide a smaller number by the larger number. An interesting class discussion of this issue ensued! Significantly, the division rule emerged as something generated by the students themselves rather than something presented by the teacher.

At this point in the curriculum, students had been introduced to the following ideas about density: Density is an intensive property of materials that does not change as one changes the total amount of material; the density of an object can be obtained by dividing the weight of the object by its volume; the relative densities of objects and liquid are relevant to predicting the behavior of an object in the liquid; and density can be modeled as number of weight units per volume unit. In addition, we stressed two qualitative rules for inferring relative density: (1) if two objects have the same volume, the heavier object is made of a denser material; and (2) if two objects are the same weight, the smaller object is denser. What was the relative importance of these different ideas for students? Some clues about how students put this all together came from watching them reason about a new phenomenon: thermal expansion.

Part 2: Expanding Student Thinking: Thermal Expansion

The experimental phenomenon: Class demonstration

Students were introduced to the phenomenon of thermal expansion by observing the following metal ball and ring experiment. First, they were shown that a cold metal ball could easily pass through a metal ring. Then they watched while the metal ball was heated and saw that it would no longer pass through the metal ring. They concluded that the heated ball must be larger (we introduced the word "expanded"). We asked them to consider whether it had also changed in weight. We then showed them by using a balance scale that the weight of the heated and unheated ball was the same.

Exploring students' intuitive ideas: Model building, class discussions, and manipulation of conceptually enhanced computer simulations

Students found this demonstration very interesting and surprising and were excited to discuss what had happened. We focused the discussion by asking them to draw models of what had happened—first, in any way they wanted, and then (if they had not spontaneously tried to use a grid and dots representation), to think of a way of adapting this kind of model.

While only about one-third of the students attempted to use the grid-and-dots model spontaneously, most students were able to think of ways of adapting the model to apply to this situation. More than half the students were able to convey accurate information about the relative size and weight of the metal ball before and after heating. That is, their models showed that the ball increased in size but remained the same weight. However, there were interesting differences in the ways students modeled this situation. Some of these students retained a standard size unit representation and showed that the number of size units increased, the total number of dots remained constant, and the dots per box decreased. Other students represented the size globally (a small box versus a large box), with the number of dots remaining the same in the small and large box, and the crowdedness of the dots in the entire box lessening (see Figure 13-3).

The responses of the rest of the students showed that they failed to encode accurately both weight and size information. Two patterns that occurred for these students were either increasing both the number of size and weight units, or increasing the number of size units but decreasing the size of each unit so that the overall size of the object remained the same. Clearly, asking students to model a situation is a cognitively demanding task. Yet pedagogically it seemed highly useful, for as teachers walked around the room and looked at the different models, they could immediately see the differences in how students were viewing the situation.

At this point there was class discussion of various models, not in terms of judging whether some models were right or wrong but, rather, in terms of what facts were relevant and whether they accurately showed the basic

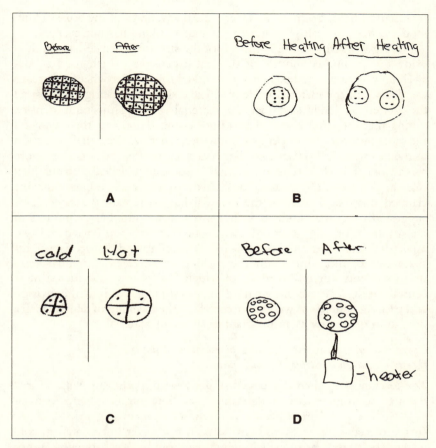

Figure 13-3 Examples of student models of changes in the ball (in the ball and ring experiment) when the ball is heated. (A) and (B) involve increasing the number of standard size units, and decreasing the number of dots per box, while (C) and (D) involve swelling a fixed number of size units, and decreasing the overall dot crowdedness.

facts. (Some of the students' models were faulted on this criterion if, for example, they erroneously showed that both size and weight were changing.) Further, it was also agreed that there was more than one way students could choose to represent the same facts: The box-swelling model and the standard size unit model were both accepted as legitimate models in the class discussion, because they both accurately represented the relevant facts. The class discussion stressed the way we see models, not as truth but as instruments to use in thinking about reality. The advantages and disadvantages of each representation were also discussed. An advantage mentioned for the standard size unit model is that it gives a quantitative representation for both size and weight. An advantage of the box-swelling model is that one can portray that the material kind has not changed.

Having worked to develop models of the situation themselves and then using our computer models of thermal expansion (which used a box-swelling notation), students were next asked to consider what happens to the density of the material in thermal expansion. Interestingly, almost all the students initially said that the material still had the same density, noting that the kind of material had not changed and that there was still the same number of dots per box. However, when we drew their attention to the fact that the box itself got larger and, therefore, the dots were more spread out, a lively discussion followed. Some now ardently maintained that the density of the material must have lessened, while others staunchly claimed that the density of the material had to remain the same. This suggested to us that students in fact internalized different definitions of density from our first unit. Although our first unit had considered two aspects of density (density as property of materials and density as weight-size ratios or more intuitively the packing of weight in a standard size unit), students differed in terms of which feature they considered most central. In our discussions, we tried to help students see how the division and packing definitions were more central to the meaning of density than a definition of density as an invariant property of materials.

Coordinating the two experimental phenomena of flotation and thermal expansion: Student model building

The teaching unit then challenged students with a problem that required them to coordinate their understanding of flotation and thermal expansion. In the problem, students were shown that an egg-shaped object (made of clay-covered Styrofoam) sank in hot water but floated in cold water. Their task was to explain why they thought that happened and to draw a model of the situation.

About two-thirds of the students (those who had given evidence on the interim pretest of having successfully differentiated weight and density) gave explanations showing that they were able to coordinate thinking about sinking and floating with thinking about thermal expansion and to accompany their explanations with some relevant model. Most of these students assumed that cold water was denser than hot water and that the density of the egg was in between the densities of the hot and cold water and remained unchanged. The most common model students used imposed a grid of constant size units on the object and liquid, and then showed the density differences directly in terms of different numbers of dots per box, a version never used by our computer program on thermal expansion. Other models included a box swelling model (where density had to be inferred in terms of dot crowdedness) or intensity shading models.

In contrast, those students who had not clearly differentiated weight and density at the time of the interim posttest tended to try to simplify the problem in one of two ways. One simplification was to focus only on the effect of hot or cold water on the density of the egg (ignoring the densities of the water entirely as well as the issue about the relation between the density of the water and egg that is crucial to sinking and floating). In keeping with their focus only on the egg, their models of the situation only represented their idea about the density changes of the egg. The liquid was shown merely as background, with no explicit representation of density. The other strategy of simplification was to focus only on the relation between object and liquid in the two situations considered separately. These students noted that the egg was denser than the hot water (because it sank) and that the egg was less dense than the cold water (because it floated). They made no attempt, however, to model the situation or talk about the effect of temperature changes on density. Finally, two students had difficulty formulating any coherent hypothesis or model about this situation at all.

The nature of models: Class discussion

In concluding the curriculum, we involved students in a general discussion of models. We began by giving students four different maps of the Boston area (a street map, a highway map, a subway map, and a tourist map) and asking the following questions: What does each map show? Do they all show the same things? How do they represent things? Is one map better than the others? Students enjoyed this activity immensely and immediately saw our main point—that because each map was designed for a different purpose and because the different maps were good for different purposes, there is not one best map. We also discussed the point that no map can provide all the information about something. The map-maker needs to decide what is the relevant information and then to present it in a clear, accurate, and accessible manner. Using maps as an introduction, we then turned to a discussion of models in science and our use of models in the curriculum.

We gave students a final worksheet in which they were shown multiple models of thermal expansion and asked to evaluate them vis-à-vis different purposes or uses. All students were comfortable with having more than one model for a phenomenon. At the same time, they did not find all models equally satisfactory. Although their initial choices did not always coincide with ours, the fact that they understood the activity and were willing to engage in a discussion of this complex issue suggested that they had begun to understand an important metaconceptual point in the curriculum—namely, that models are representational tools that must be evaluated with respect to how well they convey relevant observations, fulfill particular purposes, and help one think about a given problem.

Analyzing the Elements of Instruction in the Teaching Unit

In this section we analyze the main types of activities that were employed in the unit: laboratory experimentation, student model building on paper, class discussions, and manipulating conceptually enhanced computer simulations. Although each type of activity is described separately, their power lies in the way they are interwoven into a coherent whole. Within the unit, students made observations (laboratory activity), built a model of what they did in the lab, and then participated in a class discussion and/or manipulated conceptually enhanced computer simulations. For example, they did real-life sinking and floating experiments, followed by drawing models to describe the density of the materials and then manipulating computer models to focus their attention on the concepts needed to understand what was done in the laboratory.

Laboratory Experimentation and Classroom Demonstrations

Natural phenomena as they occur in everyday life are often very complicated and hard to understand. For example, most everyday objects are made of a combination of materials of different shapes and sizes. When studying flotation, it would be quite complicated to analyze the phenomenon of flotation regarding these nonhomogeneous objects with irregular shapes and holes or cavities, especially given that most students start with an undifferentiated concept of weight/density. Thus we made choices in how to constrain and design the laboratory experiences of students. We assumed the experiments should be as simple as possible to help students focus on key concepts and contrasts. At the same time we wanted the experiments to be interesting, rich, and representative of the whole set of concepts we were dealing with.

In our flotation unit, we chose a set of laboratory activities with an eye to our explicit purpose of helping students differentiate weight from density. Students were asked to keep records of the flotation of different sized objects made of different homogeneous materials. All the objects were made of chunks of pure materials, with no holes or hidden cavities. The size differences between objects could be estimated by viewing the objects and the weight differences determined by comparison on an equal arm balance. Another activity in the lab included ordering sets of objects by weight and density and then testing the behavior of these objects in water, in order to call students' attention to the difference between the two variables and highlight the importance of density in flotation.

The laboratory experiments were designed to give the students the foundation for the first two levels of science learning. Through the experiments students learned certain facts about flotation (e.g., large and small pieces of oak float, large and small pieces of clay sink) and described some of the properties of these objects (e.g., noting the relative size, weight, kinds of material, color, and texture of the objects). They also began to wonder about how to explain these facts and relate their descriptions.

Thus the laboratory was used to begin to construct a descriptive language that would be employed throughout the unit and to provoke students' curiosity about the subject matter on which we wished to concentrate. For example, when we taught students about weight, we wanted them to think about what they meant by weight, what procedures they used to find the weight of an object, how they compared the weights of two objects, and how the absolute weight of an object was different from the density of the material the object is made of. We built a vocabulary of words connected to the reality students encountered in the laboratory, which, once established, would be later used for further thinking and discussion about the phenomena and concepts in computer simulations.

In the laboratory activities, we preferred whenever possible to have students do the experiments themselves. But when safety problems arose or when we wanted to review quickly what students had already observed, we typically used class demonstrations. For example, the ball and ring thermal expansion experiment was done as a class demonstration.

It is important to emphasize that we used the laboratory for qualitative purposes, not to achieve some predefined quantitative goals, such as measuring some constant to a certain degree of accuracy. When measurements were taken, they were designed to help the students make comparisons, not to find absolute values. For example, students were asked to find which of two objects was larger or had more weight or to order a set of objects by relative weight and density, rather than measure accurately the values for any specific object. Our aim was to make students aware of basic facts about phenomena in a qualitative way that would enable them to move to the second stage: reflecting on the findings obtained in this first stage.

To conclude, we believe laboratory activities give students the opportunity to use all their senses and obtain the indispensable direct experience of sensing materials and observing phenomena. We believe that nothing can replace this direct contact with phenomena in science learning. But, as stated above, learning some basic facts and procedures concerning observable phenomena does not by itself ensure an understanding of the underlying set of concepts needed to explain those phenomena. In the next section, we describe other tools we used for achieving this deeper goal.

Model Building: A Tool for Reflection and Concept Construction

To start students on the work of understanding a phenomenon, we asked students to interpret the phenomenon they had observed in the laboratory work by creating and drawing a model of the phenomenon on a worksheet. They were free to convey information by whatever means they chose—graphic, symbolic, numeric, or pictorial. However, it was important that their model accurately captured certain basic facts about the phenomenon, and we encouraged students to think of ways to show their ideas visually. These worksheets were then collected and used as the basis for class discussion.

These modeling activities had two aims. The first was to elicit students' intuitive thinking about what they saw in the experiments. This activity gave both them and their teachers the opportunity to learn about their initial conceptions of the phenomenon in a noncritical atmosphere. Once acknowledged, these initial conceptions were then used as a starting point for the process of conceptual change.

The second aim of these modeling activities was to provide students with firsthand experience as model builders and designers. Such experience offered students a basis for participating in a discussion about the model building process itself. In such discussions, they confronted fundamental questions concerning models themselves, such as: What is a representation? What is a model? Why do people make models? What are the purposes of making a model? What makes something a good model? Can there be more than one good model? This discussion process is described in the next section. In our unit, we held such "meta" discussions about modeling at three different points in our unit: when students first created models to clarify their conception of density of materials, when students created models to understand how thermal expansion affected the density of materials, and at the conclusion of the unit when students explored map making and alternative model building.

Class Discussion: There Are No "Wrong Models" But There Are Criteria by Which Models Can Be Evaluated

In class discussions, we gave students the opportunity to present their models and evaluate their own and their peers' work. Sometimes the students themselves presented their models, and sometimes we collected their work and presented it in an organized way. The fundamental aim here was to create a situation in which we did not judge students' models as right or wrong. Instead, we repeatedly raised questions that are fundamental to evaluating any model: Is it adequate? What aspects of the phenomenon can be explained by the model and what aspects cannot? In this way, we involved the students themselves in the process of model evaluation. We encouraged them to begin to build criteria for evaluating models and to accept or reject models based on how well they met their criteria, rather than on the basis of authority or how similar they were to accepted scientific models. Consequently there were always a multiplicity of models that we accepted as "good models" consistent with a given purpose throughout the unit, and these included some student-generated models that were quite different from our computer models or the kinds found in textbooks.

We also confronted them with the fundamental limitation of all models: their ability to tell only part of the truth. In our discussions, we encouraged students to find out what part of the truth their model conveyed, and ultimately challenged them to devise a model that could tell a larger part. Issues about criteria for evaluating models were first broached when students devised models for representing the density of materials. Students' next opportunity for generating and evaluating their own models was in the context of explaining the phenomenon of thermal expansion. In this context, students needed to think about how to adapt and modify their models to account for a new phenomenon. They experienced both model building and model revision. As a capstone experience, we discussed these metaconceptual points about the criteria for model building in the more familiar context of evaluating different maps of Boston. Here it was clear to students that different maps had different purposes and that, while it was important for a map to be accurate and consistent, it had to be evaluated with respect to how well it served its given purposes.

Other researchers have used student model building as an effective means of eliciting student ideas in the classroom. For example, in one report (Nussbaum and Novick, 1982), a teacher showed students a beaker of gas, and then used a bicycle pump to remove air from the beaker. Students in this situation were asked to model their ideas about how the gas molecules in the beaker were distributed before and after the pumping. The student models were then collected and grouped, and each group of students was asked to explain their drawings. In the class discussion that followed, the students' models were ultimately judged by pointing out the differences between their models and the scientific one.

Our approach to using and evaluating student models is different from Novick and Nussbaum's in that the relevant question is not whether a particular student model is right or wrong but rather what aspect of the phenomenon at hand it does and does not account for. If this approach had been adopted in the Novick and Nussbaum experiment, some of the "incorrect" student models might be accepted as adequate in depicting the beaker with less gas because they could not be ruled out without further experimentation. For example, some students showed that after pumping there are fewer molecules in the beaker, but all the remaining molecules are in the lower part of the beaker. This model cannot be ruled out as wrong on the basis of the above demonstration alone.

Conceptually Enhanced Computer Simulations

The fourth component that we used, interwoven with the other three previously described, involved conceptually enhanced computer simulations. A detailed description of the structure and design of our most recent conceptually enhanced simulations and their role as a tool for science teaching is provided elsewhere in this volume (see Chapter 7). Here we outline only the main ideas that guided us in designing this kind of tool.

We believe computer simulations should be based on scientific models and laws. The power of a scientific model lies in its ability to predict new events and explain a network of relationships derived from analysis of the real system in question. When the running of a computer simulation is based on physical laws (e.g., our flotation simulation had the physical laws of conservation of matter and the equivalence of hydrostatic pressure built into the program code), then it can create novel situations that were not directly programmed. Such a case of deepened understanding was actually experienced by one of us after creating this program. In particular, working with the computer simulation he had developed, Snir noted he could make a large heavy object float in a small container of liquid, where the total weight of the liquid was less than the total weight of the object. This is understandable when one thinks of flotation in terms of pressures but seems to contradict the way that Archimedes' law is typically formulated in textbooks and in Archimedes' writings (see Snir, 1991, for further details about how this contradiction should be explained and its historical roots).

Although most computer simulations typically use screen visuals that provide simply a cartoon-like picture of a laboratory phenomenon (what we call pictorial representations), the program designer can choose to create other kinds of visuals as well: visuals that make "observable" what is in nature "unobservable." One important kind of "unobservable" is a set of interrelated concepts. In a conceptually enhanced simulation, we add a visual representation of the concepts used in explaining a specific phenomenon (the theoretical level) to the representation of the observable features of the objects (the object level). This enables the students to switch between two levels of thinking about the same phenomenon and to live in (or experience) the conceptual space in which the expert thinks.

For example, the different programs that we designed for this teaching unit involved a progression of conceptual visual models for density. Both our programs concerned with sinking and floating and with building objects used a basic grid-and-dots model (see Figure 13-2). In this conceptual model, each box stands for a standard unit of volume (size unit), each dot represents a standard unit of weight (weight unit), and the number of dots per box corresponds to the density. Material kind is represented in two ways: by the color of the material (orange, blue, green, etc.) and by the density of the material (green material has 1 dot/box; purple has 2 dots/box and so on).

Using these programs, students can switch back and forth between viewing the object (or liquid) with either pictorial or conceptually enhanced models. In the pictorial representation, objects are displayed as rectangles of varying sizes (without internal grids) filled with different colors corresponding to the type material they are made of. However, there is no explicit visual representation of weight or density. In the conceptually enhanced representation, objects are displayed using the grid-and-dots model that provides explicit and interrelated visual representations of size, weight, and density. In this way, the model offers a distinct visual referent for density, and helps students "see" how density and weight are distinct yet interrelated quantities.

One of our programs (the thermal expansion program) gives students a choice of two conceptually enhanced models for understanding this phenomenon (see Figure 13-4). The first model is basically a revision of our basic grid-and-dots model. In this revision, individual boxes get bigger when the material is heated. Thus, the student can see that the same amount of weight is now distributed in a larger volume. Dots per box still stand for material kind, but no longer represent density since the size of

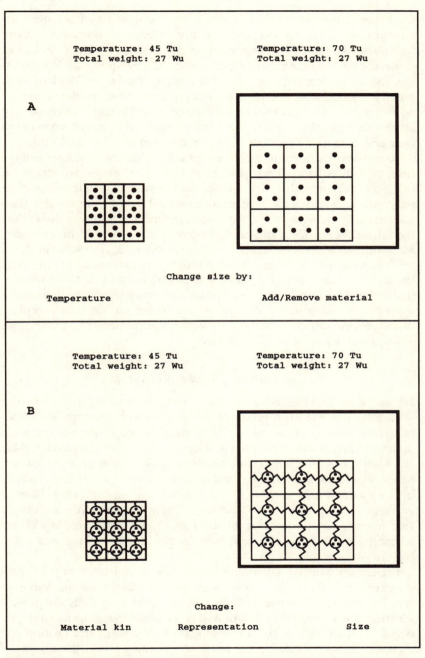

Figure 13-4 The two models of thermal expansion used in our computer programs.

the boxes is not constant. This motivates a discussion of the need for standard units. The second model returns to standard units and is more "atomistic" in flavor. It represents material kind by dots per circle, but shows the circles some distance apart (connected by squiggles). With heating, the circles stay the same size, but move further apart. Working with multiple models with different kinds of representations for the same phenomenon may help students to understand an important metaconceptual point about modeling: it is important for models to represent attributes in clear and consistent ways but there is more than one way to do this.

To summarize, our unit used conceptually enhanced computer simulations as well as hand-drawn student models. The specific advantages of using computer-based models include the fact that: (1) students can independently alter two of the elements of the visual model, with the computer automatically changing the third visual element in a way that shows how the three elements form an interdependent system; (2) students can interact with the simulations and try to discover the rules embodied in them; and (3) students can begin to link multiple representations for the same situations (verbal, pictorial, conceptual, and numeric data representations). Further, using computer simulations, students can easily perform experiments that in the real world would be hard to do with precision, would involve difficult numbers, or would involve unsafe materials, thus aiding their discovery of basic patterns.

Integration of Teaching Elements

We have described the various components of the teaching unit. However, we believe that the main power of the unit lies in the way these components are interwoven so that each illuminates the other and enhances understanding at a different level of scientific instruction. In practice, there are many ways this interaction can be managed by a creative teacher; hence, we are not advocating a fixed or invariant cycle of activities. Indeed, in our own teaching unit we found it natural to use somewhat different sequences among activities at different points in the unit, with class discussion interspersed throughout all activities. And there were some classes where it was natural to include at least three different elements in one class period.

Laboratory work or classroom demonstrations were often used to introduce students to new phenomena, while the modeling work and computer simulations were often used to help students clarify their ideas and provide for themselves a deeper explanation of those phenomena. To illustrate, we began the unit with a student investigation of sinking and floating and then moved into modeling materials and working with a simulation of sinking and floating using conceptually enhanced models. Similarly, we introduced students to thermal expansion with the ball and ring demonstration, followed by activities in which we asked students to model what they had observed about what happened to the weight and size of the ball, and infer what happened to the density.

However, this was not the only function of laboratory work in our teaching unit and we did not feel rigidly compelled always to introduce new phenomena in this way. Indeed, sometimes new aspects of a phenomenon were first explored in a simulation and only subsequently verified through laboratory work. For example, students first explored the effects of different liquids on sinking and floating in the computer simulation (because it is easier to do a range of experiments with liquids of different densities in this environment) and only subsequently confirmed through classroom demonstrations that the same object would behave in different ways in different liquids. Similarly, the phenomenon of level of submergence was first focused on in the computer simulation, and once students thought they understood this concept and had a way to predict level of submergence, they followed it up with classroom experiments.

Thus, there were two-way interactions between the laboratory and modeling: laboratory work informing the modeling, and ideas developed through modeling informing one's laboratory work.

Learning from Students

It is important to note that the process of building and implementing a teaching unit designed to construct concepts though a cooperative effort of students and the teacher has an impact on the two partners: the students and the teachers. While the students go through a cycle of changing and clarifying their concepts by using models, for example, or class discussion, we the curriculum designers and teachers go through cycles of refining and improving our materials based on what we have learned from the students. For example, we have learned that intuitively many students used shading intensity as a technique for modeling density. Thus, in the next version of our software, we provided multiple conceptual models for density (in addition to our basic grid-and-dots model), including an intensity shading model. In addition, we have come to more fully appreciate how students' undifferentiated concept of weight/density is supported by alternative conceptions about matter itself. Thus, we have expanded our teaching unit to include a unit that allows students to confront some fundamental questions about matter. Both examples illustrate how constructing understanding with students works two ways: We teachers and curriculum designers construct our understanding of students' ideas and needs, and learn how to negotiate this conceptual terrain with them, while our students construct deeper understandings of matter, density, and the process of modeling in scientific inquiry.

References

Barton, R. F. 1970. *Simulation and gaming*. Englewood Cliffs, NJ: Prentice-Hall.
Brown, D., and J. Clement. 1987. *Overcoming misconceptions in mechanics: A comparison of two example-based teaching strategies*. Paper presented at the AERA Annual Meeting, Washington, DC.

Carey, S. 1985. *Conceptual change in childhood*. Cambridge, MA: MIT Press.

Grosslight, L., S. Smith, C. Unger, J. Snir, and C. Smith. 1988. *Weight and density: Lesson plans*. Curriculum Materials No. TM88-23. Cambridge, MA: Harvard Graduate School of Education, Educational Technology Center.

Nussbaum, J., and S. Novick. 1982. Alternative frameworks, conceptual conflict and accommodation: Toward a principled teaching strategy. *Instructional Science* 11 (3): 183–200.

Smith, C., S. Carey, and M. Wiser. 1985. On differentiation: A case study of the development of the concepts of size, weight and density. *Cognition* 21: 177–237.

Smith, C., J. Snir, and L. Grosslight. 1992. Using conceptual models to facilitate conceptual change: The case of weight-density differentiation. *Cognition and Instruction* 9 (3): 221–83.

Snir, J. 1991. Sink or float? What do the experts think? or: The historical development of explanations for flotation. *Science Education* 75: 595–609.

———, C. Smith, and L. Grosslight. 1993. Conceptually enhanced simulations: A computer tool for science teaching. *Journal of Science Education & Technology* 2(2): 373–88.

Strike, K. A., and G. J. Posner. 1985. A conceptual change view of learning and understanding. In *Cognitive structure and conceptual change*, edited by L. West and A. L. Pines. New York: Academic Press.

Viennot, L. 1979. Spontaneous reasoning in elementary dynamics. *European Journal of Science Education* 1: 205–21.

White, B. Y., and P. Horwitz. 1987. *ThinkerTools: Enabling children to understand physical laws* BBN Report 6470. Cambridge, MA: Bolt, Beranek, & Newman.

———. 1988. Computer microworlds and conceptual change: A new approach to science education. In *Improving learning: New perspectives*, edited by P. Ramsden. London: Kogan Page.

Wiser, M., and S. Carey. 1983. When heat and temperature were one. In *Mental models*, edited by D. Gentner and A. Stevens. Hillsdale, NJ: Erlbaum.

Wiser, M., and D. Kipman. 1988. *The differentiation of heat and temperature: An evaluation of the effect of microcomputer models on students' misconceptions* Tech. Report TR88–20. Cambridge, MA: Harvard Graduate School of Education, Educational Technology Center.

Wiser, M., L. Grosslight, and C. Unger. 1989. *Can conceptual computer models aid ninth graders' differentiation of heat and temperature?* Tech. Report TR89–6. Cambridge, MA: Harvard Graduate School of Education, Educational Technology Center.

14

Teaching the Metacurriculum: A New Approach to Enhancing Subject-Matter Learning

STEVEN H. SCHWARTZ and DAVID N. PERKINS

Studying BASIC is Jeff's first experience with computers. He finds it kind of interesting and kind of hard at the same time. In fact, he can't seem to make up his mind how much he really likes it. "So often," he says to himself, "you don't quite know what to do."

A case in point for Jeff happened when the class had been studying the FOR/NEXT loop. The next day, there was an exercise to program that did not seem to have a place for the FOR/NEXT loop. Jeff scratched his head over the dilemma. Finally, he wrote this:

FOR N = 1 TO 1

And, after that line, Jeff continued with the rest of his program.

Jeff deserves congratulations for his cleverness. He found a neat resolution of a perennial dilemma for students: How do you use the concept that was just taught, even though you don't appear to need it to solve the problem at hand? Still, that Jeff should feel pressed to adopt such a tactic points to something odd about the typical conduct of instruction.

And this tactic of Jeff's is only the tip of a chilly iceberg of difficulties concerning typical instruction in mathematics, science, and programming. Over the past several years, research in these areas has disclosed that instruction leaves students with a great variety of misconceptions and shortfalls in problem solving (Clement, 1982, 1983; Driver, Guesne, and Tiberghien, 1985; McCloskey, 1983; Novak, 1987; Perkins and Martin, 1986; Perkins and Simmons, 1988; Schoenfeld, 1987; White, 1983;

Wiser and Kipman,1988). The prevalence both of lack of understanding and of odd misunderstandings challenges investigators and educators to fathom why present instruction so often teaches such subject matters poorly and to frame possible solutions.

Responding to these and other concerns, researchers and educators working at the Educational Technology Center have evolved a form of instructional intervention called a "metacourse." Now a metacourse is not a course at all in the conventional sense, but rather a set of supplementary ideas and activities that rides piggyback on the regular course (for instance, beginning BASIC), augmenting it in ways that deepen student understanding and improve problem solving. As the name "metacourse" suggests, an intervention in this style provides metacognitive and metaconceptual support to students as they strive to master a new subject matter.

Perhaps a metacourse to go with Jeff's instruction in BASIC could give him and other students a different and deeper take on programming. And perhaps metacourses for other subject matters such as algebra could be helpful as well. In the following pages, we will discuss the general idea of metacourses and articulate two particular examples. However, first let us return to Jeff's dilemma to draw out its implications further.

Jeff's resolution of his dilemma discloses some disturbing aspects of his picture of programming. Plainly and understandably he feels that it is important to include whatever has recently been taught. Also, he may have a notion that a proper program comes about by including the right forms or templates in the program—in this case, a FOR/NEXT loop with whatever pretext. He may not see a program as a functional entity with each part justified by the job it does—with no place for a part that does nothing. Still, Jeff has done quite a bit better than several of his classmates. Extraneous command or not, his program ran.

If Jeff and many of his classmates think in too "syntactic" a way about programs, not attending enough to what they tell the computer to do, the same can be said about students' understandings of other formal languages, the language of algebra rather than BASIC, for instance. Suppose, for example, Jeff encountered the well-known "students and professors" problem (Clement, Lochhead, and Monk, 1981; Ehrlich, Soloway, and Abbott, 1982; Soloway, Lochhead, and Clement, 1982). You are asked to write an algebraic expression saying that, at a certain university, there are six times as many students as professors. Jeff, as with many others, would probably write an expression like this:

$$6 * S = P$$

A careful look at this response reveals that something is very wrong. Suppose, for example, that the university has 1000 students. Then, according to the formula, there are 6000 professors—a truly exceptional teacher/student ratio. An examination of the instructions suggests what has gone wrong. People who give this answer have composed it by literally translating the surface language of the instructions: "six times as many students" gets coded as $6 * S$. Unfortunately, this puts the multiplier of six on the wrong side of the equation.

There are some notable similarities between Jeff's supposed response to the students and professors problem and his handling of FOR/NEXT. In both, Jeff takes a template-like approach to the task at hand, attempting to deal with it by plugging in expressions that seem to have a suitable surface pattern.

So how can we conduct instruction in these subject matters so that students take a more "semantic" and less "syntactic" approach to them, attending to what symbolic expressions mean, not just their rules and forms? How can we conduct instruction so that students adopt a more strategic and insightful approach to problem solving? So that students are more reflective about the subject matter and their own learning of it?

In this chapter, we first discuss a general stance toward improving instruction in mathematics, science, and programming that has evolved at the Educational Technology Center. Then we describe an example of the form of intervention mentioned earlier, a "metacourse" designed to enhance students' learning of the BASIC computer language. We profile briefly the rather positive findings yielded by several evaluations. Then we characterize the general features of a metacourse, with suggestions about how these principles can be applied to the design of metacourses for other subjects including one for beginning algebra now under construction. Finally, we turn to the more encompassing issue of substantive wide-scale change in educational practice, drawing morals from our experience that go beyond the particulars of metacourse design.

A Perspective on Improving Education

From the inception of ETC the researchers and educators involved have focused on a "pedagogy of understanding" wherein students would develop a genuine comprehension of key concepts, an improved ability to formulate and solve problems, and an overall grasp of the nature of science and mathematics . The overall approach might best be summarized in terms of the following five broad recommendations.

Focus on Specific "Targets of Difficulty"

For educational interventions to be effective, they must emerge from careful investigation of particular examples within content domains rather than from broad generalizations. While students do exhibit similar learning difficulties in diverse content areas, they also face unique problems within particular domains. Heat and temperature, or weight and density in science, or fractions and ratio quantities in mathematics, are examples of such concepts. Likewise within the content area of computer programming, a subject many students find difficult to learn, a number of key conceptions seem critical.

Have a Clear Understanding of Student Models and Theories

It is clear from research summarized in earlier chapters that students do not undertake various academic courses with a "tabula rasa" concerning scientific and mathematical phenomena. Instead, they come with existing theories, models, and misconceptions of key concepts, based on their everyday experience and previous instruction. In particular, many students enter a high school programming course with misconceptions about precisely what a computer and computer programs do. We have to identify and understand these misconceptions if we are to devise effective means of encouraging students to accommodate more sophisticated understandings.

Use Technology Selectively

Technology is most effective in the classroom when it makes a distinctive contribution to learning and teaching as indicated in the second section of this volume. A number of studies have confirmed the value of concrete visual representations in helping students understand concepts and phenomena that otherwise might remain highly abstract and inaccessible (Gentner and Stevens, 1983; Kurland, Clement, Mawby, and Pea, 1987; Mayer, 1985; Perkins and Unger, in press). The computer is particularly well suited in realizing both static and dynamic visual representations of such concepts and phenomena. At its best it presents models and interactive learning environments that can be easily infused into existing curriculum and practice. Thus ETC's Programming Research Group designed a dynamic model of a computer and the actions that take place therein—the "Data Factory."

Integrate a "Meta-Level" of Instruction

Many studies suggest that students' learning increases when they become more explicitly aware of the nature of knowledge and evidence in a discipline, how to go about pursuing such knowledge, and how they can more closely monitor their own progress (Campione, Brown, Reeve, Ferrara, and Palincsar, 1991; Glazer, 1991; Perkins, 1992; Perkins and Salomon, 1989). Such "metacognitive" skills are emphasized in all the ETC curriculum interventions, from science and math groups through programming. Many of these seem likely to prove useful across disciplines. For example, considering the appropriateness of a model, or whether a problem is appropriately conceptualized, is sound practice in almost every content area.

Combine Collaborative Research and Implementation

The research teams at ETC have always included content area specialists, learning specialists, graduate student assistants, and subject-matter teachers in order to bring a broad perspective to the research and maximize chances for improvement of educational practice. Thus, our research on programming has focused on teachers' central concerns, and our interventions are designed to be readily implemented by teachers.

A Metacourse for Beginning BASIC

The research model previously described has been implemented most extensively by the programming group through the development of the "Metacourse for learning BASIC." The metacourse comprises 10 lessons, or about 15% of a one-semester high school course. The materials are designed to be like a vitamin shot integrated into the regular course, not a substitute for usual course content.

We use the prefix *meta* to mean that the materials focus on *skills* and *mental models* needed to learn particular content in a course rather than on the content itself. The metacourse stresses fundamental concepts and strategies students need to program successfully in BASIC, and it encourages them to reflect about what they are doing, why they are using those procedures, what progress they are making, and so on. The goal is to provide students with a conceptual framework and strategies they can use in organizing and implementing their programming knowledge. This framework includes (1) a schematic model of the computer—"the Data Factory"—(Figure 14-1) to help students understand what takes place in the computer and how to hand-execute the actions of various statements, (2) a systematic approach to understanding and producing code—in terms of a "Purpose, Syntax, Action" schema—(Figure 14-2), and (3) a set of strategies (metacognitive questions and prompts) to use when learning a new statement and designing or debugging a program.

The Data Factory is realized in a dynamic interactive format (on the IBM PC) wherein a robot performs operations in the Data Factory based on the instructions (program) it receives. The robot is called NAB, an acronym for "Not Awfully Bright." The name is used to emphasize to students the point that the computer does not know or understand what a program is supposed to do, a common student misconception; the computer just follows a small set of instructions in a mechanical manner. The model depicts variables and their values, characters on the screen, and the flow of control and information in the computer.

Next we introduce an analytical scheme for comprehending commands and command lines in terms of (1) the purpose of a command, (2) its legal syntax, and (3) its action in the computer as shown in the data factory. Teachers are encouraged to present, and students to utilize, this framework as a way to organize their learning of each new command. The metacourse

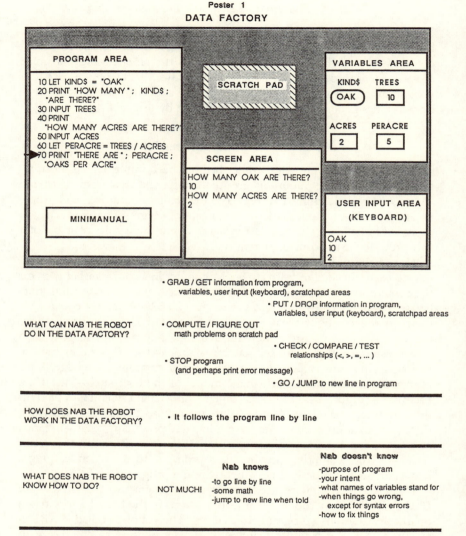

Figure 14-1 Poster 1—DATA FACTORY.

emphasizes the utility of employing the purpose-action-syntax schema when trying to understand the lines of a program during checking and testing of program parts or whole programs.

Finally, the metacourse enables teachers to provide students with a number of (1) metacognitive and metaconceptual heuristics, and (2) resources to help them understand and generate BASIC programs. For example, the problem-solving nature of comprehending and producing programs, in-

Poster 2
How To Understand What Code Does

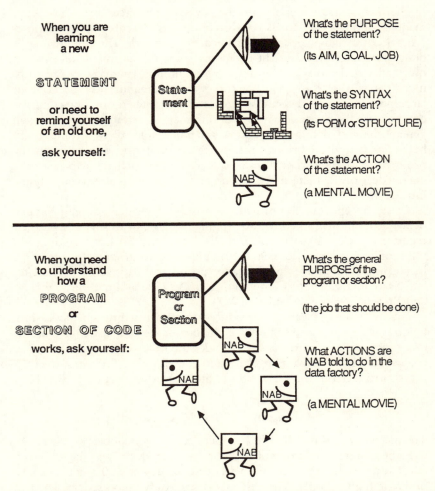

Figure 14-2 Poster 2—HOW TO UNDERSTAND WHAT CODE DOES.

volving multiple rounds of modeling, planning, or conjecturing, writing code, debugging or inferencing, emphasizes further conjecturing and testing. We suggest the strategy of looking for frequently occurring lines or chunks of code that work together to accomplish a particular job. We call such recurrent schema "patterns" (i.e., a summing pattern, a counting pattern), a term roughly synonymous with the "programming plans" described by Soloway and colleagues (Soloway and Ehrlich,1984). The metacourse stresses the importance of patterns for efficient comprehension of programs and program segments as well as their utility and portability in the construction of programs.

The metacourse materials also include such resources as: (1) a "Mini-manual" of quick easy-access BASIC commands presented in the purpose-syntax-action framework, accompanied by examples. The minimanual is designed to help the student overcome some of the initial information overload associated with learning a programming language. Seven common "patterns" also appear at the end of the minimanual. (2) A set of four large posters constantly on display in the computer room, depicting the data factory, the purpose-syntax-action framework, strategies for program generation and debugging, and a general "toolbox" of prompts and heuristics to use at various times when encountering difficulties in the programming enterprise. These posters are designed to help keep the major ideas of the metacourse salient, and in use, long after their original introduction.

These concepts in effect provide students with elementary self-prompts, or metacognitions, tuned to the programming context, that add to their repertoire of elementary problem-solving strategies. Such self-guiding and self-monitoring heuristics help them in learning to program, as they have helped improve student performance on other cognitive tasks (Bereiter and Scardamalia, 1986; Campione, et al., 1991; Larkin, 1985; Palinscar and Brown, 1984; Schoenfeld, 1987).

The metacourse ideas are introduced to students through the lessons, taught about one per week toward the beginning of a semester and one every two weeks toward the end. Besides the lessons themselves, teachers receive sample homework problems and guidelines for "infusing" the concepts introduced in the lessons throughout their instruction in BASIC.

Testing the BASIC Metacourse

The metacourse in BASIC was first pilot tested by members of the development group in the spring of 1986. It was then revised and the following fall 9 teachers field tested the metacourse with over 300 students in 17 different high schools. The results of that study (reported in detail in Schwartz, Perkins, Estey, Kruidenier, and Simmons, 1989) were quite positive. Its impact as evaluated by a fairly conventional test of comprehension, hand-execution, debugging, and program generation problems was considerable. The metacourse groups compared to control groups produced overall gains of about half a standard deviation, with gains on different types of problems from one-third to two-thirds of a standard deviation. While the metacourse stressed mastery of BASIC rather than transfer to general cognitive skills, significant "near transfer" was observed in the experimental groups on a task that most closely resembled programming (formally describing a series of actions in a story in terms of a sequence of "repeats" and "decides").

The experimental groups in this study came from high schools that had agreed to participate in an intensive laboratory site research and implementation experience, entailing considerable support for teachers directly involved in testing curriculum materials. Therefore it was possible that the gains we observed might have been attributable primarily to the unusual support provided teachers, not to the metacourse itself. Thus, it was quite reassuring when nearly identical results were obtained the following spring with a new group of students whose teachers received minimal training and support.

The instructors in the spring 1987 study were given a brief two-hour introduction to the philosophy of the BASIC metacourse and received the 10-lesson package. The only other support provided was two-page "Metacourse Memos" containing additional teaching tips formulated by the instructors who had used the metacourse the previous semester. One "memo" for each of the 10 lessons was mailed to the instructors prior to the presentation of each lesson. The teachers in this study were able to elicit performances from their students on a variety of types of BASIC problems that were indistinguishable from those obtained in the previous study where teachers had more extensive supports. Thus there is evidence that the metacourse in BASIC can provide teachers with a powerful pedagogy for improving student performance, without requiring extensive faculty development time (Schwartz, Perkins, Estey, Kruidenier, and Simmons, 1989).

Beyond BASIC: Metacourses in General

The metacourse in BASIC can be taken as one exemplar of a class of interventions in the same general style and promising the same spectrum of benefits. For example, in collaboration with colleagues in South Africa, we have developed and conducted field testing of a metacourse in algebra, designed to help disadvantaged nonwhite South Africans understand algebra and solve problems better. Although we are not at the point of formal testing, the general architecture of the algebra intervention offers an opportunity to generalize about the design of metacourses. In general, we suggest that, for any curriculum in mathematics, science, programming, or, indeed, humanistic subject matters, there is a "metacurriculum," a range of metacognitive and metaconceptual ideas that get little attention in normal instruction and invite cultivation (Perkins, 1992).

What, then, are the general properties that characterize a metacourse and how do they appear both in the BASIC metacourse and the algebra metacourse under construction? While we cannot provide an algorithm that will guarantee easy development of a worthwhile metacourse in any area, we can indicate some general guidelines based on research in cognitive psychology that should increase the chances of success. It is useful to profile the idea of a metacourse under four categories: content, structure, materials, and teacher education.

Content

First, we should emphasize what a metacourse is *not:* A metacourse does not seek to supplant the existing text, although it may challenge some ideas in that text. Instead, a metacourse strives to provide kinds of "higher order" content—mental models, problem solving and learning strategies, and so on—that (1) are not normally addressed in the subject matter in question, and (2) address known student difficulties in ways likely to be effective according to research on learning and problem solving.

Thus a metacourse should contain concrete visual models of the phenomena under study. Ideally these should be dynamic and manipulable so that changes in the state of the model occur as a result of a certain limited number of legal operations. This can be done through concrete materials, software implementation, and often rather well through students' "mental animation" of images presented statically. Naturally, a model should behave in a fashion analogous to the target phenomenon while referring to the relevant variables. For example, the "robot" in our Data Factory can only perform some half dozen or so simple actions (e.g., store, compare, go to),which correspond to the limited number of fundamental information manipulations that occur in the computer.

Like the BASIC metacourse, the algebra metacourse provides visual mental models to help students with concepts known to puzzle them. For example, various uses of letters in algebra are clarified through a running metaphor of a letter in algebra as a box with a number in it. For another example, the entire structure of algebra is characterized as a workshop, with parts (e.g., numbers, operations, letters), tools (e.g., distributivity, commutativity, adding the same thing to both sides of an equation), and structures that you build and modify (e.g., algebraic expressions and equations). This image fulfills the same integrative role as the Data Factory image for the programming metacourse.

Research by Richard Mayer (Mayer, 1976,1981,1989), as well as our own experience with the BASIC metacourse, testifies to the efficacy of imagistic mental models in clarifying hard concepts. Further, students encountering a concrete visual model are more apt to compare it with their own naive model and change toward a more appropriate conception (Joshua and Dupin, 1987).

In addition to visual models, a good metacourse should contain some simple category systems that help learners to organize their knowledge in the domain. Thus, the Purpose, Action, Syntax schema in the BASIC metacourse aids students in learning commands meaningfully. Because students can get confused about the different roles of letters in algebra, the algebra metacourse distinguishes four specific roles: unknowns (to solve for), variables (as in a function), constants (pi, e), and parameters (A, B, C in the quadratic formula, for example). It's also emphasized that sometimes a letter can play more than one role or shift roles in the course of a problem.

Both the BASIC and algebra metacourses teach problem-solving strategies involving heuristics that force an examination of the student's ongoing cognitive processes and the nature of the task they are attending to. In the BASIC metacourse, we encourage students to ask themselves constantly, "What is the purpose of this section of code?" "Have I seen a pattern like this before?" "What actions are actually taking place?" "What code accomplishes such an action?" And so on. (Perkins and Martin, 1986; Perkins, Martin, and Farady, 1986.)

Likewise, an interesting feature of the algebra metacourse is a generic self-monitoring strategy with the mnemonic slogan "What? Why? Something else to try?" Students are encouraged to stop periodically, asking themselves what they are doing at the moment, why they are doing that, and, if it's not yielding progress, what else they might try instead. This reflects research showing that students often perseverate in ineffective approaches to problems, failing to monitor and redirect themselves (Schoenfeld, 1987).

Structure

A metacourse involves (1) occasional lessons spotted throughout the period of instruction, designed to introduce mental models, problem-solving strategies, and other metacourse content; and (2) an infusion plan for keeping the ideas alive as the regular instruction proceeds. Both (1) and (2) are distinctive characteristics: Most supplementary materials are taught all at once rather than spread out, and most have no plan for keeping the ideas alive once the instruction has occurred.

To exemplify, like the programming metacourse, the algebra metacourse consists of a number of lessons introducing key ideas: in the case of algebra, the "workshop" integrative model, the concept of a variable, mental monitoring, the concept of an algebraic expression, and related matters. Metacourses include plans for keeping the ideas alive once they are introduced. For instance, once students have learned the "number in a box" mental model for the uses of letters in algebra, the teacher is encouraged to utilize this metaphor on a number of specific occasions: when setting up an equation and choosing variable names, when deriving a solution on the blackboard, and so on. Thus, the ideas of the metacourse are designed to infuse the instruction.

Materials

Important premises of the materials side of metacourse design are: (1) Materials should be mostly for the teacher, to minimize costs; we believe that, to see wide use, innovative materials must cost substantially less than a textbook per student per year. (2) Certain carefully selected materials should be visible in the classroom, for instance, in the form of posters, to stimulate attention to the metacourse concepts; without visual reminders, infusion of the ideas throughout the subject matter is unlikely to occur. (3) The materials should minimize classroom management and "front end hump" problems of incorporating the metacourse into instruction. Thus, the materials do not depend on a strong support structure for teachers, in whose absence innovations that make substantial extra work for teachers are routinely and understandably rejected.

Thus, for example, most of the BASIC and algebra metacourse ideas are contained in the teacher's guide. However, in both metacourses, large posters displayed prominently in the classroom convey mental models and key problem-solving strategies. Also, in both metacourses, students receive a "minimanual" that characterizes important aspects of the subject matter in terms of the central integrating image. For the BASIC metacourse, the minimanual profiles the most common BASIC commands in terms of the Purpose, Syntax, Action schema, as well as giving simple examples of code. For the algebra metacourse, the minimanual reinforces the "workshop" metaphor by organizing into categories the basic algebra "tools" commutativity, transposition, and so on—as well as explaining and exemplifying them.

Teacher Education

An important question for any instructional innovation concerns how teachers learn about and gain skill with the innovation. Metacourses are designed to have minimal in-service demands, because cost bottlenecks prevent any innovation that requires several days of in-service from propagating widely. As reported earlier, experience with the BASIC metacourse has shown that it indeed has relatively modest in-service demands. The field-testing of the algebra metacourse suggests that many South African teachers in nonwhite settings would benefit from a more extended period of teacher development. These teachers are often less familiar with the kinds of ideas advanced in the matacourse as well as with students' problems of learning the subject matter. With this in view, the algebra metacourse is still designed to reduce in-service needs.

Metacourses also are designed to be resonant with teachers' concerns in facing an innovation, as detailed, for example in the Concerns-Based Adoption Model (Hall and Hord, 1987; also see related concepts in Fullan, 1991). This research-based stage model of teachers' work with innovations profiles teachers' shifting concerns about an innovation as they first encounter it, begin to work with it, and become experienced in its use. For example, when teachers commence work with an innovation, according to the model they are most concerned with practical issues—how to conduct lessons competently, how to manage seatwork, how to ensure reasonable student conduct. Thus, metacourse materials are crafted to speak to these concerns directly, with lesson plans that are easy to follow and activities for students that are clearly defined. Or, for another example, the model emphasizes that a principle concern of teachers, and a strong motivator, is payoffs for students. Accordingly, both the BASIC and the algebra teacher materials put clear characterizations of expected payoffs for students near the front of every lesson.

Another concern of metacourse design is to invite teachers to actively interpret and extend the metacourse materials. In this way the metacourse encourages the sort of active sense-making on the part of teachers that it strives to support in students. In the BASIC and Algebra metacourses, this is handled through infusion activities. Whereas the metacourse lessons that introduce key concepts and models are specified step by step, appropriate infusion activities are only sketched. Teachers are explicitly encouraged to innovate, to find their own opportunities, to do whatever they can to infuse throughout their instruction the ideas introduced in the metacourse lessons. Indeed, they are invited to extend those ideas, adding mental models and strategies of their own, for example.

Beyond Metacourses: The Problem of Lasting Change in Education

While we believe that the "metacurriculum" is neglected and that metacourses are a valuable approach to develop toward change in education, we certainly do not believe that they are the only such approach. Indeed, our work on the metacourse concept has helped us toward a more overarching perspective on what substantive change in education requires, by way of metacourses or any other style of innovation.

It appears that several factors highly constrain viable designs for wide-scale change in education. To put the matter metaphorically, often developers seem to view an occasion for educational innovation as the artist's blank canvas: Any of a great variety of solutions might serve. Instead, we suggest that an occasion for educational innovation is much more like the mathematician's blank page: What gets written there is highly constrained by all sorts of considerations, else the results will not prove out.

To be more explicit, a number of conditions appear to be necessary for educational innovations with the potential of effecting widescale change (Perkins, 1992). Some concern content of the innovation but others involve quite different matters. For a sample of conditions regarding content, the innovation should take account of student misconceptions, otherwise many students will maintain their misconceptions despite the instruction. The approach should respect limitations of human working memory, which can make complex concepts inaccessible (e.g. Brainerd, 1983; Case, 1985, 1992). The approach should highlight semantics and the meanings of abstract symbolic expressions, because students will fall into "syntactic thinking" where they try to use ritual patterns of symbol manipulation to deal with problems (Resnick, 1987).

Considering matters other than content, the innovation should cost an order of magnitude less per student per year than a textbook, because otherwise it will be too costly to propagate. Understandably, decisions of the order of cost of a textbook tend to be conservative, since they are major budget commitments; one implication is that a substantial innovation probably cannot consist in a textbook. Also, the innovation should not create dramatically more work for teachers than they now undertake; teachers are overloaded as it is and are likely to reject innovations that burden them. Of course, in settings that support and reward special effort on the part of teachers, the story may be different; indeed, teachers who make a special effort may see that as an "investment" in the innovation and hence develop all the more commitment. However, it must be remembered that we are considering conditions for wide-scale change, and, in the great majority of school settings, supports and rewards for extra effort are scanty.

In addition, the innovation should interpenetrate the subject matter, otherwise it will just lead to an isolated "fix" of a few aspects of student learning. Many educational supplements occupy a few class periods and perhaps help students with a particularly troublesome concept or area of skill, but do little to enhance students' understanding or mastery of the subject matter in general. Finally, the innovation must respect teachers' priorities and concerns, even as it tries to expand and shift those priorities and concerns somewhat. Otherwise, teachers will feel uncomfortable with it and will reject it.

Although just a sample, these principles give some flavor of what we have in mind. They play out the analogy that educational development work is more like filling the mathematician's page than the artist's blank canvas. Unlike the artist, the mathematician *and* the developer designing for widescale change must meet a number of *necessary conditions*, in the sense of the logical distinction between necessary and sufficient conditions. In other words, if even one of these conditions is not met, the innovation is not likely to succeed on a wide scale. Or, to put it yet another way, the problem space in which the developer navigates has a conjunctive rather than a disjunctive character: An effective innovation pretty much must satisfy this condition *and* this *and* this, rather than this condition *or* this *or* this.

Is such a point too obvious to be worth making? We don't think so. In fact, a scan of the landscape of educational innovation suggests that innovations that hold the seeds of their own failure are a common pattern. We are struck by how often immense resources will be invested in the development of materials that, whatever their instructional merits, have a cost to users in dollars, effort, or risk that forbids their wide-scale adoption.

Metacourses may be one tool among many that produce viable models of change. They explicate key concepts and strategies of subject matters along with simple but powerful metacognitive prompts. They attempt significant, modest, manageable change. In certain ways, they challenge the standard curriculum even as they partner with it, raising questions about certain practices and nudging attention in new directions. Perhaps, by incremental extension, the metacourse can even take over the course, fundamentally changing both teacher and student behavior and ultimately our conception of what constitutes an acceptable course.

References

Bereiter, C., and M. Scardamalia. 1986. *The psychology of written composition.* Hillsdale, NJ: Erlbaum.

Brainerd, C. J. 1983. Working-memory systems and cognitive development. In *Recent advances in cognitive-developmental theory: Progress in cognitive development research,* edited by C. J. Brainerd, pp. 167–236. New York: Springer-Verlag.

Campione, J. C., A. L. Brown, R. A. Reeve, R. A. Ferrara, and A. S. Palincsar. 1991. Interactive learning and individual understanding: The case of reading and mathematics. In *Culture, schooling, and psychological development,* edited by L. T. Landsmann, pp. 136–70. Norwood, NJ: Ablex.

Case, R. 1985. *Intellectual development: Birth to adulthood.* New York: Academic Press.

———. 1992. *The mind's staircase: Exploring the conceptual underpinnings of children's thought and knowledge.* Hillsdale, NJ: Erlbaum.

Clement, J. 1982. Students' preconceptions in introductory mechanics. *American Journal of Physics* 50: 66–71.

———. 1983. A conceptual model discussed by Galileo and used intuitively by physics students. In *Mental models,* edited by D. Gentner and A. L. Stevens. Hillsdale, NJ: Erlbaum.

———, J. Lochhead, and G. Monk. 1981. Translation difficulties in learning mathematics. *American Mathematical Monthly* 88: 26–40.

Driver, R., E. Guesne, and A. Tiberghien, eds. 1985. *Children's ideas in science.* Philadelphia, PA: Open University Press.

Ehrlich, K., E. Soloway, and V. Abbott. 1982. *Transfer effects from programming to algebra word problems: A preliminary study.* Report No. 257. New Haven: Yale University Department of Computer Science.

Fullan, M. G. 1991. *The new meaning of educational change.* New York: Teachers College Press.

Gentner, D., and A. L. Stevens. 1983. *Mental models.* Hillsdale, NJ: Erlbaum.

Glazer, R. 1991. Intelligence as acquired knowledge. In *Intelligence: Reconceptualization and measurement,* edited by H. Rowe. Hillsdale, NJ: Erlbaum.

Hall, G. E., and S. M. Hord. 1987. *Change in schools: Facilitating the process.* Albany: State University of New York.

Johsua, S., and J. J. Dupin. 1987. Taking into account student conceptions in a didactic strategy: An example in physics. *Cognition and Instruction* 4(2):117–35.

Kurland, D. M., C. Clement, R. Mawby, and R. D. Pea. 1987. Mapping the cognitive demands of learning to program. In *Thinking: The Second International Conference,* edited by D. N. Perkins, J. Lochhead, and J. Bishop. Hillsdale, NJ: Erlbaum.

Larkin, J. 1987. Understanding problem representations and skill in physics. In *Thinking and learning skills. Vol. 2. Research and open questions,* edited by S. F. Chipman, J. W. Segal, and R. Glaser, pp. 141–59. Hillsdale, NJ: Erlbaum.

Mayer, R. E. 1976. Some conditions of meaningful learning for computer programming: Advance organizers and subject control of frame order. *Journal of Educational Psychology* 68: 143–50.

———. 1981. The psychology of how novices learn computer programming. *Computing Surveys* 13(11): 121–41.

———. 1985. Learning in complex domains: A cognitive analysis of computer programming. *The Psychology of Learning and Motivation* 19: 89–130.

———. 1989. Models for understanding. *Review of Educational Research* 59 (1): 43–64.

McCloskey, M. 1983. Naive theories of motion. In *Mental models*, edited by D. Gentner and A. L. Stevens, pp. 299–324. Hillsdale, NJ: Erlbaum.

Novak, J., ed. 1987. *The proceedings of the Second Misconceptions in Science and Mathematics Conference*. Ithaca, NY: Cornell University.

Palinscar, A.S., and A. L. Brown. 1984. Reciprocal teaching of comprehension-fostering and comprehension-monitoring activities. *Cognition and Instruction* 1: 117–76.

Perkins, D. N. 1992. *Smart schools: From training memories to educating minds*. New York: The Free Press.

———, and F. Martin. 1986. Fragile knowledge and neglected strategies in novice programmers. In *Empirical studies of programmers*, edited by E. Soloway and S. Iyengar, pp. 213–29. Norwood, NJ: Ablex.

——— and R. Simmons. 1988. Patterns of misunderstanding: An integrative model of misconceptions in science, mathematics, and programming. *Review of Educational Research* 58(3): 303–26.

———, and G. Salomon. 1989. Are cognitive skills context bound? *Educational Researcher* 18(1): 16–25.

———, and C. Unger. In press. A new look in representations for mathematics and science learning. *Instructional Science*.

———, F. Martin, F., and M. Farady. 1986. *Loci of difficulty in learning to program*. Tech. Report TR86-6. Cambridge, MA: Harvard Graduate School of Education, Educational Technology Center.

Resnick, L. B. 1987. Constructing knowledge in school. In *Development and learning: Conflict or congruence?*, edited by L. Liben, pp. 19–50. Hillsdale, NJ: Erlbaum.

Schoenfeld, A. H. 1987. *Mathematical problem solving*. New York: Academic Press.

Schwartz, S., D. N. Perkins, C. Estey, J. Kruidenier, and R. Simmons. 1989. A "metacourse" for BASIC: Assessing a new model for enhancing instruction. *Journal of Educational Computer Research* 5(3): 263–77.

Soloway, E., and K. Ehrlich. 1984. Empirical studies of programming knowledge. *IEEE Transaction on Software Engineering*, SE-10(5): 595–609.

Soloway, E., J. Lochhead, and J. Clement. 1982. Does computer programming enhance problem solving ability? Some positive evidence on algebra word problems. In *Computer Literacy*, edited by R. Seidel, R. Anderson, and B. Hunter. New York: Academic Press.

White, B. 1983. Sources of difficulty in understanding Newtonian dynamics. *Cognitive Science* 7(1): 41–65.

Wiser, M., and D. Kipman. 1988. The differentiation of heat and temperature: An evaluation of the effect of microcomputer models on students' misconceptions. July 1988. Educational Technology Center draft article.

15

Integrating Computers into Classroom Teaching: Cross-National Perspectives

MARGARET VICKERS and JANE SMALLEY

In most industrialized countries throughout the world, the availability of microcomputers in elementary and secondary schools increased rapidly during the 1980s (Cerych, 1982; Vickers, 1988). Yet many teachers ignored this new technology, and progress toward integrating computers into the teaching of existing subjects proceeded more slowly than might have been expected, given the rate of increase in the availability of hardware. Cross-national surveys conducted in the mid-1980s suggested that teachers of separate computer science courses were the main computer users, that few regular elementary and secondary school teachers were actual users, and that mathematics teachers were more likely to use computers in their lessons than teachers of other subjects (Becker, 1986; Pelgrum and Plomp, 1991).

Why did this gap arise between the level of supply of computer hardware and the level of computer uptake in classrooms? Possible answers to this question emerged as psychologists, ethnographers, and policy analysts showed how microcomputer use unsettled the normal routines of classroom life. Careful ethnographic studies suggested that profound changes in classroom dynamics followed the introduction of microcomputers to this delicately balanced environment. For example, researchers such as Sheingold and Hawkins found that regardless of the teacher's orientation, the use of computers in the classroom tended to result in higher levels of peer interaction and greater student control over their own learning. They also found that there is more student collaboration on computer-based tasks than on other classroom tasks (Hawkins et al.,1982). This comparative difference was consistent over time and for different classrooms. They found that some students acquire particular expertise with computer use and become "expert consultants" who advise other students on programming problems. This kind of role differentiation was also observed in Australian classrooms (Firkin et al., 1985). These dynamics can be a source of anxiety for teachers who feel they are no longer in charge of their classes, and that the students know more than they do. In addition, policy makers found that teachers did not know how to integrate computer applications into the existing curriculum.

Throughout the 1980s, a number of strategies for encouraging the integration of computers into classroom teaching emerged. This chapter provides a cross-national overview of this recent history by describing policies aimed at promoting the educational use of computers in elementary as well as secondary schools, and in language studies and history as well as mathematics and science, in four countries—Australia, France, Norway, and Scotland. Key elements of these policies included the development of software and complementary curriculum materials, participatory approaches to teacher development, and support for changes in school organization.

The first section of the chapter sets the scene by outlining broad patterns of classroom computer use in Europe, the United States, and Australia. The second section presents case studies of policies for educational computer use, indicating what has been found to work best in particular settings, and illustrating the complexity of developing programs that make teachers feel comfortable, if not enthusiastic, about the use of new technologies in their classrooms.

Patterns of Computer Use: An Overview

In the early 1980s, most industrialized countries launched major programs for introducing microcomputers into schools. Early activities were experimental and future directions for the innovation were not clear. The controversy over "computer science" emerged early, and at the Organization for Economic Cooperation and Development in Paris, an international debate among educators failed to resolve the issue of whether computers should be seen, essentially, as a learning tool, or whether programming should become a new element of the curriculum in its own right (OECD-CERI, 1986).

During this period, the OECD member countries divided themselves into two groups: those that developed "restricted" policies, aimed at introducing computer science into the vocational and academic upper-secondary schools only, and those that developed "comprehensive" policies endorsing the use of computers as a learning tool for all subject areas at all levels of schooling.

Countries with a strong "dual system" of apprenticeships—Austria, Germany, and Switzerland—fell into the first group. In those countries, computer science and computer literacy became compulsory subjects during the 1980s. While computer use in other subject areas remained permissible, the scarcity of hardware outside computer laboratories restricted the integration of computers into other curriculum areas in these countries.

The second group of countries—especially the United States, the United Kingdom, Australia, and certain provinces of Canada—endorsed both computer literacy courses and integration across the curriculum from the very beginning. But integrated approaches were slow to develop, because in most places the hardware found its way into the schools before sufficient attention had been paid to the curriculum development and teacher education that would be required to make it effective.

In Norway, Scotland, and the Netherlands, government-mandated programs supporting integrated computer use were launched in 1986/87 (Nagtegaal and Scholtes, 1987c; OECD-CERI,1987c; SED,1987). In each of these countries the central government funded the creation of subject-related software packages and supportive curriculum materials. Their approaches to in-service teacher development at both local and national levels are described below. But France was the first country to commit itself to integrating the use of microcomputers across the curriculum, and the lessons from the French experience are still salient for countries seeking to follow this path.

A Cross-National Sample of Case Studies

France: Integration by Decree

From the beginning of the 1980s the French Ministry of Education took a firm position on educational computing. Integrated use across the curriculum was declared as policy, and computer awareness was not to be taught as a separate subject. The National Government provided substantial resources for equipment and software. In 1981, the plan called "10,000 Micros" was implemented, followed by the "100,000 Micros" plan in 1983. Then, in January 1985, the Prime Minister announced the plan "Informatique pour Tous," under which every lower secondary school in France was provided with at least one professional and six domestic-type microcomputers, and each upper secondary school obtained a network of one professional and eight domestic-type microcomputers, plus three independent professional computers. Under this ambitious plan, over 157,000 teachers received a 50-hour initiation course in computing by the end of 1985.

Despite increases in equipment *provision,* a report of l'Inspection Générale, Ministère de l'Education Nationale (France, 1985) found that actual microcomputer *use* in classrooms remained steady or even declined, equipment was underused, and teachers were disaffected. Although lack of quality software was cited as a partial cause, the main reasons given for teachers not using the microcomputers related to pedagogical organization and teacher training. One-quarter of the teaching force had been trained in how to use the machines themselves, but these courses did not provide the necessary experience in actually applying computers in classroom settings.

To begin with, teachers had no idea what effect the computers would have on learning interactions and dynamics in the classroom, and their tentative experiments confirmed their fears. The Inspectorate report found that teachers were reluctant to use the networks they had been given because the number of workstations was inadequate for whole class teaching, and the problems of organization resulting from this were regarded as insurmountable.

The introduction of microcomputers seemed to disturb the prevailing pedagogical culture of French secondary classrooms. Teachers complained about the organizational problems of using microcomputers. Because they did not have one computer for every child, whole-class management strategies could not be used, and many teachers seemed to be unfamiliar with group work or individualized classroom management techniques. An alternative approach, which eliminated the need to adapt classroom management to the computer challenge, emerged in many French schools. The computers were assigned to a laboratory where students could use them on a "self-serve basis" to do basic skill practice in their own time or when released from classroom lessons.

For teachers socialized into a tradition of whole-class teaching, computer use may demand a complete reconstruction of their strategies for classroom management—a complex and time-consuming task. In addition, the presence of microcomputers can be a source of anxiety for teachers who feel they are no longer in charge of their classes, because the students often know more than they do about how to use this technology. Taken-for-granted assumptions about "being a teacher" are thus called into question. It is not surprising that the early French initiative, in which teacher education was seen as basically a computer skill issue, did not result in the widespread and integrated use of microcomputers in French classrooms.

Under the new "Plan National Informatique," which began in 1986, the Ministry announced that an emphasis on the *pedagogical* aspects of computing should replace the earlier technological emphasis, and that in the future teachers should be given more time for *auto gestion* (a combination of self-teaching and peer-supported learning) within the schools. This new approach, combined with an energetic program for creating subject-related software, seems to have increased the level of computer use in French classrooms well beyond the levels reported in 1985 (Dumont, 1988; France, 1985; Pelgrum and Plomp, 1991). Yet according to a survey conducted in 1989, computer use in France still seemed to be dominated by technological commercial studies and by mathematics (Pelgrum and Plomp, 1991).

Scotland: A National System for Teacher Participation

Beginning as early as 1982, the Scottish Education Department and the Convention of Scottish Local Authorities began to craft a National Plan for computer education in Scottish schools. The plan proposed three key objectives: to develop software packages for each subject area, to help teachers understand *how* new software might be used to teach particular topics, and to support teachers as they grappled with any changes in attitudes and behavior that might result from the integration of computers into their classrooms. Intrinsic to this plan was the conviction that the knowledge base for educational computing could be best developed by promoting high levels of teacher participation in the development of teaching kits and in the provision of in-service education throughout the local areas.

Scotland is about the size of the state of Maine and with a population of 5.5 million people it houses roughly as many people as Indiana or Virginia. The Scottish Office Education Department (SOED) plays a role similar to that of many state departments of education in the United States, with one major exception. While funding in the United States is dependent on a local tax base, and therefore varies from school district to school district, funding in Scotland is centralized through the SOED. Local education authorities in Scotland carry out many of the same personnel, administrative, and curriculum functions as do the school district authorities in the United States, but because local authorities in Scotland are funded through the SOED, the playing field among the local authority areas is more level than in the United States.

By combining national coordination with local authority involvement, the Scottish Education Department has promoted high levels of teacher participation in three key aspects of the development and implementation of technology-enhanced curricula. The approach encompasses:

- Development of software for particular topics.
- Development of curricular kits to support the software.
- Implementation of teacher-based "train-the-teacher" programs to support the use of particular software items and curricular kits. In train-the-teacher programs, a selected group of teachers is trained and then given release time to train other teachers.

Teachers need to know how a particular piece of software can be used to teach particular topics, as well as the effect its use may have on classroom practice. Recognizing that the expertise involved in developing materials for successful classroom use lies with teachers, Scottish policy makers have decided that the most effective way to develop technology-enhanced curricula is to give innovative teachers time to develop teaching kits for software use, and then have those teachers provide in-service education throughout their region. In this approach, the goal is clearly teaching with computers rather than teaching about computers. An important and interesting feature of this process is that both the software production and the interpretation of how software might be used are treated as teacher education activities (SED, 1987).

The production of software through teacher partnerships is now a well-established model in Scotland. National needs assessments identify areas and topics for which new products are required. Teachers who have developed creative proposals for dealing with these topics are recruited into working groups where they are supported by professional programmers. Through an iterative process, the software is drafted, field tested, improved, and, finally, packaged into a teaching kit that includes supporting materials. This process is orchestrated by a part-government, part-private company known as SCET—the Scottish Council for Educational Technology. SCET derives it funding partly from the Scottish Office Education Department and partly from commercial ventures, including the sale of software and educational kits (Hunter, 1987; SED, 1987).

A variety of schemes for the release of teachers for such work has been organized. The most common one is for staff release to be paid for by SCET, while field testing is organized free of charge by schools. SCET also has a major information dissemination role in this area, publishing a free newspaper that draws attention to effective uses of information technology in schools at all levels of the Scottish education system. Until recently, local schools received SCET software free of charge through local authorities, but, more and more, schools are being asked to purchase directly from SCET because the rising costs of material production must be recovered (Turnbull, 1993).

Over the last decade, Scotland has achieved a considerable increase in microcomputer use in a wide range of subjects across the secondary curriculum, and Scottish policy makers are confident that much of this can be attributed to the involvement of teachers in software development and in-service activities (SED,1987; Roebuck, 1993). Creating a classroom culture that leads to increased student interaction and participation has been an explicit goal of Scotland's educational leaders, and they have used the introduction of microcomputers to promote hands-on exploratory learning and problem-solving approaches.

Scottish educators estimated that by 1987, technology-enhanced curricula were being used in at least half the humanities departments in Scottish secondary schools (SED, 1987). This represents a considerable change from the early 1980s, when mathematics and science teachers dominated the use of microcomputers in schools. Scotland's achievement in this area also contrasts with that of continental Europe and the United States, where a 1989 IEA survey showed that mathematics, science, and technology teachers were still the predominant users of microcomputers (Pelgrum and Plomp 1991).

Scotland's commitment to this participatory model is continuing into the 1990s, as educators seek to exploit the potential of the latest generation of interactive multimedia technologies. Another part-private, part-public company—the Scottish Interactive Technology Centre (SITC)—is playing the leading role in this area. The cost of multimedia technologies makes it highly undesirable simply to hand out equipment and software to teachers who may be unaware of its value. To give teachers direct experience with these technologies, the SOED has invested heavily in delivering in-service education to teachers and principals in the form of interactive multimedia simulations. These simulations are used to develop the interviewing skills teachers need to conduct staff appraisals, skills in teaching high school mathematics, and time-management skills for principals. As with earlier initiatives, SITC is developing these materials by assembling working groups in which classroom teachers, temporarily released from their local schools, play leading roles.

Australia: Teacher-Based Teams Build Software and Peer Support

Two different projects in Australia illustrate ways in which teams of teachers have worked together, producing technology-enhanced curricula that aim to put students in charge of their own learning. One of these programs was based on a sophisticated interactive simulation, while the other used a simple database. What the projects had in common was the inclusion of practicing teachers in the development of the materials.

The Australian Computing History Project (CSC, 1986) illustrates the importance of encouraging and enabling all teachers to use software in their classrooms. Before the inception of the project, Australia's schools already had a significant amount of curriculum material that used standard software, such as database and word-processing applications. For example, the database "First Fleet" represents a compilation of the criminal and personal data of the 548 male and 188 female convicts who were exiled to Australia in 1788. Using this database, students can explore numerous questions, such as which crimes most commonly led to transportation, which were committed by women, the ages of the youngest and oldest convicts, and so on.

Surveys suggested, however, that very few history teachers were using this material; in fact, it was mainly being used by computer awareness teachers to teach computing rather than by history teachers to teach history (Wills et al., 1985). The central goal of the Computing History Project was to increase the use of computer software by the reluctant history teachers. The project deliberately selected twenty teachers who traditionally had not had access to their school's computing facilities. All the teachers chosen were strong in curriculum writing; they were not selected for their computing expertise. By focusing on history, the project also made inroads into a subject in which the majority of teachers are female.

The project involved the formation of a specialist team of practicing history teachers who supported each other in developing ways to integrate existing history software into the curriculum. Over a period of twelve months this group produced a curriculum kit containing case studies, curriculum units and teaching ideas for a range of history software, and a professionally produced videotape depicting four different school environments and four different software applications. Although the members of the team came from many different schools, the team members kept in touch with each other, and held several weekend retreats at which they compared notes and improved on their work.

In the Computing History Project, outlays for expensive technology were small, but expenditures on teacher release were large. The point was to give teachers time and maximum control over developing their own curriculum. Unlike teachers described by Michael Apple, who are deskilled because they must use prepackaged materials developed by outsiders (Apple, 1983), the experience of these teachers was an empowering one because their voices and ideas were incorporated into the materials. Because the software and microcomputers available to them were fairly standard applications like databases and word-processing packages, the teachers' expertise about what works in the classroom, along with the time provided throughout the project, became the most important components in creating innovative curricula to give students more control over their learning.

The second Australian example of including teachers in the development of technology-enhanced curriculum materials is a project known as "Christopher Columbus—Down Under." This project is a joint partnership among the University of Wollongong, Apple Computer Australia, and a local high school, Keira Technology High School (Harper et al., 1993). A working team whose membership includes practicing teachers and professional technicians has been assembled in Wollongong, and their production strategies reflect many of the features of the Scottish model previously described.

One product of this collaborative has been an interactive multimedia CD-ROM-based disc called *Investigating Lake Iluka*, which is a science package for junior and senior high school students that allows them to simulate a number of related ecosystems. Students choose from a range of tools to learn about the ecosystems and make their own connections among pieces of information that are presented in Hypermedia format. This program allows students to create their own pathways through the complex navigational information available, giving them increased control over what and how they learn.

The programming expertise of software experts was clearly necessary to develop a sophisticated multimedia program such as this one, but the teachers' expertise about how students learn and how they are likely to fare in this unstructured learning environment was equally important. Because such packages are still fairly new, research on how students navigate and learn in Hypermedia is somewhat conflicting. In this case, even with very sophisticated software, teachers' knowledge and participation were just as important as in the Computing History Project, which involved much simpler technology. These two Australian cases illustrate how technology can be used in very different ways to support hands-on learning, but no matter how the technology is used, teacher participation in developing ways to use the technology is essential.

Norway: Developing Project Schools

Projects such as those developed in Scotland and Australia tend to promote computer use in a wide range of subject departments. While this is desirable in itself, it can lead to logistical problems within high schools. One such problem is that the more widely microcomputers are used by different subject departments, the more competition for access to them will grow. If the total number of computers is small, sheer logistics may prevent their widespread use. As more teachers become interested, staff development needs also increase rapidly, and the burdens on a single computer-resource person to support teachers who have no experience in classroom computer use can become quite unreasonable.

In Norway, this problem is being tackled by selecting a limited number of pilot schools for intensive development each year, and phasing in additional schools over successive years. (OECD, 1987c). The Norwegian "Program of Action" was launched in 1984 not only to promote the development of technology-enhanced curricula and better training of teachers in the use of computers, but also to ensure effective coordination of the use of computer resources, by locating decision making at the school level. The idea here is that if all teachers in a school (not just traditional computer users like math and science teachers) work together to develop a plan for technology use, the school's computer resources will be more widely used.

A further goal of the program is to use teachers' experiences and school-level research to develop understandings of the most appropriate ways to use computers throughout the Norwegian school system. Since the Norwegian Parliament has explicitly adopted a decentralization policy under which the responsibility for school reform lies with the schools themselves, all the pilot schools in the program were required to establish their own specific project ideas. In each pilot school, all the teaching staff completed a 40-hour intensive school-based training program, and the entire school staff was required to agree on a concrete policy for computer applications across all areas of the curriculum. The goal was to develop high levels of competence within these schools, to use the schools for software evaluation, and to involve them in a continuing process of development and evaluation of effective classroom strategies for technology-enhanced curricula. The experiences gained in these schools has provided a knowledge base for the entire Norwegian school system.

Along with the Scottish and Australian models, the Norwegian plan provides a third example of an approach to policy development in which teachers are becoming full partners in curriculum change and in the specification and evaluation of software. Furthermore, the Norwegian program provides models not only for software and curriculum development in teacher training, but also for organizing schools and coordinating computer resources so that the maximum number of teachers, from all subjects, can benefit from them. This model illustrates how educational computing has led teachers to take on new tasks and roles, and has given them greater control over professional knowledge and decision making.

Conclusion

The cases described in this chapter demonstrate that the changes in teachers' knowledge and skills associated with microcomputer use are enormously broad. While all the applications described demand at least elementary competence in using microcomputers, the new learning required for effective computer use goes much deeper than this.

Many teachers will have to master new subject matter, and most will need to develop different strategies for managing classroom organization and interaction. Some applications (but not all) challenge teachers to reconstruct the practical theories they use for understanding the learning process itself. Teacher's practical theories, for example, embody all that they "know" on the basis of their stored past experience, about how to teach their subject, manage the classroom, and deal with individual learning problems. The reconstruction of such procedural knowledge is a slow and painful process. Withdrawal from the school for a short formal course at best provides a starting point. If this is not followed by opportunities to practice the new skills in a supportive school environment, the initial effort can easily be wasted.

Overall, the strongest policy implications of the analyses presented here relate to the critical role that teachers are playing in areas such as software design and the development of effective strategies for computer use in the classroom. In many of the programs described in this chapter, teachers are directly involved in applied research into what is taught and how it is learned. Their knowledge of classroom practice and student behaviors has played as important a role in developing materials as that of programmers and technology experts. This process, however, is not always easy and may require teachers and administrators to break routines and step outside traditional roles. To formalize and disseminate the knowledge they develop, expert teachers will require time release to work with professional programmers and teacher educators. By extension, this implies that teachers would become full partners in the development of curriculum, exercising greater control over the production and legitimation of professional knowledge.

References

Apple, M. W. 1983. Curricular form and the logic of technical control. In *Ideology and practice in schooling* by Michael W. Apple and Lois Weis. Philadelphia: Temple University Press.

Becker, H. J. 1986. *Instructional uses of school computers: Reports from the 1985 National Survey.* Issue No. 1(June) Baltimore: Center for the Social Organization of Schools, John Hopkins University.

Cerych, L. 1982. Computers in education: Major problems and key policy issues. *European Journal of Education* 17, (4), 421–23.

Commonwealth Schools Commission, Australia. 1986. *Computing history: Teaching with a new technology.* Videotape, CSC, Canberra.

Dumont, B. 1988. Aspects of the introduction of new technology into education in France. In *Interactive learning and new technologies: A report of the Educational Research Workshop in Eindhoven,* edited by C. Harrison. Published for the Council of Europe, 2–5 June, 1987, by Swets and Zeitlinger, Amsterdam.

Firkin, J, M. Davidson, and L. Johnson. 1985. *Computer culture in the classroom.* Melbourne: Victorian Institute of Secondary Education.

France. Ministère de l'Education Nationale, Inspection Générale. 1985. *Note sur les applications pedagogiques de l'informatique dans l'enseignement secondaire.* June 15.

Harper, B., J. G. Hedberg, and C. Brown. 1993. *Information landscapes, user interface and simulation: Improving learning outcomes.* Paper presented at the First International Conference on Multimedia Modelling, Singapore.

Hawkins, J., and K. Sheingold.1986. The beginning of a story: Computers and the organization of learning in classrooms. In *Microcomputers in education: 88th yearbook of the National Society for the Study of Education,* edited by J. Culbertson and L. Cunningham. Vol. 1. Chicago: University of Chicago Press.

Hawkins, J., K. Sheingold, M. Gearhart, and C. Berger. 1982. Microcomputers in schools: Impact on the social life of elementary classrooms. *Journal of Applied Developmental Psychology* 3(4): 361–73.

Hunter, L. 1987. *Teaching an old dog new tricks.* Paper presented at the SED-OECD seminar on Microcomputers and Teacher Education, Glasgow.

Nagtegaal, C., and P. Scholtes. 1987. *Computers in Dutch secondary education.* Paper presented at the SED-OECD seminar on Microcomputers and Teacher Education, Glasgow.

Organization for Economic Cooperation and Development (OECD). Centre for Educational Research and Innovation. 1987a. *Information technologies and basic learning: Reading, writing, science and mathematics.* Paris: OECD.

———. 1987b. *Microcomputers and secondary teaching: Implications for teacher education.* Appendix to Secretariat Report. Restricted. Paris: OECD.

———. 1987c. *The introduction of computers in schools: The Norwegian experience.* Examiners' Report. Paris: OECD.

———. 1986. *Changing work patterns and the role of education and training.* Secretariat Report. Restricted. Paris: the Organisation.

Pelgrum, W. J., and T. Plomp. 1991. *The use of computers in education worldwide.* Oxford: Pergamon Press.

Roebuck, M. 1993. Director of Research, Scottish Office Education Department, New St. Andrew's House, Edinburgh. Personal communication.

Scottish Education Department (SED). 1987. *Learning and teaching in Scottish secondary schools: The use of microcomputers.* Report by HM Inspectors of Schools. Edinburgh: HMSO.

Turnbull, G. 1993. *Scotland structuring teacher participation.* Report of the Scottish Council for Educational Technology. Glasgow, SCET.

Vickers, M. 1988. *Microcomputers and secondary teaching: Implications for teacher education*. Report of an International Seminar convened by the Scottish Education Department and the OECD, Glasgow, October 1987. Edinburgh: Scottish Education Department.

Wills, S., A. Bunnett, and T. Downes. 1985. Convicts and bushrangers: Educational databases brought alive. In *Education: Issues and applications*, edited by J. Oakley. Sydney: NSW Computer Education Group.

Subject Index